"I'm Edwards, Charlie Edwards," he said as he stepped forward. He sat down, crossed his legs, squinted at me a little and began grilling me. "What makes you think you can bring my granddaughter back when no one else has been able to?"

Still standing, I planted both boots firmly into the nap of the carpet, crossed my arms and answered him flat out. "Mister, let me tell you something. I didn't ask for this job . . . I didn't go out looking for it. I ain't looking to string you along for money. I got a family of my own, I ain't here for my health. I want this ugly thing over and done with as much as you do. I got no problem going into Mexico for that sorry son-of-a-bitch son-in-law of yours and I'm gonna take real pleasure in being the man to flip on the switch. Mr. Edwards, I'll be damned if I'm gonna back out now."

We just kind of froze there and glared at each other for what seemed like an hour but, more likely, was only two or three seconds. A big grin started to melt his stone-faced expression. He cocked his head and in a gruff, yet friendly voice said, "Son, I think we're gonna get along just fine. How soon can you get started?"

Books by Ray "Tex" Brown

18 Wheels of Justice (with Stephen C. Lynch)
A.K.A. Narc (with Raymond Angus)

Published by POCKET BOOKS

18 WHEELS OF JUSTICE

RAY "TEX" BROWN
with
STEPHEN C. LYNCH

POCKET BOOKS

New York   London   Toronto   Sydney   Tokyo   Singapore

An *Original* Publication of POCKET BOOKS

POCKET BOOKS, a division of Simon & Schuster Inc.
1230 Avenue of the Americas, New York, NY 10020

ISBN: 0-671-70890-2

First Pocket Books printing February 1992

10 9 8 7 6 5 4 3 2 1

POCKET and colophon are registered trademarks of
Simon & Schuster Inc.

Cover art by Jeff Walker

Printed in the U.S.A.

Dedication

Many men and women who drive eighteen wheelers coast to coast have contributed greatly in making drug busts, both knowingly and unknowingly. In recognition of their hard work and devotion to their families, their profession and their nation . . . and in tribute to all the law enforcement officers as well as their loved ones who have spent untold hours worrying whether a phone call was bringing bad news . . . to these courageous individuals, I dedicate this book.

Acknowledgments

There are many, many people I want to thank. The following is only a partial roster of those whose efforts to support and preserve law and order have made this book possible:

Mrs. Bonnie V. who has received many late night calls relaying messages, never knowing what to expect; Roy B. of District 7 of the Department of Public Safety; Mr. Bob S., Deputy Sheriff of Fort Worth, Texas, who was a major influence for good in my formative years; the late Judge John Woods of San Antonio, Texas, who, up until his final day, waged war on drugs; the late Jimmy Kelner who worked for the Texas Department of Public Safety and for the U.S. Drug Enforcement Agency . . . the man who saved my life.

Ray "Tex" Brown

18 WHEELS OF JUSTICE

PROLOGUE

Just about every kid in America, at one time or another, holds a fascination for trucks—especially the big rigs. Many a small boy's fantasy includes a dream that someday he'll be big enough to handle a colossal eighteen-wheeler. This is a book about trucks and about a trucker, but it's not a story about the sort of child's play many of us fondly recall from our carefree youth. Rather, it's the saga of a modern-day bounty hunter and narc whose cover is that of a good o' boy and long-haul tractor-trailer jockey.

Ray "Tex" Brown is well known among law enforcement agencies on both sides of the U.S.-Mexican border, yet his shroud was so convincing that for twenty-five years even his closest family members did not know him to be anything but the epitome of his CB radio handle, "The Texas Outlaw."

This book is unlike any other about eighteen-wheelers. It is more detailed than anyone has yet dared. You will feel as though you are riding shotgun and absorbing every shock wave of the pavement, pulsating with every shift of the mighty gears. As you bounce down farm market roads and across pastures, gliding over major thoroughfares, every fiber of your being will vibrate to the thundering rhythm of the big rig's stacks. From your vantage point inside the cab, you will witness just how an eighteen-wheeler and its rough-and-tumble incognito driver waged relentless battle after battle against interstate and international crime—crimes like drug smuggling and dealing, kidnapping, black marketing, rape, murder, and more.

Much of what you experience on these pages will read like the musings of a creative writer of fiction— farfetched, even outrageous. Be assured—it is anything but the inventions of an overactive imagination. Far from it. These are the true chronicles of dope hauled amid loads of lettuce and electronics—sometimes with, more often without, their drivers' knowledge. These are faithful reenactments of one man getting the goods on the bad guys, tracking truckloads of stolen merchandise, busting crack and cocaine houses, stalking kidnappers, rescuing their victims and making enforceable cases against perpetrators of heinous crimes.

On reading these pages you will be privy to the tactics of an undercover agent who hustled hot freight by making certain he was overheard when he called his "broker" to complain that he wasn't making enough money running ordinary loads. You will also be exposed firsthand to real-life horrors like battery acid being pawned off as narcotics to addicts who were hooked on getting high, but instead ended up going blind.

What you are about to read are the bona fide recollections of a wildcatter dodging DOT (Department of Transportation) inspection stations without permits or tags and the fast company of outlaw truckers and lawless reprobates he kept as he pulled into all-night truck stops and back-road rendezvous under the pretext of being one of them.

These are the ugly, sometimes lurid facts behind many a sensational news headline. How am I so certain of the authenticity of what you are about to read? Because I am "The Texas Outlaw."

Ray "Tex" Brown

CHAPTER 1

It was late morning on a warm spring day in southeast Texas and I was daydreaming as I rolled down the interstate in my black Mack B61 diesel truck. Towering over traffic at breakneck speed, I felt like I was galloping along atop some huge prehistoric beast. My fantasy was abruptly ended when my CB radio crackled, "How about you, Southbound? Come back to Double T."

Grateful for the company, I replied, "You got the Texas Outlaw here southbound. Where the heck are all the smokey bears? Come back."

"They're about thirty miles south, five or six carloads, on your side," the husky voice drawled.

Surprised, I asked, "What the hell's going on there?" The FCC doesn't like to hear profanities on citizens band radio, but for something to get the attention of that many troopers, I knew instinctively that it had to be mighty serious. Politeness was the last thing on my mind.

"I don't know, but it looks like they got one smokey in the air and he be right over your truck, man."

His reply sounded kind of left-handed. Craning my neck to catch a view skyward, I pressed the mike switch. "My truck? This black Mack?"

He didn't hesitate to confirm. "Ah, yup. That's the one for sure." His response told me he was glad he wasn't in my shoes.

I'd spent too many years driving a truck not to know that the Department of Public Safety (DPS) used single-engine aircraft to patrol long stretches of highway. This one, however, didn't look like it was on any such milk run. It seemed I was headed straight for the hornets' nest. I flicked my Cat radio scanner on to try and get some idea of what I was getting into. The police frequencies I picked up were a jumble of frantic voices. It was a sharp contrast to the typical monotone chatter between too-serious professionals.

Finally the LED sweep caught a DPS channel. My heart damn near stopped at the transmission, "Officer down! I repeat! An officer has been shot!" I got a sickening feeling in the bottom of my gut. Most of the people I can truly call friend are involved in law enforcement. They're folks who are in many ways closer than family to me. They're hardworking, honest professionals who are out there on the line, risking their lives every day. And they've got wives, husbands, mothers, fathers, daughters, and sons all praying to God that they don't end up just another statistic or a mere memory.

I stomped on the accelerator so I could cover real estate as quickly as possible. It's safe to say I was well over the posted speed limit as I thundered past a black-and-white police cruiser. As the cruiser faded off in my right rearview mirror, the trooper ripped his microphone from the dashboard. Just as the vehicle vanished from sight, my Catscanner caught his call. "Ten forty-two to one-sixty. That agent, the guy the captain told us about in this morning's briefing—I just spotted his vehicle heading south on Highway Seventy-seven. He's north of Ricardo. Please advise." The answer came back like a shot.

"Ten forty-two, pull him over! Advise him of our situation and await further instructions." I wanted to hear the story worse than they wanted to tell it. In a flash, I kicked the clutch pedal, throwing gear levers, leaning on the brake, and edging onto the shoulder of the pavement until the big black Mack came to a screeching halt. All I could do now was wait for the officer to arrive. At the speed I'd been humping it, I figured he'd be a few minutes.

The scanner didn't really tell me much more than I'd already picked up. I was antsy just sitting there listening, as if my hands were tied, so I grabbed the mike on my trusty Cobra citizens band and dialed onto channel 19. Keeping an ear cocked at the CB, I opened the door and firmly planted a boot between the frame of the cab and the doorsill. Just as I was inhaling a welcome cool spring breeze, I caught the glint of blue light in my rearview. Instantly, I swung myself out of the cab onto the running board and damn near did a half gainer to the pavement. An exaggeration maybe, but I'll bet most folks are a whole lot less enthusiastic about being confronted by the police.

As I watched the patrol car heading smack for me, it seemed to catch air as it came over the distant rise and bounced, swerving slightly to correct for a bend in the road. I wasn't sure if he recognized my rig, so I held my Stetson out. The officer immediately slowed down, tires chirping as he changed lanes. Then he fishtailed to a halt in the gravel several yards ahead of my left headlight.

Through a thin cloud of dust, the young patrolman jogged toward me as he kept a light grip on his holstered sidearm. As he came to a bouncing stop, he pulled out a notebook and asked, "Are you Tex?"

At the time it seemed inappropriate to give him a smart-ass response, but there I was, big as life, standing next to painted letters damn near a foot tall that spelled out TEX on the side of my cab. As some wise man once said, "There are no dumb questions, just dumb answers." Though this seemed an exception to that statement, and since the patrolman was obviously here to involve me in some powerfully serious business, I played it straight.

"Yeah, I sure am. I heard you on my radio. What's all the commotion?"

The officer flipped his hat off, wiped his brow with his

sleeve, and began spelling it all out in an accent that said I was in the company of a fellow native Texan.

"Some lunatic stole himself a car and come up Highway Seventy-seven to the checkpoint station at Riviera. Well, he must have got nervous, I guess. He up and shot a border patrolman!"

Under my breath, which I was barely able to catch, I uttered, "Oh, shit!"

The officer plopped his hat back on and continued. "He took off and he's got the patrolman and a woman held hostage! They wouldn't give me any ID over the air. We think he's going to run south and he's real skittish, so we can't get too close. If he's crazy enough to shoot a cop . . . well, we can't take any chances. We got the Matamoros bridge covered and Progreso's been secured, too. My boss says you might be able to help us out with that truck of yours."

In spite of already suspecting the answer to my next question, I still asked. "You got any snipers set up anywhere?" It was standard operating procedure and about the only blasted thing they could do at this point.

"We got teams being sent out right now, but I don't have any details, mainly 'cause the gunman's got himself a police radio."

"All right. I know I can run this truck right along with the son of a bitch and he'll figure me for just another trucker, but I don't want to run him down to just sit on my hands and have a look-see at him. I want you to get a sharpshooter to make this here run with me."

"You mean shoot the guy while he's driving? They might all get . . ."

I cut him off in midsentence. "Well, my friend, we can't let this cowboy get himself and his hostages into Mexico, now can we?"

I think the officer knew by my tone that I was getting more than a little impatient. He shut up, began jogging back to his cruiser, then stopped dead in his tracks. "Shoot, man, I'm gonna have to get to the call box at the rest stop so's this S.O.B. don't hear what we're up to."

He jogged off and I decided to check out a few things on my rig. It was probably just me, but it seemed like I had enough time to rebuild nearly my whole blessed truck before he finally returned and found me underneath one of the axles. He squatted down and filled me in.

"Okay, Tex, they're sending a man by helicopter. He'll be landing in a pasture in Ricardo. That's just south of here and they might get there the same time we do."

Well, they didn't. By this time, though, I was getting used to waiting. I kicked back with the door open, feet up, arms folded, and the brim of my Stetson pulled down just off the tip of my nose. But I was too fidgety to take a nap, so I reached under the seat and pulled out the leather case that held my Colt Government Model .45 automatic pistol. I popped the clip out, racked back the slide catching the round that was in the chamber, cranked off the barrel bushing, and took the weapon apart. It was something to do.

I was startled by the thunderous chopping roar that announced the helicopter's arrival as it dipped into a clearing like a giant locust that had jumped over the nearby tree-covered hill. The aircraft swooped past to our left at spitting distance, then gracefully swung around to face us. With a slight twist, it plopped down and sat there all peaceful-like in the tall grass in the middle of a whirling cloud of dust. It looked like it was suspended in the peaceful eye of a raging hurricane. I was nearly mesmerized by the impressive sight, but quickly reassembled my autoloader, slapped the clip in, drew the slide back, and let it slam forward to push a live shell into the chamber. After snapping the safety on and stowing the weapon, I jumped down out of the cab.

Holding the brim of my Stetson, I ducked and ran through the torrents of air, dust, and grass kicked up by the chopper's spinning blades. From the far side of the machine, a man stepped out. I put him in his late forties or early fifties. He had a silver crew cut and a trim, matching mustache. He was sporting a pair of mirrored, gold wire-rimmed aviator glasses and holding the meanest-looking high-powered weapon and scope setup I'd ever seen. It was a bolt-action rifle with a scope damn near as big as the gun itself. It had all sorts of dials and switches, a flip-up protective lens cap, and a contoured, cushioned rubber eyepiece to block out any distractions. I later learned that it even ran on batteries and could read a license plate at three hundred yards on a moonless night.

The man approached me and presented a handshake that clamped onto my paw like a bear trap. With an emotionless nod, the grizzled veteran officer barked out his introduction in competition with the noise of the aircraft engine. "My name's Jim."

I returned the greeting and motioned for him to follow me. We sprinted across the pasture. When we reached my truck, I opened the passenger door for him. Jim handed me his rifle. He climbed in as I gave the weapon a long, slow stroke before passing it up to him and slamming the door. As I hopped up behind the wheel and was getting ready to crank up the engine, Jim's voice boomed at me like a Texas drill sergeant.

"Tex, is that a Drug Enforcement Agency frequency I'm hearing on your scanner? That's some heavyweight shit, boy! They don't just hand those babies out like candy and I sure as hell never ran across any civilians with one of 'em."

My response was pretty much matter-of-fact. "Well, Jim, I do get myself into some pretty wild shit now and again. I work with the DEA."

My companion kind of shook his head as if he'd just lost a bet. Next he looked me square in the eye and, with some reluctance, told me, "I never have approved of bounty hunters before but I s'pose you're the exception. I've heard a lot about you, but I never dreamed I'd ever really meet up with you." Without another breath Jim changed the subject. "Say, how fast will this rig go?"

With the straightest face I could muster, I said, "Normally I don't like to take her over ninety-six on the straights, but she'll hold at a hundred and two if need be."

He gave me a hard, sideways glance. He took a deep breath and let it out hard. It seems like he didn't have much confidence in my old Mack. "Man, I hope we don't have to run that fast."

I stifled most of my grin. "We will if we have to!" I fired up the engine, pulled a few knobs, flicked some switches, shifted up and taxied the beast up the dirt road, and headed for the highway.

Neither of us seemed to be much for talking, but since we had a ways to go, I thought I'd draw him out a little and maybe learn more about the situation. He wasn't able to tell me a whole lot that I didn't already know about the checkpoint shooting, but he did fill me in on the wicked-looking rifle he was toting. It fired a .220 Swift cartridge, which any experienced hunter knows has to be the fastest caliber currently in factory production, bar none. The slug it fires moves out at least four times faster than my .45, and at two hundred yards it's stepping out about as quick as an M16's .223 does at the muzzle. Before Jim got done running down all of that fine weapon's features, I knew I had to have one for my own collection.

We were roughly thirty-five miles down the road when we came up over a rise and I geared down, pulled over, and rolled forward just enough to see the Riviera checkpoint station. It was beyond a short man-made cliff that had been left when workers blasted through a rolling hill to clear the way for the road. I reached into the back of the cab, pulled out a bag, and rifled through it till I found my binoculars.

Jim was slinging up his rifle, popping open the lens cap and adjusting for parallax. His voice sounded like gravel sliding down a tin roof. "You got a pillow I can rest this thing on?"

My rig was as much my home away from home as it was my transportation and my meal ticket. It had a sleeper cab and a pillow was standard equipment. I climbed into the back, grabbed it, and passed it forward to him.

"You got it made here," he said with a wink. "All the comforts of home."

I climbed back into the saddle and dialed my binoculars into focus.

About a half mile down the road I spotted an old four-door sedan with a tired paint job and a crooked rear fender. The trunk was open and one extremely nervous-looking dude was hunched over, leaning into it. As the guy righted himself and turned, I caught a glint of sunlight off something in his hand. I couldn't quite make it out, but Jim said it was a large-frame Colt revolver. Through his scope, Jim also had a clear view of the border patrolman handcuffed inside the trunk. I knew this was no time for joking around, but in all my years of man hunting I had found a sense of humor helped relieve a lot of tension. I forced a smile and said, "Hell, man, I bet you can read a newspaper at that distance with that thing." Jim just snorted and barely turned up one side of his mouth in a smug grin. He kept his crosshairs on his target as the kidnapper slammed the trunk shut.

Now we could see the female hostage sitting sideways in the backseat of the sedan. She was bent over a bit and didn't look all too comfortable. With a puff of blue-gray exhaust smoke the gunman laid a patch of rubber and sped away from the checkpoint. Jim unlocked his rifle bolt, caught the shell, popped the round back in the magazine, and then set the weapon in my gun rack while I geared up and edged onto the pavement. My partner used binoculars to keep an eye on the culprit as I got the Mack up to speed. Jim watched as the gunman made his demands into the wounded officer's hand-held radio. And on the scanner we heard, "Like I told ya before . . . if I see any cops, people are gonna start dyin'!"

By now the sedan was cruising a little over sixty-five miles per hour. Few folks would suspect a tractor-trailer rig of being a police vehicle, but this guy had to be some kind of head case. I didn't want to take any chances that he might make us, so I dropped her down to forty-five miles an hour on a long flat stretch of road. I hung back just enough for Jim to keep an eye on the sedan as I brought the rig back up to speed. The first town we came to was Serita, barely more than a wide spot in the road—one of those tiny towns where, if you blinked while buzzing through at ninety, you'd probably miss it.

It was a little early to set up a road block. The only course of action officials could take was to block every possible exit and side road, so they did. That action created a stir of excitement among residents of the small town we were bypassing on the highway. Hordes of curiosity seekers lined the roadside as if they were anticipating a passing spectacle like the Tournament of Roses Parade. Keeping him just on the edge of the horizon, I hung with the sedan as it passed through the outskirts of three small Rio Grande Valley towns. Jim, peering through field glasses about every other minute, kept an eagle eye on the vehicle.

Just as we were approaching Raymondsville, Texas Jim yelled. "Shit! We're losing him, boy! Step on it!" I stood on the gas pedal. In response, the diesel's stacks belched white smoke with a near-deafening roar. Jim nervously cinched his safety belt a little tighter and clenched his fist around the grab bar above his door.

The DPS had put a negotiator on the horn to try to smooth-talk the gunman into at least giving up the wounded officer before he bled to death. The kidnapper steadfastly refused. By his anger, threats, and the tone of his conversation, it was plain that the kidnapper was confused and desperate. We were getting closer and closer to Mexico and I knew something had to be done real quick.

I kept my foot pressed hard against the pedal, started closing the distance between us and the sedan, and alerted Jim. "I got an idea. Hang on." I kept pouring it on. "Look, you need a real steady rest to make a good shot, right?" Jim gave a quick nod of agreement and forced a smile while maintaining a white-knuckle death grip on his grab bar. "Tell you what . . . you reach back there and grab your rifle, brace that pillow up against the door, buckle up as tight as you can, then hold on."

He shot me a puzzled look that told me he wasn't real sure about my plan. "Yeah, but . . . ," he began.

Countering his hesitancy, I cut him off abruptly. "'Yeah, but' my ass! We ain't got time to fuck around here, man. Okay?"

This wasn't my usual mild-mannered tone, but there were lives at stake here. Shaking his head, Jim unfastened his seat belt, cautiously stretched back, grabbed his rifle, and then sat back down. While he was rehitching his safety belt, he gave me a glare that clearly questioned my sanity.

"Okay, Jim, we're only gonna do this once. I'm going to get as close as I can, then lock 'em up. When we come to a full stop, lean that rifle of yours out the window and take your very best shot. I don't care how you do it, just stop that vehicle."

Now he was looking straight ahead and I could tell he was playing the upcoming scene over in his head. He swallowed hard, turned, and, with absolute determination in his voice, gave me the only response I wanted to hear. "All right, Tex, let's do it."

The big black Mack was zooming down the highway. Suddenly, the sedan loomed up in front of us. We sped toward it. When we were close enough to read the license plate, I swung the big rig to the right and steered her onto the gravel shoulder. Standing on the brake and letting the clutch out, I threw it down a couple of gears to slow the engine and us down. Then, just as fast, I pulled the wheel as far around to the left as I could. The front tires started skidding out of the dirt, then screeched as they hit pavement. I don't think I'd ever pulled this maneuver before and I could only pray that my rig didn't jackknife as we fishtailed to a grinding halt.

What happened next seemed like it occurred in slow motion. The cab came to a stop in the right lane with the passenger side half facing the suspect's vehicle, which sped away past a few small buildings on both sides of the road. Jim threw his sunglasses from his face, twisted himself to the right, hung the rifle out the window while wrapping the sling twice around his left arm. He racked the bolt back with his right. He took a long, deep breath, let it out slowly, then took another and held it for what seemed like eternity. Sitting motionless, the rifle seemed to be an extension of the man. With a thunderous clap, the weapon spit an orange-red tube of flame nearly a yard wide and twice as long. The shock wave damn near knocked my hat off. At that very instant, a puff of white smoke blew out from under the left-rear quarter panel of the getaway car. The rear end dropped down, swung right, and the car came to a halt in front of the Harlingen Motel.

The passenger door of the sedan flew open and the female hostage and the gunman emerged. He had her in a half-nelson and held a revolver to her head. Jim racked back his rifle bold for another shot and leveled the weapon a second time. After a long pause, he growled. "Man, I can turn him off like a switch right now, but he's got the hammer of that pistol cocked and if I zap him, his muscles could tense up and she'd be a goner."

Still pointing the gun at her head, the gunman let go of the woman, opened the trunk, and pulled the officer out. The woman helped hold the wounded man and tried to see how badly he was hurt. The vehicle had stopped just to the left of a room where two of the motel maids were working. As one maid popped her head out of the open door in response to the commotion, the gunman ran toward her waving his revolver and kicking over laundry carts. The maids then scattered. Half dragging the semi-conscious patrolman, the woman and the kidnapper hustled into the room.

I'm sure all this happened in less than twenty seconds,

but it seemed like time had stood still. Jim had already signaled all units to converge on the motel. And converge they did, along with nearly half the reporters in the great state of Texas, complete with camera crews and vans sporting satellite dishes. Microphones and lenses were jammed into the faces of anyone and everyone who looked like they knew anything about the situation.

We ended up parked about a good stone's throw and six doors down to the right of the room where the trio was holed up. Just behind the police barricade, we must have blended in pretty well because none of the reporters paid any attention to us. I'm glad they didn't. After being on the road since before daylight, then taking a roller coaster ride in a semi, I didn't feel like playing celebrity. Besides that, if the face of this good ol' boy appeared in the newspaper or on TV along with this story, my cover as a dope hauler would be blown. Coverage like that would most likely have prompted my life insurance agent to reclassify me as a very high risk.

Nobody can truly say that they know what another person is thinking, but it seemed like the kidnapper was getting a real kick out of all the press coverage he was getting, and he must have wanted to see himself on television, too, because one of his demands, besides food, was to have a reporter with a video camera sent into the room so he could tell his side of the story, whatever the hell that was.

For hours the negotiators tried unsuccessfully to convince the gunman to release the patrolman, who by this time was close to death. Now, where all logic had failed, they had a bargaining chip that appealed to the desperado. A deal was struck and paramedics were permitted to enter the motel room, but not before the gunman made them take their shirts off and roll up their pant legs to make sure they weren't carrying weapons. After a few agonizing minutes, the paramedics emerged from the room with the unconscious patrolman on a stretcher. Suspending the intravenous apparatus that had been hooked up to the officer onto a mobile stand, one of them gave a sober, but hopeful, nod as the patient was whisked into a waiting ambulance.

Even though some might think twice about being on the business end of a big-bore handgun wielded by a lunatic who'd just shot and kidnapped a cop, I'll bet a lot of journalists would drool at a chance to get the kind of interview that had been promised to the kidnapper. Several reporters drew straws for the honor, or maybe I should say sentence.

The barricade situation was far from being one of those colorful, fast-paced, dramatic scenes from a Hollywood movie where the hero drives a car through a window and saves the day. It was a waiting game—long hours, a lot of coffee, and even more knuckle biting.

The reporter who went into that motel room knew he was risking his life and the officer in charge of the operation instructed him that under no circumstances was he to try any heroics. To do so would not only be jeopardizing his own life, but the life of the lady hostage. The reporter nodded, then shrugged with a forced laugh, turned to look at the motel room, paused, and sucked in two great big lungs full of air. He looked like a man who was about to jump out of an airborne plane for the very first time wearing a parachute the devil had packed for him. It was a very long hour before the reporter came out of the room. He was met by the DPS captain and a sergeant who debriefed him in an effort to learn as much about the mental and physical states of both kidnapper and hostage as well as the layout of the room. Any detail, no matter how small, could give them a great tactical advantage.

From what I overheard, the gunman acted out of panic and desperation when he shot the patrolman. He carried on like a wild man during the interview, pacing around as he talked and, with his revolver in one hand, thrashing both arms in all directions whenever he tried to make a point. The woman was alive and unharmed, tied up with bed sheets and lying on the floor in the far left corner of the room. When food was sent in, her captor made her sample each and every item in case it had been poisoned.

After another hour of quiet anger and frustration, the sun finally set and Jim decided to put away his weapon and call it a night. He unwrapped the leather sling from his arm, stretched and yawned, twisted his neck a few times, then climbed into the sleeper for a few winks. Several minutes had passed when an officer climbed up the left side of my rig and handed me a fresh thermos of coffee, which I gratefully accepted. I was in this too deep to sleep and the strong "stakeout brew" helped see to that.

Just before Jim dozed off, I asked him if I could keep an eye on the room through his infra-red rifle scope. Reluctantly, he agreed, but only if I kept the chamber empty. I was like a kid in a candy store, admiring the almost blue and orange wood grain of the stock, the contour of the comb and cheek piece, the finely detailed hand checkering on the grips and the tight, butter-smooth metal-to-metal fit of the action. It didn't make me forget the gravity of the situation but it sure made the waiting a lot easier.

I shouldn't have looked at my watch just then because it made me realize that the standoff had been going on for nearly twenty hours.

As the sun began to show itself, I climbed down from the cab and stretched so hard I thought I was going to pull a muscle. It took a minute or so to get my legs working again before I could walk over to the motel café to get more coffee and something to eat.

I was carrying a breakfast tray back to the truck when I slowed down to hear what the negotiator was saying to the gunman over the phone. Maybe the kidnapper had worn down and didn't function too well in the morning —or maybe it was just because he had scrambled eggs for brains—but it didn't sound like the conversation was going too well. I started heading back to my rig so Jim's coffee didn't get cold.

Suddenly, there was a startling blast as the window of a police car ten feet in front of me shattered. I tossed the tray and flattened myself on the pavement as all hell broke loose. The captain frantically shouted the order. "Return fire to suppress only! Shoot high! I want a man over here with tear gas right now!" Sixteen officers opened fire at ceiling level to give another with a grenade launcher time to set up.

Instantly, the window of the motel room burst inward tearing the heavy curtains off their rings. Huge chunks of brick facing exploded onto the sidewalk. An officer in full riot gear and flack vest, carrying a small case, darted past me in a crouched run and stopped behind a car thirty feet to my left. He set the case on the ground amid the broken glass and took out a single-shot, break-action, forty-millimeter gas-grenade launcher. Cracking the barrel open, he took out a massive grenade shell that made it look like he was loading the weapon with a D-cell flashlight. The officer slammed the rifle shut and paused, still crouched behind the bullet-riddled squad car. Next he swung the barrel up onto the hood, took aim, and with a hollow pop and a puff of smoke the grenade rocketed into the dust-filled motel room.

With a flash and a heavy thump, the grenade went off, sending clouds of noxious fumes rolling out through the smashed window. The door flew open and through the toxic fog came the barrel of a handgun and the half-blinded, choking kidnapper.

He was wearing a black T-shirt printed with the full label of a Jack Daniel's bourbon bottle across the front, faded jeans, and ragged-looking sneakers. Screaming as he staggered across the sidewalk, the gunman frantically rubbed his eyes as two streams of mucus ran from his nose down the front of his shirt. Just as his foot hit the pavement, in rage and panic, he began to raise his Colt revolver in the direction of the marksmen who, with their M16's, shotguns, and Magnums, held ready and awaited the signal.

The captain stood stone still, his right hand on a microphone and his left held high, palm open in readiness to give the order to drop the hammer. As the seconds ticked by, the captain's gaze quickly shifted from the gunman to the floor above, where three troopers in full riot gear and gas masks were posed and ready to pounce.

A rope brace had been fastened to the guardrail of the balcony to support their combined weight. All three men crouched outside the railing with autoloading pistols in hand. As the gunman seemed about to fire, the captain calmly said one word into his microphone. "Go!"

At that instant, the three men dropped in perfectly orchestrated unison. Two of the officers landed directly on the outlaw, one on each shoulder, and dropped him like a sack of potatoes. Just to the right, the third officer landed in a tuck and rolled forward and to the left, bounced to his feet directly between us and the perpetrator, turned and leveled his nine-millimeter automatic from a crouched, two-hand hold directly at the kidnapper's face.

After all those hours, it was over in seconds. No sooner had the assault team hit the ground than two men with gas masks stormed the motel room to rescue the woman. The captain barked commands into the radio and to all the men around him. An ambulance screeched to a halt at the right side of the room and four paramedics rushed to attend to the woman, who was being carried away from the fumes in the arms of one of the gas-masked officers.

Throughout the long siege, I thought for sure that somebody was going to die, and in this last minute, when the shit hit the fan, it looked like the kidnapper would be the one. I don't know why, but I'm glad they got him alive. I do believe in getting an eye for an eye, but more strongly I believe in the laws of this great land—due process and justice for all.

According to the paramedics, the female hostage was, under the circumstances, in good shape, and as standard procedure dictates, she was rushed to the hospital for examination and observation. As me and Jim followed the convoy of squad cars back to the county lockup, I tried not to think about the fact that I'd now been awake for seventy-two hours or more. All I wanted to do was get a nice quiet room with a huge firm bed and a nice soft pillow. Next I wanted to put out the DO NOT DISTURB sign, fasten it down with a staple gun, then lapse into a three-day coma.

We arrived at the county jail and so did the prisoner, who was booked into custody on two counts of kidnapping, one count for the attempted murder of a federal officer, plus a list of secondary counts too numerous to mention. The instant I got through the heavy glass doors of the entrance, I made a beeline for the men's room. As I entered, I wearily pulled off my shirt, walked over to the sink, cranked the cold water on full blast, and thoroughly drenched my head. I probably would have spent more than ten minutes under the faucet, but I started laughing as I envisioned a newspaper headline reading TRUCKER FALLS ASLEEP AND DROWNS IN POLICE STATION LAVATORY. I pulled my head out of the sink, blotted my face, my beard, and shoulder-length hair with a fistful of paper towels, slipped my overripe shirt back on, took care of the rest of my businesses, rinsed my hands, and walked out into the hallway.

I was reluctant to drink any more coffee at this point since my plans did not include staying up any longer than I had to, but I had reports to fill out. Even though I wasn't officially on any roster or payroll, I was still an employee of the United States Government, and the government runs on paperwork. So I chugged a cup of hot black coffee to take the edge off my numbness and saddle sores. After getting through all the red tape, I asked one of the detectives handling the case if there was anything else I needed to do. Fortunately, he told me exactly what I wanted to hear, which was to go on and get some rest. As I dragged myself back down the drab hallway, I was half tempted to just crawl into the sleeper cab of my truck and get unconscious.

CHAPTER 2

As I got toward the end of the corridor, I heard high-pitched screaming. It sounded like a woman was being attacked. When I approached the desk sergeant's station, I saw an attractive brunette lady in her midthirties pleading with the officer. "Isn't there anything you people can do to get my daughter back? He's sexually abusing her, goddamn it! Look at these photos! Isn't this proof enough?"

The stoutly built sergeant barely glanced at the photographs, handed them back to her, and said, "Ma'am, I'm truly sorry, but my hands are tied. The United States can't send officers into Mexico. We just can't."

The woman stood frozen for a moment, hands covering her mouth as she slowly shook her head. Finally, heaving breathlessly, she broke down and sobbed.

The sergeant spotted me as he came out from behind his desk to console the woman. He wrapped his arm around her and gave her his handkerchief. "Now, you just wait here one minute, ma'am. I think I might just know somebody who can help you." He turned in my direction. "Hey, Tex!" I was almost at the door and I realized that slowing down out of curiosity had been a big mistake. Even in my barely lucid state, I could see it coming.

"Hold up there a second, Tex," came the burly voice.

"I want you to meet somebody. Tex, this is Mrs. Byrd. She's in a real bind. Her ex-husband kidnapped her daughter and took off to Mexico." He ducked down slightly to catch her gaze and, with a hopeful look, explained. "This man is a professional bounty hunter, and since he has no badge, he can track them down in Mexico."

The woman wiped her nose with the handkerchief. Her eyes were red and watery and her lips trembled as she shook my hand. She could hardly speak through her tears as she mumbled something about not understanding why the police couldn't handle the job. She was too shaken to make a lot of sense. The sergeant, in a soft yet commanding voice, again went into what was beginning to sound like a used-car sales pitch. "Tex knows what he's doing, ma'am. If there's anybody can get your daughter back, he's the man."

Barely able to keep my eyes open, I smiled half-heartedly. "I hate to be rude, but I've been awake for the last three days, and if I don't get some sleep real soon, I'm afraid I won't be no use to anybody, including myself."

Tears welled up in the lady's eyes. Furious, she stomped her foot into the floor several times and lashed out verbally. "You don't care either! Y'all just don't care!" Her head sank as she turned away and broke down again.

In frustration, I turned to the side, took my Stetson off and swatted it against my leg. I felt as if I'd just dropped my favorite wristwatch down the one-holer of a well-used outhouse. I knew that if I didn't help find her daughter it would haunt me for life.

In my growing exhaustion, I tried to sound as reassuring as I could. "Now, now, Mrs. Byrd. Take it easy. I promise, I'll do whatever I can to help. Tell you what, let's go talk it out over a cup of coffee."

The distraught woman pulled herself together somewhat. She blew her nose a couple of times, turned, and gave me a skeptical once-over. Her tone was more than a little sarcastic. "Far be it from me to put you to any trouble."

Under other circumstances, if anybody had talked to me like she did, I'd have just said, "Terrific!" and turned on my heels and disappeared in a cloud of dust. I couldn't blame her for acting the way she did and I think if I had been in her shoes I'd have been a whole lot more ornery.

I looked her square in the eyes. "I said I'll help in any way I can, but first I need to get me some coffee and something to eat just to get my brain cells functioning right." I motioned for her to accompany me and she led the way. As I held the door for her, the afternoon sun hit me square in the eyes.

She paused and turned to me. "Call me Gloria . . . my first name's Gloria."

We stepped outside and walked, not saying a word until we reached the faded, sun-cracked blacktop parking lot where her late-model Cadillac Seville was parked. The sunlight flashed off a paint job that had "showroom" written all over it. I pointed out my truck and told Gloria to follow me just a ways down the road to the Highway 83 Restaurant. We parked our vehicles out front, entered the restaurant, found a table in the far right corner, and slid into opposite positions on the well-worn vinyl benches of the rustic booth.

The waitress was right on our heels, so before settling in I ordered coffee, two eggs over well, hash browns, a double order of bacon, Texas toast, and a large orange juice before I turned my attention to Gloria. I was starved. Gloria asked for a cup of tea, nothing more, and reached into a thin burgundy leather briefcase. She rummaged through it furiously, ripped out a handful of eight-by-ten color glossy photos and shook them at me. "This is what he's doing to her!" I grabbed her wrist so I could take them out of her hand. I wasn't prepared for what I saw.

The pictures stunned and repulsed me to where I forgot how bone tired I was. The first showed two prepubescent girls lying side by side, nude, on a bed, with their legs spread. The second showed the woman's ex-husband, also naked, in bed with the girls. One child was straddling him and the angle of the shot graphically illustrated the penetration of intercourse. He was fondling the genitals of the other child, his own daughter, lying to his right. I briefly glanced at a few of the other photos, but I was so disgusted by what I saw I had to put them down.

Even though I'm just a country boy, I'm far from naive. At that point I'd seen more than my share of the dark side of humanity in more than twenty years of working undercover in the fight against drug trafficking, smuggling, white slavery, and perverse satanic dope cults. I figured by now I was hardened to a lot of the sickness and depravity of some people, but this hit me like I'd been kicked in the gut by a crazed horse. I raised my eyes slowly and solemnly swore, "If she's in Mexico, I'll find her. Count on it."

When the waitress arrived with my bacon and eggs, I held up my hand and apologetically told her that suddenly I wasn't feeling too good. I told her to leave me the coffee and bill me for the food but get it out of my sight. The thought of eating anything at that moment turned my stomach something fierce.

"Okay, Gloria, tell me everything you can. First of all, how long has your daughter been missing?" Recalling the whole incident, Gloria trembled and choked up sporadically, but she managed to fill me in.

"It was nine months ago, three months after the divorce. We had joint custody of Sara. Gene—he's the no good monster I was married to—took her on weekends. Sara wouldn't say why, but she didn't like going to her father's. After finding the pictures I can . . ." She paused while her body convulsed with a very visible shiver. "Anyway, nine months ago I went to Gene's office to give him some important documents. He's had the same office since we were first married. Well, he wasn't there so, out of curiosity, I tried opening his wall safe. I thought that surely he would have changed the combination by then. Well, he hadn't and it opened. I was just going to close it, but it was filled with pictures and I was . . . well, I was just plain nosy. At first I thought they were just plain old trashy, mail-order photos, then I recognized . . ."

Gloria broke down and began crying again. I didn't think it would be a good idea to offer her the handkerchief I'd had in my back pocket for three or more days, so I emptied the napkin holder on our table and handed her the whole bunch. She blew her nose a couple of times, wiped her tear-stained face, and continued.

"I took the pictures, closed the safe, and raced home as fast as I could. I was going to take Sara and the photos straight to the police, but when I got home the babysitter told me that Gene had picked up Sara. I didn't know what to think or what to do. The police did what they could, I guess. Later we found out Gene had a video camera installed in his office, for security I guess. He was monitoring his office and saw me when I found the photos. He immediately rushed to the house, kidnapped Sara, then closed out his bank account and skipped town."

She stopped long enough to blow her nose a couple more times and went on.

"We hired a private investigator, who found out that they went north to Dallas, where Gene sold his Mercedes for cash. An employee of the car lot told the investigator that he and Sara had left in a cab. The P.I. traced the cabby and he said he took them to Plano, Texas, and another car lot, where Gene bought a different vehicle. Then Gene took Sara into Mexico."

I was baffled. "Well, it sounds like this investigator sure took himself a long time. Why didn't he finish the job?"

Gloria let loose with a laugh of irony and disgust. "Your guess is as good as mine. Frankly, this has been one of the biggest screw-ups you could imagine. That investigator's been collecting two hundred dollars a day plus expenses. It seems to me he's just trying to bleed my father dry. I suppose he did all right for a while. I mean, he did give us written reports on where they had been, but it was always too little, too late." Gloria excused herself and went to the telephone while I finished my coffee.

In my line of work one of most important tools I have are my ears. That's how I've made cases. I'd overhear somebody talk about dope or hot cargo and, since I look less like a cop than about anybody, folks would just open up to me. Hundreds of criminals have bent my ears every which way blowing off about their slick dope connections and their dirty, illicit dealings. I guess it was just force of habit, but I was able to hear part of Mrs. Byrd's half of the phone conversation. Other parts I missed in the midst of a great Waylon Jennings tune blaring from the antique fifties-style jukebox, the endless clatter of dishes, and the noisy chatter of road jockeys jaw-jacking in nearby booths. All I could make out from her call was that Gloria was telling her father, who apparently held the purse strings and ran the show, that she had found somebody who would go into Mexico.

It was plain that Gloria was at her wits' end and I understood that after being burned by a P.I. she'd be slow to trust anybody. My good-ol' boy looks and manner may not have raised her level of confidence any and, from her body language and the way the conversation had gone by then, I could tell she was still a little hesitant. She returned to the booth as the waitress came to refill our cups.

Now, I'd been driving trucks since I was old enough to shave, and even though I may not see them but once or twice a month, I make it a point to get to know as many truck stop waitresses as humanly possible. Not in the Biblical sense, mind you, but when you're on the road pretty near round the clock, it's nice to have a friendly face to talk to. These gals also have a real special inside track when it comes to knowing exactly what's going on in the tight-knit trucking community.

That afternoon our waitress was a lady named Patricia. She was an attractive woman on the early side of thirty, and after three years I guess I knew her well enough to small-talk with her about personal things, both good and bad. Patricia was real concerned over Gloria's troubles and asked if there was anything she could do to help. It wasn't my place to let her in on somebody else's personal business, but not to be rude I told her, "Mrs. Byrd's daughter has been kidnapped, but I don't think right now is a good time to talk about it. Thanks for your concern."

Something, but I'll be damned if I know what, triggered Gloria and she got really hysterical. She wailed so loud every head in the house turned. They probably thought I'd hit her. Patricia came over with another handful of napkins, sat down next to Gloria, and did her best to console her. It took a couple of minutes for her to catch her breath, but when she did, Gloria opened up and told her the whole story.

I'm sure that sharing her pain with another lady helped. After listening in horrified sympathy, Patricia gave Gloria a reassuring squeeze on the arm. "My God, I have a daughter about that age and I just don't know what I'd do if something like that happened to my Becky. I can't even begin to imagine." She shuddered at the thought. "I do know one thing, though—you should thank the good Lord that you found Tex here, 'cause he will find your daughter. And I'll tell you another thing— I'd trust this man with my daughter's life under any circumstances."

Still very distraught, Gloria managed a faint smile. It was hard to tell whether she was about to laugh or to choke, but she did seem a little calmer. As we left, I threw a couple of bucks down on the table, looked up at Patricia, and silently thanked her for her confidence with a smile and a wink. Gloria agreed to meet me in the lobby of the Holiday Inn at Brownsville. Her Caddy hung right with me every step of the way.

When I got done parking my big rig around back,

Gloria was waiting for me in the lobby and we talked a little as I was checking in. She said she would call her father again and have him come meet with me. I wrote down my room number along with my name, not just my handle, and asked her to call after she got settled in her room and after giving me a few minutes to grab a quick shower.

It couldn't have been more than twenty minutes later when she rang my room. I was trying to loosen up under the man-made downpour of water. I gradually raised the water temperature to just below the point where human skin starts to bubble up and peel off. Through a cloud of steam, the muffled ringing seemed like it was in my head. Then I snapped back to reality. I would have liked nothing better than to let it ring, but all I could think about was that little girl and the desperation and anguish of her mother. I shut the water off, grabbed a towel, and left watery footprints in the pea-green shag carpeting as I ran to the phone. Dripping wet, I grabbed the receiver while water streamed off my shoulder-length hair and beard and flooded the faded veneer nightstand. Gloria told me she had made reservations at the motel for her father and that he'd be arriving the next day. Matter-of-factly, she added, "And Daddy's bringing enough money to start a war in Mexico."

I told her, "We don't need a war—just good street sense and plenty of guts."

After I hung up the phone, I cranked up the air conditioner, got myself dried off, and collapsed on the bed. As tired as my body was, my mind wouldn't slow down. My brain raced through the horror of that helpless, pretty little girl held in some grimy hell hole, being sexually assaulted by her own deranged father. It was hard to imagine the kind of psychological scars it would leave on the child at her tender age.

I don't know how long I lay there tossing and turning, shutting, opening, and reshutting my eyes. I tried hard to concentrate on sleep, but every little noise, every itch, every thought drove me nuts. The longer I stayed in bed, the more outraged I got. Four hours later, I called room service and ordered three eggs over well with bacon and toast. I also told the man who took my order to bring me the largest container of coffee one person could carry on a tray.

I don't think lack of sleep usually affects me that bad, but those past few days my adrenaline had been working overtime. I jumped into the shower again and that seemed to clear my head. As I dressed, I instinctively tucked my .45 automatic into the back of my belt and a .38 snubnose on the right. It was second nature wearing my pistols in a way most lawmen would consider too uncomfortable for everyday carry. I probably had the imprints of two guns permanently pressed into my body, but in my business, it was necessary to safeguard my image. The guns were covered by my vest or my jeans jacket, as I had to look as low key as possible—with both the police and with criminals. If too many officers got to know me, my cover would eventually be blown. If the bad guys made me, it would be curtains.

The sun had just started to show itself as I stepped out the door of my room to get a breath of fresh air and stretch my legs a little. I've always loved mornings— especially mornings down in the subtropics of the Rio Grande Valley, where sometimes when the wind's just right you get a nose full of salt air as the wind blows over from the Gulf and crosses the rich farmlands. The sound of birds waking with the sun always brings me a sense of wonder at the power and beauty of mother nature. I walked around for a while, then went back inside, leaving the door open so the morning breeze could fill the room. After finishing breakfast, I opened up a small leather satchel and laid the contents out on the bed to see if I had everything I would need. I made sure my camera was loaded and that I had extra film, then I saw to it that my cassette recorder was ready to go. As I checked the equipment, I started getting really pissed off at the thought of the P.I. who'd been on the case and how his fear of going into Mexico had prolonged the torment of Gloria and her family.

I had just put the last of the gear back in the bag when I realized that I had promised my wife I'd get home in time to join three other couples and take our horses out to the local brush track for a quarter horse match race. I really didn't give a hoot about winning the purse or that my friends wouldn't understand why I had to miss the race. My only real concern was that I had been neglecting my family time and time again. Fortunately, my wife was very understanding, and I knew in this case she'd be happier about me doing the right thing.

I was always an early riser, but this morning was a little too early considering how little sleep I'd had the past week. By now I was chomping at the bit, so I picked up the phone just about the time the sun came up full over the top of a distant hill. I thought to myself, *The sooner the better. I'll be damned if I'm going to cool my heels any longer.* I dialed Mrs. Byrd's room thinking for sure she'd still be sound asleep at this hour. It turned out her night had gone like mine and, as impatient as she seemed to be, she said she wanted to give me plenty of time to sleep. Gloria told me her father had arrived about half an hour earlier and the two of them had just ordered breakfast. I said I'd call room service and have them send their order, along with more coffee, to my room. That way, I figured I could meet her father and get going. About two minutes later, she showed up in my doorway shadowed by her father.

He was a tall, stately-looking man who must have been in his mid- to late sixties. He was broad shouldered, with a full head of near-white hair. It was very neatly trimmed. He carried himself with an air of dignity and importance, and by the way he dressed I knew he was no ranch hand. Gloria started to introduce us, but he quickly took control.

"I'm Edwards, Charlie Edwards," he said as he stepped forward. He was warily sizing me up as he cautiously extended a well-manicured hand. In contrast to his skeptical frown, he gave me a firm, enthusiastic Texas-sized handshake. I invited them both to have a seat in the room's two easy chairs.

Edwards sat down, crossed his legs, squinted at me a little and began grilling me. "What makes you think you can bring her back when no one else has been able to?"

Still standing, I planted both boots firmly into the nap of the carpet, crossed my arms, and answered him flat out. "Mister, let me tell you something. I didn't ask for this job . . . I didn't go out looking for it. I ain't looking to string you along for money. I got a family of my own, I ain't here for my health. I want this ugly thing over and done with as much as you do. I got no problem going into Mexico to see to it the shit hits the fan for that sorry son of a bitch and I'm gonna take real pleasure in being the man to flip on the switch. Mr. Edwards, I'll be damned if I'm gonna back out now."

We just kind of froze there and glared at each other for what seemed like an hour, but more likely it was only two or three seconds. He reached into his coat pocket and pulled out a cigar and a big grin started to melt his stone-faced expression. He cocked his head and in a gruff, yet friendly voice said, "Son, I think we're gonna get along just fine and I'll tell you why. You speak your mind. You don't try to bullshit folks or tell 'em what they want to hear. I respect that in a man. How soon can you get started?"

31

CHAPTER 3

Mr. Edwards asked again, this time in a less threatening manner, just how I thought I could rescue his granddaughter. I poured myself a cup of black coffee, sat down, and laid it all out for him.

"Just over the border, I have two friends I've worked with for over fifteen years. My work takes me into Mexico a lot . . . maybe too much. It's a place where you ain't got too many rights—if you got any at all—and you need all the friends you can get. I hear that in Mexico money is the only thing that can buy loyalty, but I'll tell ya, these two men are like family to me. Money's got nothing to do with it and I'd trust them with my life."

Charlie sat forward in his chair a little, then rested his chin on his fist and stared at me intently while I continued.

"I'll need some equipment. Most of it I can find myself. I'll need to get some wiretap gear, and when I get down there I'm going to buy some pistols—it's too risky to smuggle them across. Now, when we get your granddaughter, we got to get her back here as fast as possible. We don't know if he's got local Mexican officials on his payroll who might throw a monkey wrench in the works so I'm gonna need a plane. I got to have it waiting at the Brownsville airport—ready to go at any time. I know where we can rent an old Cessna one eighty single-engine that'll hold together."

The old man sat up straight, thought silently for a second, then nodded and leaned back. "Son, money is no problem, just do whatever you have to."

I turned to Gloria. "I'll need a good picture of your daughter, a recent picture. And something else. She's pretty scared as it is right now and when she gets a load of me . . . well, hell, I even scare myself looking in the mirror sometimes. What I mean is, do you know of anything I can say to her that she'd recognize? 'Cause I'll tell you what—if she don't trust me, this deal could go sour in a heartbeat."

Gloria bit her lip, crinkled her forehead, and stood up. She began pacing back and forth across a sunlit patch of carpeting just inside the motel room door. With her head slightly bowed, she tapped a clenched fist against her temple. Her answer, she knew, could mean the difference between her daughter's life and death. There was absolute silence as she wracked her brain for something that would tell her daughter instantly that I could be trusted. Suddenly, Gloria clapped her hands together in excitement and shouted. "Cookie! That's it! Cookie—that's the nickname I gave her. Nobody else ever calls her Cookie—just me!"

Almost as an afterthought, she reached into her small Gucci handbag, fished around for a second, then pulled out a small jewelry box. "This is a locket I gave her for Christmas two years ago." Gloria's hand was trembling slightly as she handed me the box. As distraught as she was, her face still lit up with a hopeful smile.

There was a long silence again until Charlie, sounding a bit impatient, broke it. "Well, what the hell happens now?"

I grabbed a small wooden desk chair from under the dressing table, swung it around, and sat facing the old man and Gloria, who had plopped down on the edge of the bed. I folded my arms across the chair back and let out a heavy sigh. "Well, my operatives and me are in for a lot of legwork. We'll start by asking most anybody we can find if they've seen your little girl or that son of a. . . . That reminds me, I'm gonna need a recent picture of your ex-husband, too."

Gloria dug through her purse while Charlie puffed on his Havana cigar and listened.

"Okay, the way we execute this rescue will depend on a lot of things—where they are, who they're with, what kind of routine they have, things of that sort. Now if you'll excuse me, I need to use the phone a minute."

I called Pete Paredes, a friend of mine down in Progreso, Texas. I asked him to gather up some supplies and drive them down to me in my K-5 Blazer. Pete was more than a neighbor. He was like a brother to me. I'm not the type to leave my door unlocked, even living as far away from the city as I do, but for years me and Pete have had an open-door policy with each other. Both of us had the keys to damned near everything the other owned, and more times than I can count Pete's been a real lifesaver. Pete said it would be no problem—all he'd have to do was find somebody to follow him in his own truck so he'd have a way back home. I then dialed my house to tell my wife what was going on, but got no answer. I hung up and sat back down.

"That was a good friend of mine. He'll be here in about two hours with my Blazer and some equipment."

On the edge of his seat now, Charlie was getting antsy. "I want to go with you." It wasn't a request—it was a demand—and I wasn't crazy about having him tag along during the whole investigation. There was no way I was going to let him be there for the actual rescue. I figured I better cool him off slowly.

"As a matter of fact, as soon my friend gets here with the Blazer, you and me will take a little ride."

About an hour and a half later Pete showed up at the room. He peered in to check the number on the open door, then tapped on the hollow wood as he called out a greeting. I stood up, walked over to him, introduced him to Charlie and Gloria, and they shook hands. As Pete and I walked out to the truck to check the gear, I filled him in on the situation.

Pete's concern showed. He also loved the idea of getting involved in what he affectionately called my "Mission Impossible" adventures. "Is there anything I can do to help?" I looked at him and nodded.

"Well, when it comes time, I might need somebody with flashlights on the U.S. side of the river to mark the crossing."

Pete nodded back, smiled, and grabbed one end of a large wooden ammo box. I got the other end and we hoisted it out of the Blazer and set it on the ground.

The old man walked over as I was lifting the lid to check its contents. His eyeballs darn near fell out of his head. The big box held four army field radios, infrared night-vision goggles, flare pistols, and a good supply of military gear, some of which could be mistaken for explosives if you didn't know better. I tested out the walkie-talkies to make sure the batteries were in good shape and also checked out the batteries on the night-vision goggles. Finally, I took a quick inventory and scribbled down a list of things I needed to buy.

After loading the box back on the truck, Pete told me to give him a call and let him know one way or the other about the river crossing. I gave him a big-as-Texas handshake in gratitude. I slapped him on the shoulder with my left hand, grabbed him by the scruff of the neck, and gave him a little shake. Just then his buddy drove up and as he jumped in I remembered something else. "Hey, Pete, I tried to reach my wife but got no answer. When you get back, would you have her call me?" I scribbled the number on a piece of paper, handed it to him, and waved as they headed out to the highway. Charlie and me jumped into the Blazer and drove up to Los Fresnos to rent an airplane.

On the way to the airstrip, I talked it over with Charlie and we decided to rent the plane for a month so it would be there when we needed it. A husky young man handled the transaction. We completed all the paperwork and Charlie paid in advance. As we were leaving, I stopped in my tracks, walked back over to the young man, and looked him square in the eye. "Now, boy, if I come back here and that airplane ain't fueled and ready to go, you and me are going to have us a serious little talk. Do I make myself clear?"

I wasn't trying to be ornery and I sure wasn't looking to tangle with the kid. He was no ninety-pound weakling; in fact, he bettered me in both height and weight. But in all my years of experience I had learned that fear is the deciding factor in any conflict. When I was just a kid, somebody told me that dogs can sense fear—they can smell it. If you face them down they will fear you, or at least respect you. I apply the same principle to my dealings with human beings. It's the only way I can survive in my line of work.

The young man's eyes got big as saucers and he bobbed his head up and down real fast. "No problem! She'll be gassed and greased and ready to fly! You got it, mister!" I smiled, shook his hand, and followed Charlie out the door.

We headed back down a lonesome old military highway that was sun-bleached and crumbling. The road ran parallel to the Rio Grande River and as we traveled I pointed out a few spots where I had helped make some drug busts. When Charlie and me got back to the motel, I noticed how out of place Gloria's fancy Cadillac was. Just to be on the safe side, I told her to park out back where it wouldn't be seen so easily.

When I said I was on my way to meet my two friends in Mexico, Charlie wanted to go with me, just like I figured. I understood how frustrated he felt—itching to do something to help somebody in trouble but forced to put the brakes on. I took my Stetson off, dragged my fingers back through my hair, and scratched my head a little as I sized him up. Then I reluctantly agreed. "Okay. I don't see why you shouldn't come. But it's going to be pretty boring for the most part—I'll tell you that right now. But when show time comes, if Gene Byrd sees your face, he's gonna panic and somebody could get hurt."

Charlie gave me a real sober look. "I see what you mean. Believe me, I wouldn't do anything to jeopardize Sara's safety. Okay, Tex, you're the boss."

We both got into the Blazer, said good-bye to Gloria, and headed for the bridge that spans the Rio Grande and leads into Matamoros on the Mexican side.

About twenty minutes later, we pulled in at a small auto body shop in Matamoros that was owned by my good friend, Chuy Catalano. The garage had an antique gas and diesel pump outside that still worked and in this border town was probably considered state of the art.

Border town body shops normally don't rely on local trade to stay in business—many are notorious for dealing in stolen cars. But Chuy was also a qualified pilot and from time to time supplemented his income by dusting crops out of Raymondsville, Texas. The man had been my friend for many years and as far as I knew he was honest, but I made it a point not to pry into his affairs. As the wheels of the Blazer crunched to a stop in the dirt in front of his shop, I saw Chuy step out of the shabby building with a bottle of Coca-Cola in one hand. He was surprisingly tall for a Mexican, built like an athlete, and was in his early thirties.

Just as Charlie and I stepped out of the truck, Chuy looked up and I caught a glint of sunlight as it shot off the gold tooth at the front of his big smile. It had been a long time since I last saw him and I didn't always look forward to his greeting. He yelled at me across the dirt driveway. "Tex!" Then he bolted toward me like a linebacker with his arms extended and two five-fingered meat hooks ready to grab me. Sure, I was happy to see him, too. I just wasn't quite as enthusiastic about it. Chuy skidded to a halt and damn near slammed into me as he picked me up, spun me halfway around, then grabbed me by the back of the neck and shook me from side to side. He was laughing and at the same time cursing about my ancestry and saying how great it was to see me.

The three of us went inside the building, where I told Chuy why I was there. Under the gruff exterior, he's a really good family man, and I could tell that the situation with Sara upset him. He swore he would do everything he could to help me find Sara. He also told me that Tico Tapia, the other good friend whose help I wanted, would be in town later that evening and that he was sure that Tico would also join us. Chuy closed up shop, and as the three of us headed for the center of town, I explained my game plan.

"I figure Byrd will still be taking those pictures, being the sick dog that he is. I figure the first place to start looking is everyplace that sells or develops film." I gave Chuy copies of the photos of Sara and her father. I also pressed a handful of bribe money into his hand to help loosen people's jaws. It's not that I didn't want to ask around all by myself—I'm no stranger to that sort of thing. I've had to track men down in Mexico plenty of times, but this time was different. There was an innocent child involved and I wanted to make sure we got nothing but straight answers. I knew my Mexican compadres were more likely to get the information I needed.

We must have questioned more than a dozen shopkeepers that afternoon with no luck. Well, we did have luck, but all of it was bad. The three of us had covered a lot of ground that afternoon and by now the last of the sunlight was nearly burned away. Charlie Edwards was trying his best not to look discouraged and tired. I'd been on enough bounty hunts to know that these things take time. We stopped at a pay phone so I could call Mrs. Byrd to let her know what was going on. As I picked up the receiver, I glanced upward and said a prayer. The telephone system, sometimes jokingly referred to as Taco Bell, is anything but reliable. I got lucky, got the operator right away, and Gloria answered on the first ring. She sounded anxious.

"Nothing? You haven't found out anything at all?"

I was damned if I was going to stretch the truth and get her hopes up.

"Look, I hope you're not expecting me to find your daughter overnight. This may take a little time, considering how long the trail's been cold. Just hang on, okay?"

I could tell she was close to tears, but she managed to sniffle out a faint, "Okay."

I put her father on the phone for a minute, then we set off to check all the cantinas. As we got to my Blazer, I stopped short and turned to Charlie. "Hold on a minute. There has got to be something we can go on. Charlie, what else can you tell me about Gene Byrd?"

Charlie stopped and frowned thoughtfully. "I'm not sure I follow you."

I moved a couple steps closer to Charlie and leaned on the hood. "Any other vices you can think of—you know—drugs, alcohol?"

His eyes widened. "Say, now that you mention it, during the divorce proceedings there was talk of Gene using cocaine."

I squinted and the corner of my lip curled up in a grin. I stood up straight, swung my right arm across Chuy's shoulders and my left across Charlie's, and began walking away from the Blazer. "Gentlemen, I do believe we've got him!"

What we had to do was talk to dope dealers, something I did damn near every day in my line of work. It was shortly after my eighteenth birthday that I first started my career as a bounty hunter. It wasn't too much later that major law enforcement agencies took notice of the number of bail jumpers I'd recovered and how effective my cover was. Then one day some folks with the Drug Enforcement Agency decided it might be a good idea to put this long-haired good ol' boy to work for them. I had a clean record, I was already an officer of the court through my work for bail bondsmen, and I was a familiar face in nearly every truck stop in the country. I had no badge to prevent me from building cases in Mexico and stopping drug traffic at the border.

I explained to Charlie and Chuy that when I talked to the dopers, I couldn't let on that the man we were looking for had kidnapped his daughter. I had to continue to play the bad guy so I wouldn't blow my cover with any connections I'd met before or any I might meet up with again in setting up drug busts. If any of them even suspected I had anything to do with the police, I was as good as dead. I decided to make people think that Gene Byrd owed me money. We began by talking to a few local Matamoros snitches who had helped me make important dope connections in the past.

It was close to three o'clock in the morning when we hit pay dirt. An informant of mine named Ramone lit up when he saw the photo of Gene Byrd. No doubt the fact that there was money in it for him helped loosen his tongue, and since he never had steered me wrong before, I had no reason to doubt him now. I trusted the information he gave me. Ramone said he had seen Byrd hanging around a gay bar near the southeast corner of town. Somehow that didn't surprise me. I handed Ramone four twenty-dollar bills and I headed back to my truck, where Charlie and Chuy were waiting. At that point, it was getting a little late to follow up the lead. We were all dog tired so I drove Chuy back to his place, told him to fill Tico in, then we arranged to meet back at his garage at four in the afternoon. Charlie and I headed back over the bridge into the U.S. and stopped at the Kettle Restaurant for a quick bite to eat. Charlie had no intention of eating anything in that Mexican border town and I can't say that I blamed him one bit.

The old man sat quietly as we waited for our food to come. He looked real drawn out, which was exactly how I was feeling. Charlie broke the silence. "Goddamn it, that was a long day."

I looked up at him and shook my head. "Man, I told ya it'd be boring as hell. And to be real honest, we're lookin' at more of the same this afternoon. We gotta take it real slow. If we start flashing Byrd's photo around and asking a lot of questions in that gay bar my snitch put us on to, somebody might try to warn him. We don't want him running scared, so we gotta play it real cool."

Charlie tried to look the picture of cool. His voice, however, was a dead giveaway. He was angry and he was frustrated. "So, are you telling me that we're back to where we started?"

I tried to keep from yawning, but I did stretch a bit. "No, now, I didn't say that. We've got a good start, and just like I told you back at the hotel, I will get your granddaughter back. That's a promise. And I'll tell you something more—it ain't gonna take no nine months!" Charlie leaned back and relaxed. Our meal was delivered, we damn near inhaled our food, and he picked up the check.

As we walked out of the diner, the first hint of morning was visible in the sky to the east. Somehow that made me even more tired than I already was. I fired up the Blazer, turned to Charlie, and said, "Let's get us some sleep," then, with all the energy I could muster, drove back to the Holiday Inn.

The noise of my 427 engine announced our arrival and Gloria ran to the truck as we rolled into a parking slot. Expectation quickly turned to despair when she saw that her daughter wasn't with us. Without a word she turned and began slowly walking away, her head and shoulders bowed. I dragged myself out of the Blazer and went after her. In spite of the fact that I'd told her on the phone not to expect the world, I felt obliged to offer her some comfort. "Ma'am, I know that yesterday ain't soon enough for you to get your daughter back, but we did find somebody who knows one place where your husband . . ." She cringed at the word *husband*. I knew the thought of having been married to the rat was painful. I continued. "I mean ex-husband . . . where your ex-husband hangs out. We're one step closer, but it's still gonna take some time. I can't promise when, but I will promise you this—I will stick with it and I will bring your daughter back—no matter what."

She turned, took my hand in hers, and looked up at me. Silent tears streamed down her cheeks. "Thank you," she whispered.

Charlie caught up with us and the three of us walked toward our rooms. Gloria kept a light grip on my hand until we reached her room. She gave her father a good-night hug, then turned and gave me one, too.

"Tex—look, I'm sorry I was so hard on you when we first met. This has been a grueling ordeal and I haven't always handled myself real well."

I could almost feel the pain she was going through. I bit my lip, but I couldn't hide my feelings. I gave her a brotherly squeeze around the shoulders. "Think nothin' of it. Y'all get some sleep now. I'm leaving a wake-up call for ten." As I backed away and headed for my room, I told Charlie and Gloria to give me a call when they got up so we could all have breakfast together.

My wake-up call came earlier than I expected. My wife, Becky, had got the message from Pete Paredes that I was trying to reach her. It was about eight thirty when I was startled back into reality. The phone was about a foot from my ear and it had a loud, industrial-strength bell that rattled the nightstand. I damn near snapped my neck when I reached over to silence the thing.

Becky was worried that she hadn't heard from me in a few days. I was still half asleep and I told her to hang on for a second. I hoisted my carcass out of bed, splashed my face with cold water, and grabbed a glassful to drink. When she was sure I was alive and well, Becky made it real clear that she was pretty put out that I hadn't made it home in time to go to the races with our friends.

Once I explained where I'd been and told her the whole story from the time I started on the hostage case to the point where I was waylaid by this hysterical woman whose daughter had been kidnapped, she changed her tune. She asked if there was anything she could do to help.

"For starters," I said, "you can hang up and let me get some sleep." She did and I gratefully slumped back onto the pillow and went out like a light.

Later that morning, after breakfast, I handed Gloria one of my field radios and showed her how to use it. "These radios have a range of about fifteen miles or so. They'll allow me to keep in touch with y'all, but I don't want you calling for no reason. I'm going to be real busy and the people I'm going to be talking to might get the idea that I've got a police radio. I'll check in with y'all about every two hours to keep you posted." I told her that not because I was anxious to talk to her a whole lot, but to keep her calm. I realized that all the waiting must have been driving her nuts. The radio, I figured, would give her a little piece of mind.

I asked Charlie if he was ready to go and was thankful for his answer. "Tex, I've seen enough. I think I'll just sit this one out here with Gloria." I knew the old man trusted me.

I headed back into Matamoros by myself and met up with Chuy and Tico, who I hadn't seen in a long time either. My reunion with Tico was a happy one and, fortunately, a lot less vigorous than Chuy's greeting the day before. I gave both Chuy and Tico photos of Gene Byrd and little Sara. I also handed each of them enough cash to get people talking. The three of us set off to cover different areas of town and agreed to meet back at my truck in an hour.

We got a late start on purpose because the places we were headed for didn't get busy till late in the evening. Since I had the tip on one of Byrd's hangouts, I parked the Blazer at the opening of a dark alleyway almost directly across the street from the place and watched with binoculars. Chuy and Tico spent about thirteen hours a day asking questions while I staked out the gay bar. After a few days and a lot of dollars, we had people coming out of the woodwork claiming they had seen Byrd and his daughter.

About four days into our mission, we got what seemed like a really hot lead from a local who said he could take us to a small ranch west of town where the people we were looking for lived. The lead sounded better than most. I told the guy to hop in the front seat of the Blazer while Chuy and Tico piled into the back. The sky was still bright, but the sun had just started to dip down below the tree line as we headed down a dirt road toward a picture-perfect sunset. About four miles outside town the man told me to pull over near a side road that looked like a long driveway. I stopped the car and the tipster rattled off some directions in Spanish while looking over his shoulder at Chuy and Tico. He turned and repeated some of it to me in broken English. Finally, he held out the palm of one hand and grabbed the door handle with the other.

I sat stone still and just grinned. I must have stared at the fat little man for almost a minute before I leaned forward on the steering wheel and chuckled. In my broken Spanish I calmly told the man that he was going to go down that road with us. I reached back under my shirt, pulled out my .45, and released the safety. I reassured him in his native language that he'd get his money just as soon as we went down that road and found out he was telling the truth. He got real nervous and his eyes widened as I drew the slide back halfway to expose the shiny brass and copper shell in the chamber. Without warning, I let the slide slam shut. The fat man jumped in his seat as if he'd actually felt the crack of metal shattering bone.

He also got himself a case of amnesia real quick. Seems he wasn't so sure he recognized the people in the pictures after all. As he tried to convince us he made an honest mistake, his look of innocence turned to sheer terror. I leveled the bore of my .45 at his nose, then waved it slowly, motioning for him to get out of the truck. He crossed himself, began praying rapidly under his breath in Spanish, and complied with my order. I jumped out the driver's side and ran over to the swindler, who was now visibly shaking in his boots.

The sky was deep red as the last traces of day slowly faded. There was just enough light to see trees in the distance, the barbed-wire fence posts that lined the road, and the tears pouring down the con man's face as he pleaded for his life. Holding the pistol at my side, I put my left hand firmly on the fat man's shoulder and looked him square in the eye. "You understand English real good, don't you, amigo?" He nodded anxiously and rubbed his face with his sleeve. I deliberately spoke very slowly. "Now, *amigo,* I can understand you wanting to make a quick dollar off the gringo tourists, but if you pull that kind of shit with the wrong people, you might just get this."

In one swift stroke, I raised and fired my automatic. With an ear-popping explosion and a flash of bright orange light, the weapon threw a quarter ounce of copper-jacketed lead into a wooden fence post behind the man, sending splinters the size of pencils in all directions. The Mexican stood frozen as if he wasn't quite sure if he'd been shot or not. I paused for a second. "*¿Comprende?*" I asked.

He nodded furiously. "*¡Sí, señor! ¡Sí, señor!*"

I didn't have the heart to make him walk all the way back to town at night and I figured he might even help us out in a roundabout way if he let his compadres know that I hadn't just fallen off a cabbage truck. I dropped the fat man about a quarter mile from the edge of town and let him walk the rest of the way. Even though I was basically good-natured, his efforts to deceive me left me feeling somewhat less charitable than usual.

The next day we got an earlier start. I talked to a few more of my connections—people whose livelihoods fed off others' weaknesses. They were the middle men who occupied most of their waking hours finding and selling dope to anybody who had the money to buy it. They couldn't afford to cross potential customers, and as far as they knew, that's just what I was—a very steady customer. Little did they know that every time I placed an order, I was setting up a bust.

One of the connections I tracked down that day, a tall skinny local named Alfredo, told me he had sold some low-grade cocaine to the man in the photo. Alfredo also said he'd seen Byrd recently and gave me some ideas about where to look for him. He was not able, or willing, to tell me anything more. I checked out Alfredo's clues and found myself up a lot of blind alleys and, more often than not, in the company of still more drug dealers. It got so that I was calling Gloria Byrd just so I could talk to another human being who wasn't trying to either deal or score some dope.

Nine days later, the routine was wearing on my nerves. Staking out the gay bar was about as much fun as watching paint dry. That night, as I got out of my Blazer to stretch my legs and get some air, I noticed that the two rowdy-looking Mexicans in their late teens who'd almost always been hanging out across the street were not there. I turned to get back into the truck when I heard somebody running up behind me. As I whipped around, I caught the flash of knives in the hands of the two men. Instinctively, I stepped sideways with my left side toward them and kept my right hand out of sight. The two assailants stopped about three feet in front of me and one leveled his knife at me. He shoved his free hand out and ordered me to fill it with all my money or wake up dead.

I looked at him long and hard for about eight seconds, then just chuckled. The way I reacted confused the hell out of him and he looked over at his accomplice like he was asking what to do next. In less time than it took to blink, I whipped out my .45, stuck the barrel smack between his eyes, and snapped the safety off. It made a real nice, solid click. Behind the two thieves, the dull yellow of the lone streetlight shined directly on the muzzle of my autoloader. The message was loud and clear—the banditos had just met with superior forces.

From personal experience, I knew exactly what these sleazeballs were feeling. More than once I'd been in the gut-wrenching position of having a gun held to my head. It's damn near impossible to describe the kind of horror the experience brings. First, there's a powerful numbness that comes with that kind of fear. Almost at once, it feels like a gigantic magnet is sucking every bit of life's energy out of you. At the same time, every nerve tingles and the brain, anticipating death, races out of control. I guess some people deal with these kinds of confrontations better than others. By luck or by fate, I've always been able to hold my own because, thankfully, I've always kept my wits and somehow turned the tables.

Well, this punk didn't handle it all too well. His partner turned tail and ran while he froze and let go of both his knife and his bodily functions. I couldn't help but laugh when I saw urine pouring out of his jeans and forming a puddle at his feet. I yelled a warning at him in Spanish, then waved him away with the pistol. Gratefully, he ran off, limping slightly and shaking his drenched left leg.

That night I got back to the hotel on the early side and stopped in to see Gloria and her father. I filled them in on my progress, which, considering all things, wasn't too bad. At least I knew that Gene Byrd wasn't too far off, and with Matamoros being just about the only place for miles around to get supplies, I knew it was just a waiting game. They were encouraged by the news. I started to tell Charlie that I was thinking about sending Chuy up to Los Fresnos to bring the airplane down to us when he held up his hand. In his deep, gentlemanly voice, he cut me off in midsentence. "Tex, I got a little nervous just waiting around so I went back up to Los Fresnos and bought that airplane so you'd have it handy. It's being delivered to the Brownsville Airport late tomorrow morning."

The following day, Chuy, Tico, and I decided to cover some of the shops and restaurants on the far side of town. As we traveled down the road, the buildings started thinning out so I turned down a side street, and there it was—the two-toned blue station wagon that Byrd had bought up in Plano. I slowed down as I passed it. All three of us stared in disbelief, but sure enough, the plate numbers matched. I damn near choked thinking about all that surveillance, all that legwork and all those man hours we'd spent running down a whole lot of half-assed leads. Now, here I was stumbling across Byrd's car by dumb luck. I let out a blood-curdling rebel yell and my two amigos grabbed their ears in pain.

After cruising by the vehicle one more time, I pulled to a stop about fifty yards down the road. Since we had no way of knowing whether or not Byrd had the girl with him, I decided just to wait for our target to show and then follow him. It was a real short wait. Byrd was alone when he got in the car and I ended up trailing him around town most of the day while he stopped at several stores, the gay bar, and three dives where dope dealers were known to conduct a lot of business. I couldn't afford to let the car out of my sight, but I had to send Chuy to fly the airplane down from Brownsville and I needed to have Tico get things set up for our rescue of the little girl. I gave them both instructions and sent them off on foot.

I wasn't real sure what kind of reaction to expect when I called on the radio to give Mrs. Byrd the latest news. I didn't know if she'd laugh or cry, scream or faint—or all four at once. When I told her I'd found the car and her ex-husband, Gloria was speechless. There was a long pause, then Charlie yelled so loud into the transmitter that I thought the speaker on my handset would blow. "Tex, my boy, that's absolutely fantastic! Shoot, Tex, it's only been a little more than a week. That's the best doggone news we've had in one heck of a long, long time." He rattled on like it was all over and his granddaughter would be safely tucked in her mama's arms by nightfall. I didn't want to put a damper on things, but I had to caution him.

"Now, hold on, Charlie! I haven't told y'all everything

yet. Little Sara isn't with the son of a bitch so we ain't out of the woods yet." Charlie still sounded about as happy as any man could be. I filled him in on how we found Gene Byrd, then told him what the plan was. I cut the conversation short so I wouldn't risk attracting attention by operating the big field radio.

The sun was casting a long shadow by the time Byrd took the road out of town. I was alone now and I followed him to a little hacienda about six miles southwest of Matamoros. The place was well hidden, just off a lonesome road that led deep into rural Mexico. Fortunately, as the road heads back into town, it branches off into two narrow one-way lanes that are separated by a row of buildings. That was going to make things a lot simpler. I knew we had to move fast. Without having had any surveillance on his place, we didn't know Byrd's routine or if he was in the habit of bringing the little girl into town with him. I figured the only thing we could do was plan and pray.

That night a couple of Tico's friends loaned us two vehicles. One was a bobtail, flatbed truck and the other was an old sun-bleached, wood-paneled station wagon. Before sunrise the next morning, we had everything in position. Chuy waited in the bobtail truck, which was parked just off the street in an alley about a hundred and twenty yards from where the road branched off and led into town. The road was just wide enough for one lane of traffic and there were street vendors on just about every corner. I had left the Blazer behind a building at the other end of the alley, where Chuy was parked. I positioned myself on the rooftop of a three-story building directly above my truck. With my binoculars I had a good view of the road where our target would be coming from. I had secured one end of a long, heavy rope to a railing on the roof. That was my express ride in case I had to get down to street level fast. Finally, Tico was staked out six miles away, about a hundred yards down the road from the entrance to Byrd's place.

The three of us spent most of our time watching and jaw-jacking with each other over our walkie-talkies. Waiting as patiently as we could for Byrd's car to approach, we told each other dumb jokes and recalled some of our bygone adventures together. Four and a half hours later, there was still no sign of Byrd. Then, at ten minutes after nine, Tico rasped an urgent warning over the radio.

"¡Quidado! I see the car!" He was parked on the far side of the driveway so he could pull right in behind the car without raising suspicion.

"Tico," I said. "We got to know if the little girl is in the car. We can only do this thing once. Is she with him?" It took him a couple minutes to get close enough to the car to get a good look inside. While he was closing in on Byrd, Chuy started his engine.

In an angry voice, Tico came back. "I don't see the girl! There's just a driver!" I could hear the radio bounce around as he tossed it on the seat next to him with the frequency still open. He was cussing a blue streak in Spanish. I started calling to him, hoping he wouldn't give up.

"Tico! Tico, pick up the blasted walkie-talkie!" He answered real pissed off.

"¿Qué?" In the many years I'd known him, Tico was a puzzle. He was steady and a loyal friend, but when he got angry, his hot-blooded temper erupted like a volcano and he got pretty loco. I knew I had to calm him down.

"Now, listen, Tico. The girl is very small and you might not see her sitting in the front seat. Get up close to Byrd's bumper, but don't spook him." I was talking slow and in a real even tone hoping to mellow him out. "Now, watch the driver. I want you to tell me if he looks like he's talking to anybody. Is he moving his head a lot? Is he looking down at the passenger seat?"

It seemed like a long time before Tico came back in a nice, cool voice and it sounded like he was smiling. "Hey, wait a minute. I think maybe she might be in there with him."

"All right. Tico, let me know if you do see her and stay with 'em. Ya done real good!"

As far as I was concerned, this didn't mean a damned thing. The girl was either in the car or she wasn't. *Maybe* just didn't cut it. If we stopped this guy thinking Gloria's daughter was in the car and she wasn't, well, then all bets were off.

From my rooftop vantage point, I could see the two station wagons as they rounded a bend that opened onto the long straightaway into town. They must have been at least a mile away. Even through the field glasses, they were little more than a speck on the horizon. I figured I had about a minute before they got to where I was and I couldn't afford to waste one second. I tossed the coil of rope over the edge of the building and watched it spin wildly as it fell, jerked, and swung just short of the pavement below. Heights don't usually bother me, but it was kind of spooky how watching the rope fall made the hair on my neck stand on end. I guess it was because I knew I'd be following right after it.

I looked back up at the road to see how close the two vehicles were getting. I wrapped the rope around my left arm, put all my weight on the knot to test its strength, and with my free hand pressed the transmit button of the radio. "Okay, amigos, we're still not sure the girl's in the car. So, Chuy, listen up. I don't want you to make a move until I give the word. *¿Comprende?*" He acknowledged sharply. Satisfied that the knot would hold, I let go of the rope. If I fell, I don't think my major concern was getting hurt, although I'd be lying if I said the thought never crossed my mind. I just wanted to get the girl back to her mother as quick as I could. Breaking my leg would slow things down a might.

The cars were coming at us pretty fast now and I could only see them half the time through the canopy of shade trees that dotted the roadside. I took up a position on the right-front corner of the roof that was closest to their approach but furthest from my rope. It was going to be close. I was so damned wound up I felt like punching a chunk of the brick wall I was leaning on—that or tearing my beard out. All I could do, though, was wait and watch the end of the street just a little more than a good quarterback's throw to my right.

The two cars rounded the corner and I was doing my level best to keep the binoculars focused on the front seat of the lead vehicle as it sped toward me. The morning sun was still low over my shoulder and it was a nice clear day, but the buildings shadowed the street below. I kept my eyes glued to the windshield of Byrd's car, but I still couldn't tell if Sara was in it. Suddenly, the car passed through a beam of sunlight between two buildings. I almost yelled at the top of my lungs as I caught sight of the pink socks and two little legs hanging over the seat cushion that were draped with a blue linen dress that nearly matched the car's interior. Fumbling for the talk button, I damn near dropped the radio.

"She's there! Chuy, she's there! Let's take 'em!" In a run, I hooked the radio to my belt. With gloved hands, I grabbed the rope, cinched it to a quick-release safety ring, paused, and looked skyward in a kind of silent, last-ditch prayer. Standing on the edge of the roof with my back to the alley below, I put all my weight on the rope, jumped outward, and kicked away from the wall as I flew down to the pavement.

As soon as I touched ground, I unhooked the rope from my belt and raced past the passenger side of Chuy's borrowed truck. Chuy floored it. Tires screeched and gravel and dust exploded around us as the truck lurched into the street and cut off the blue station wagon. Just as Tico pulled up and blocked Byrd's exit from the rear, I pulled my .45, stormed the driver's side, and leveled the weapon in a two-hand hold square at the bastard's forehead.

It all happened so fast, Byrd was dumbfounded. His chin dropped and his eyes almost bulged right out of their sockets. I reckon he didn't know whether to shit or go blind. Chuy was there in an instant and all but tore the hinges off Byrd's door. He handcuffed the man to his own steering wheel, stuffed a greasy handkerchief in his mouth, tied another filthy rag good and tight across his face, and grabbed the car keys. I slipped my gun back in my belt, ran around to the passenger side, and opened the door. Sara was huddled on the floor of the car, shaking like a rabbit cornered by a pack of hounds. I crouched down, slowly reaching my hand out, and spoke very softly to her. "It's okay, Sara. I'm gonna take ya back to your mommy."

With her hands covering her tear-streaked face, the little girl cried. "Mommy doesn't love me. She doesn't want me. My daddy said so. She let daddy take me away." I looked up at her father in blind rage at the thought of the physical and mental torture that he must have put this child through. I went cross-eyed with fury and started going for my gun, but caught myself. I know that the only thing that kept me from blowing that man's heart out right then and there was the horror it would inflict on Sara. She'd been through enough and I still had to get her to safety. I couldn't afford to let my emotions get the better of me. I took a deep breath and turned my attention back to Sara.

I remembered the locket and pulled it out of a pocket, then gently handed it to her. "Cookie, do you remember this? Your mama gave you this for Christmas. Remember?"

Sara looked at the necklace, then lifted her eyes up to mine and nodded. She was still frowning a little, but she seemed less frightened. "Mommy gave it to me."

"That's right, and your mommy does love you. She loves you very much and she wants you back. She's been very worried about you. Now give me your hand. Come on, Cookie, let's go find your mama." Guardedly, she reached out one very small, trembling hand. As I grabbed hold to help her out of the car, I knew I had to coax her into hurrying. "Okay, let's run and go see mommy!" The two of us ran into the alley and to my truck, where Chuy and Tico waited with the engine all revved up and raring to go. The other two vehicles still sat blocking the roadway. We'd already arranged for their owners to pick them up after we'd made our getaway.

Officially—even unofficially—this was kidnapping, and getting caught in Mexico would mean me and my two friends could end up spending the next couple decades in a Mexican prison, definitely not a pretty sight. If we got caught, it would also mean that little Sara would probably never have another chance at getting away until long after the cruel emotional and sexual abuse had permanently scarred her fragile young mind. We drove like a bat out of hell and headed for the edge of town. Tico drove, Chuy rode shotgun, and I sat in back with Sara. We made no attempt to hide the fact that we were in a very big hurry. As we tore away from the scene, you might say I wanted somebody to notice us. About two and a half miles away, we pulled down a bumpy dirt road that was overgrown with wild grass. About seventy-five yards through thick brush and dense tree cover we came to a small clearing where Tico had stashed an old four-door Chevy. Quickly, I led Sara to the other car and sat next to her in the back. Chuy hopped behind the wheel and turned the engine over. Tico, still in the Blazer, made his way for the border while we headed for the Matamoros airport. As we got back to the road and were on our way, I looked at my watch. It hadn't been but about five minutes since I had jumped off that rooftop.

I had no doubt Byrd was still bound and gagged by the time we got to the airport. I also figured that we'd have no trouble getting away, since Chuy, the official pilot, was a Mexican national and we weren't filing a flight plan that would take us over the border. I called Mrs. Byrd from a pay phone at the airport and got through rather quickly. I told her the good news. She started to cry and ramble on, but I had to cut her off to say we didn't have much time, that I needed to talk with her father. Charlie was on the phone in a flash and I instructed him to bring Gloria along with all the court documents pertaining to Sara's custody and meet me the following night at ten at the Junction, Texas, airport. Without those papers, I knew I might very well be up shit's creek with the U.S. authorities.

Junction, Texas, was a long ways from Matamoros, Mexico—as the crow flies, about three hundred and twenty miles to the northwest. Though we were just five minutes from the great state of Texas, the route I planned to take back into the States seemed pretty crazy—kind of like using three men to change one light bulb. We had to go pretty far out of our way to end up someplace where I had friends. That place was Junction, Texas, and the friends were folks who worked for the Department of Public Safety. I needed to tip the odds in my favor as much as possible. The last thing I wanted to do was risk being stopped by the border patrol or by customs agents at a stateside airport and charged with kidnapping or with trying to smuggle an alien into the country. I had no idea what kind of connections Gene Byrd might have and I had no identification or proof of U.S. citizenship for Sara.

The route we followed took us west for nearly a hundred miles, then northwest about two hundred miles to a tiny landing strip on a ranch outside San Carlos, Mexico, that belongs to an old pal named Arturo. After warm greetings and a hot meal, I got on the phone. After trying about seven times, I finally got through to Al San Angelo, a buddy who worked for the DPS up in Junction. I filled Al in on what I was doing and how the DPS sergeant in Brownsville had got me mixed up in this thing in the first place.

Al got behind me one hundred percent, but when I started getting into details like the ambush, he interrupted. "Tex, hold it right there! Don't tell me any more. I'll support you all the way, but since I'm a peace officer and sworn to uphold the law, I'd feel a whole lot better if you finished telling me the story over a beer—after the whole thing is over and done. I'll meet you at the airport like you asked, but I'll tell you what—that woman had better have those custody papers or things could get real complicated!"

I understood his concern. Things like this didn't happen every day. Crossing the Mexican border without clearance is one thing, but when a minor is involved—especially one with no ID—friendship takes a back seat. I didn't even want to think about what might happen if I didn't have a friend waiting for me.

Well before dawn, we took off to fly across the border. It was damn near pitch black with barely a sliver of the moon showing. Since we were flying low, with no running lights, I rummaged through my duffel bag for the infrared goggles I had picked up when I was on an assignment for the U.S. Customs Service. Looking for smugglers, on stakeout duty by the border, I got a real kick out of wearing the goggles while driving around at night with no headlights. It was a damned good thing I brought them along!

We had just taken off from Arturo's, up to about three hundred and sixty feet, when I spotted the dark silhouette of a massive twin-engine aircraft heading straight for us about fifty feet above us and to the left. It was closing in fast. At our rate of climb, I knew we'd collide. I took over the controls from my position in the co-pilot's seat, cut power, nosed down, and banked slightly to the right, then kicked in full throttle and held her steady as we rolled and shook in the wake turbulence of the huge aircraft. The bandit was a DC-3 and it was also flying without lights, no doubt running contraband into Mexico. We came more than close enough for me to read the plane's markings through my night goggles, but I had more important things to worry about at the time. After that, I figured we'd better turn our lights on rather than risk another incident. At least we were still below the altitude of radar detection, and even if we did get spotted and were forced to land, we'd be in much better shape than if we had a midair collision.

We flew the rest of the way without a hitch. I had to radio the tower for clearance to land. I knew I'd have more than a little explaining to do. The air traffic controllers were somewhat pissed off, but they cleared us to land on runway two, where they arranged for the police to form a welcoming committee—but I knew it wouldn't be a friendly one.

As we came in on final approach, we were hit with a searchlight from a squad car that tried to keep pace with us and follow us down the runway with its siren blaring and cherries flashing. We taxied over toward a small terminal building, but we were cut off by three sheriff's cruisers that screeched to a halt in front of our Cessna. The squad car that followed came to a stop directly behind us. The entire area was bright as daylight—flooded by blinding white spotlights and wildly flashing blue and red gumball machines. It was hard to see just how many officers there were, but there was no mistaking the fact that they all had their weapons drawn. No doubt they suspected we were dopers. Me and Chuy were ushered out of the plane and frisked, then, thankfully, I heard a familiar voice behind me.

"It's okay, guys. He's a friend of mine. He called me ahead of time to meet him here and this woman is the child's mother." Al was talking to the supervisor, showing him the court papers, which the man carefully looked over. Mrs. Byrd, held back by her father, was hysterical. An officer blocked the path between her and the plane and little Sara. Finally, the man in charge gave a nod and the officer let Gloria through. She ran to the officer who was cradling Sara in his arms and he handed the child to her.

While the rest of the officers frantically searched the plane, Charlie walked over to Sara, brushed the long blond hair from her tired face, and gave her a big kiss on the forehead. Then he walked up to me with a huge grin on his face, shook my hand till it damn near broke, slapped me on the back, and gave me big bear hug that lifted me right off my feet.

As we walked over to his car, Charlie slapped me on the back once more. "Son, let's get us somethin' to eat!"

CHAPTER 4

Sergeant San Angelo drove Sara and her mother to a local hotel. While Chuy secured the plane, Charlie and me settled into the plush front seats of Gloria's Cadillac. We sat quietly for a minute or two, then the old man looked in my direction. He turned away quickly with an embarrassed laugh and with one big leathery hand whipped a tear from his welling eyes. Struggling to hold back a torrent of emotion, his voice quavered just above a whisper. "Thanks for my granddaughter." Charlie bowed his head and pressed his face into his white knuckled fist.

The silence was finally broken by the solid steel clack of the door latch. As Chuy jumped into the backseat and slammed the massive door, Charlie turned the key. The big engine roared and then purred off into the darkness. We headed over to an all-night café for a beer and a quick bite. Over our late-night supper, Chuy, punctuating his every word with flailing arms and an array of cartoonlike sound effects, recounted the rescue for Charlie. My old friend might have been as admirable an actor as he was a mechanic. Colorful as Chuy's performance was, I was dog tired and cut the show short to get some shut-eye.

The next morning I called my wife and asked her to drive over to Junction to collect me and Chuy. Just as I put the receiver down there was a thunderous knock at my door. Spiffed up like he was setting off for the nearest golf course, it was Charlie—in white shoes, bright green slacks, and a white knit polo shirt. He handed me a thick white envelope. Looking every bit the happiest man alive, he shook my hand so long and so hard I thought he'd pull my whole arm out of its shoulder socket. His huge frame all but blocked my view of his daughter and granddaughter, who followed behind him.

Gloria, dressed in a flowing yellow summer dress, let go of Sara's tiny hand and stepped forward. A tear fell from her bleary eyes and she gave me a great big hug. Her chest heaved silently against mine. When she finally stepped away, I reached in my back pocket and handed her my handkerchief. She laughed, this time through tears of joy.

"I didn't think you had any of these left. I thought every one of your hankies was in my dirty laundry."

Just then little Sara, who was all gussied up in a cute flowered pinafore and wearing the locket that had helped cement our friendship, jumped into my arms and planted a tiny kiss square on the tip of my nose. "You got so much hair on your face, Mr. Tex, all I can find is your nose." Her childish honesty broke us all up. We said our good-byes and the happy threesome departed, leaving me there with the white envelope in my hand and a tear in my eye.

I sat down and opened the envelope. It was stuffed with green-backed pictures of dead U.S. presidents. Tucked inside the wad of bills was a folded piece of paper. As I took it out and unfolded it, my eyes damn near popped clear out of my head. I know my heart skipped a beat or two. It was the title to the airplane. The whole hotel must have heard me as I whooped out a rebel yell. The police didn't show up, but Chuy did. He bolted through my door from his room next to mine. As soon as I got my breath, I phoned Becky to tell her the good news and let her know it wouldn't be necessary for her to pick us up.

Before taking off for home, I took a quick taxi ride over to thank Al for his help. If it hadn't been for him, Lord knows what kinds of problems we would have had bringing Sara back to the States. Me and Al had coffee in the lunchroom at Junction's Department of Public Safety headquarters where I told him about the rescue.

When I finished, Al slammed his fist on the table. "Slow death in a Mexican jail's too good for that son of a bitch!" As we stood and walked toward the door, Al snapped his fingers, whirled back around to face me, and reached into his shirt pocket. "I almost forgot," he said, handing me a slip of paper. "Captain McMann called. He wants you to call him back. He wouldn't leave a number—said you'd know it. It's none of my business, but from the tone of his voice, I'd say you were in a heap of trouble."

Staring into space, I kind of tuned out the rest of what Al said. It suddenly dawned on me that I might be in deep shit for going off on my own into Mexico. Captain Bill "Duke" McMann of the Texas Department of Public Safety was the leader of a special interagency task force on drugs and I answered directly to him. When Al gave me the message, I had a flash of Duke wearing a stern frown. I could hear his booming voice warning me as he had many times before, "No free-lancing!" The fact that he knew to call for me at Junction headquarters meant he had heard about my unauthorized border crossing.

Al led me to an interrogation room with a phone. Very slowly and very deliberately, I punched out the number I had been instructed to memorize years before. That number was my only lifeline on cases where I was working without a net. It had come in mighty handy more than once for mobilizing backup units and getting me out of binds like the times I'd been hauled into the slammer in the line of duty. This was the first time I dialed that number hoping there'd be no answer. The first ring had barely stopped when I heard the receiver being ripped off its cradle. His stern, almost angry voice came through loud and clear.

"McMann here!"

I took a deep breath. "Hey, Duke, it's Tex."

There was a long, very intimidating pause. Then, in a real calm, even tone he came back to me. "You got something to tell me?"

I began telling him the whole story. Duke didn't make a sound. He listened patiently. When I finished there was another agonizingly long pause. Eventually, he spoke.

"Tex, I'm proud of you, boy!" Just as I started to breathe again, he let me have it. "But I'll promise you this—I'll have your head stuffed and mounted and hanging on the wall in my den if you pull another stunt like that again without clearing it through me first! Do I make myself absolutely clear?"

I felt my whole body snap to attention. "Yes, sir!" Somewhere behind my eyes I had a real clear picture of Captain McMann, a sneer on his face, thumbing through the taxidermy listings in his phone book.

"Tex," he continued, "I've got a job for you. A man named Hector Gomez is running a major smuggling operation out of Laredo. We've been after him for a long time but haven't been able to make a buy from him. The son of a bitch has a closed circle of connections and won't deal with outsiders. If you can get him to hire your rig to haul a load for him, we'll catch him with his pants down. You've got to make him think he's coming to you—otherwise it won't work. You know what to do."

It wasn't a question. It was a command. There was only one answer he wanted to hear so I gave it to him along with a brief explanation that I would fly back to Brownsville, pick up my truck, and head for Laredo.

He gave me a description of Gomez, then added, "And, Tex, we'll have a spotter plane over Laredo to keep an eye on you. Keep D channel open—they'll let you know where to find the subject when you arrive."

I hustled out of the interrogation room and waved as I passed Al's office. He looked startled by my sudden exit and, with coffee in hand, ran after me. "Hey, wait up, Tex! What's the hurry? You just got here. I figured you'd come to the house this evening. Doris was looking forward to seeing you. She's even fixing a special dinner just for you."

"Sorry, Al," I said. "Got an important assignment. Gotta go!" He shot me a quick departing salute.

Fifteen minutes after Chuy and I landed at Brownsville, I was back in the big Mack making my way along the Rio Grande toward Laredo. Hours went by before anything on D channel caught my attention. As I rolled up the last stretch of Highway 83, I could see the long shadows of the tall buildings of downtown Laredo. The scanner crackled. "Ah, this is Alfa Tango Foxtrot to control . . . on a heading of two zero niner . . . altitude twelve hundred feet . . . have spotted Outlaw approximately two point five miles southeast of my position, northbound on 83. Please advise." Immediately, the response followed.

"Roger, Alfa Tango Foxtrot. Message for Outlaw is as follows. . . . Subject currently code ten at high-profile refueling station. Notify home base after contact is made. Over."

I flicked my lights on and off a few times, and after a short pause, the pilot's voice acknowledged. "Roger, control, have visual confirmation from Outlaw. Message received. Over and out."

Scanners that can monitor special law enforcement frequencies like mine are hard to come by, but since we knew dopers were managing to get hold of them, we had to be extra careful. "Code ten" told me that the man was eating and "high-profile refueling station" meant a large truck stop. I knew just the one he was talking about.

Minutes later, I pulled into the truck stop. It was a monster of a place just on the edge of Laredo, a city that is another hotbed of international drug trafficking on the Texas-Mexico border. I parked my rig and made my way across the blistering parking lot, which was about the size of five football fields. By the time I hit the door of the diner, the red bandanna I was dabbing my forehead with was soaked clean through. I headed for a vacant booth toward the back, casually scanning the joint and its patrons on my way.

Luckily, the restaurant was far from crowded. I managed to get myself a booth right beside the dope smuggler I was sent to set up. Duke's description of Gomez left no doubt. He was a Mexican in his midforties with medium-length, greased-back black hair. Clean shaven, he had bushy eyebrows and sunken dark brown eyes. He was smartly but casually dressed and wore a straw hat that shadowed his dark, sharp-featured face.

I sat down, chugged a cool glass of water, ordered lunch, then swung my leg up on the seat and turned sideways. I hollered a friendly greeting at a couple of good old boys across the aisle. "Say, where y'all from?" They were built like professional wrestlers and wore T-shirts, jeans, and baseball caps. One of them had a woolly red beard and long, scraggly hair to match. It stuck out of his hat in every which direction. The other guy had a salt-and-pepper handlebar mustache and, from what I could tell, must have been hiding a real short crew cut or a bald head under his cap.

With chicken gravy on his whiskers and his jowls full, the red haired trucker answered. "Gallup . . . Gallup, New Mexico. Say, what's the best way to get to Houston from here? Should we take Highway Thirty-five or head east toward Corpus Christi?"

I couldn't have asked for a better opening. "Well, best way I know, and I reckon I know 'em all, is to head east. I've managed to find myself a whole bunch of back roads so's I can bypass all them weight and license scales." The two men snickered a little. The one with the mustache gave me kind of a sneer.

"But they move them scales around all the time. What ya haulin' that ya need to do that anyway?"

I glanced around, leaned forward, and spoke just loud enough to be heard across the aisle and, hopefully, by the man in the booth beside mine. "Well, I'll tell y'all. Years ago, when I got into this business, I had just enough money to buy me a truck. Couldn't afford no tags for my license plate so I just ran without 'em. Been driving like that ever since. Shoot, all ya need to know is the right people, the right CB channels, and the right questions." They looked at me like I was crazy, but they were real interested in what I was saying. From the corner of my eye, I could see that my target was too.

I went on a little more about the ups and downs of my adventures as a wildcat trucker and filled them in on the fastest route to Houston. Finally, I tossed out the bait. "My broker ain't got nothin' for me to haul for a couple days. You fellas wouldn't know where I could pick me up a payload, would ya?"

They just looked at each other for a minute, then the older, leather-skinned trucker with the mustache turned to me and shrugged his shoulders. "Don't get me wrong, pal, we ain't got nothin' against independent drivers, mind ya, but we're union and ya know how that goes." I nodded my understanding and tried to look disappointed.

The two men from Gallup left as my food arrived. Just as I started to dig in, I heard the deep, accented voice behind me. "Amigo, forgive me. I could not help overhear your need for work. It happens I have some freight you may be interested in carrying for me. We can talk when you have eaten, no?" My mouth was full, so I gave him a sharp, affirmative nod and turned to finish my lunch.

I pushed my plate away, took a big drink of iced tea, called the waitress over and asked for the check. She smiled and nodded in the direction of Gomez. I hoisted myself out of the booth, threw a tip down on the table, then offered my hand to the man I was determined to help put behind bars.

"*Muchas gracias,* my friend. I didn't catch your name."

He shook my hand cautiously and looked me over real hard. After a long pause, he smiled and motioned for me to sit with him.

"I am Hector, amigo. Hector Gomez. And you are?"

I settled into the booth and looked him square in the eye. "My friends call me Tex." The word *friends* almost stuck in my throat. I kept thinking how many lives the man had ruined over the years as a result of his drug trafficking ring. I had to put that out of my head and concentrate on what I was there for. Setting up a drug bust is a lot like acting except that in my business the consequences of a bad performance involve more than dodging tomatoes being tossed by an irate audience.

I cut the small talk and asked Gomez what he wanted me to haul. He glanced around for a split second, leaned across the table, lowered his voice, and answered with a sinister smirk. "Weed, my friend. Seven hundred pounds, all right? Is that a problem?"

"Nope—no problem. I'll haul damn near anything but wetbacks."

Gomez smiled, leaned back into the corner, sat sideways in the booth, and put his feet up. "*Sí*, amigo! I hate those damned coyotes as well. They care nothing for my people—only how much they put in their pockets for bringing them across the border. Those bastards—they would leave women and children to die in the desert to save themselves from arrest."

I nodded in agreement and slapped my hand on the table. "That kinda business burns my ass, man!"

I can't figure scum like Gomez, morally adamant about one kind of injustice but totally without conscience when it comes to their own brand of greed. If he'd been able to read my mind, he'd have known how much the thought of American kids getting hold of his drugs chapped my ass.

"*Sí, sí*, my friend. Such bastards should be made to face the firing squad, no?"

I just kept nodding my head. Finally, he cut the bull and got down to brass tacks. We negotiated my price for hauling the load and settled on $3,500. I thought of a lot of things I could do with all that cash if I didn't have to give it up as evidence.

"You will follow me to a place where you will wait for a day or two . . ."

I cut him off in midsentence. "Shit, man, time is money! I want to get this show on the road as quick as I can."

Hector smirked again. "Patience, my friend. These things take time. You know this, no?" I nodded, agreeing with him, but I didn't pretend to like it.

We shook hands, then got up and headed for the door. As Hector paid the cashier, I told him I was going to call my wife. "I will wait with you." This complicated things a mite, because I had to tell Duke McMann that the deal was on, but I had to tell him with the dope smuggler standing right next to me.

I hesitated and then lifted the phone off the hook, pressed zero, then the number, making sure Hector didn't see it. "Hello, operator? Yea, collect call from Tex . . . thanks." I held the earpiece close to my head and hoped Duke's voice didn't carry. "McMann here!"

"Hello, honey! This is Tex. . . ."

It sounded like he almost dropped the phone, then his harsh voice roared back. "Tex? Tex, is that you? What the hell's gotten into you, boy?"

Doing my best to talk over him and mask his voice, I immediately cut in. "Honey . . . hon . . . now, Becky, listen to me a minute. . . . I can't talk right now—I got a load to haul, and it could be a couple days before I get on the road with it, so I'll be in Laredo awhile. . . . Gotta go, dear. . . . Love ya. . . . Bye." I quickly slammed the phone back on the hook. I could only imagine the look on Duke's face at that moment.

It was late afternoon by the time I hightailed it across the scorching hot blacktop. I climbed in the cab and settled into the sheepskin-covered bucket seat. I revved the engine a little, then cranked up the air conditioning, pulled out, and was on my way. Ten minutes later, I pulled up next to Hector's pickup at a dirt-covered wide spot on the side of a road in the barrio near the northbound entrance to Interstate 35. The spot also served as a parking lot for a grungy little roadside taco stand.

I shut the air conditioning off but left the engine running before I ambled over to Hector's brand-new six-wheeled, long-bed, step-side pickup. He pulled a huge lit cigar from his mouth, clenched it in his bony fist, and pointed it at me. "My friend, this is where you will wait. The shipment will be here as soon as possible. In the meantime, just relax." Hector's truck lurched slightly as he dropped it in gear, then he turned and issued one more command. "And, amigo, no more telephone calls. We will be watching you—¿comprende?" I gave him a nod and he drove off.

I still had plenty of fuel left, so I kept my truck running with the air on. As far as anybody knew, I was just trying to keep from frying. Standing still, the Mack's old 250 horsepower Cummins engine belched out a plume of thick white smoke that, from their aerial vantage, could be seen for miles by the DPS spotter plane. In the calm summer air, they'd easily be able to tell when I got rolling.

For three agonizingly long days, I spent most of my time in the sleeper compartment with the doors locked and the windows rolled up. My biggest challenge was trying to keep from going stir crazy. From time to time I went into the tiny restaurant to eat, to use the men's room, and to wash up. My Colt .45 auto, cocked and locked on safety, went with me, tucked under my shirt. Up in the sleeper, I played solitaire and tossed cards at my Stetson, which I'd set brim up in one corner. I also read an Irving Stone novel I had started weeks before but hadn't found time to finish. I monitored D channel, too, kind of keeping track of the spotter plane that was keeping track of me.

It was the end of the third day about sundown. I'd just heard the spotter plane pilot tell control he was coming in to refuel when somebody rapped on the driver's side window. As I peered through the fiery red glow of sunset that filled the cab, I saw Gomez flashing a sinister smile and looking like the devil himself. I was happy to see him. It meant an end to my waiting and, hopefully, the beginning of the end of his ugly dope-smuggling operation. I motioned that I'd be a minute, threw on a shirt, tucked my .45 into my belt, and climbed up front. I looked out and checked both sides of the truck to see what I was getting into and prayed my spotter plane would get back in the air before I hit the road. I popped the lock, opened the door, hopped out, and walked over to Gomez, who was now leaning against his pickup. As far as I could tell, he was alone.

Our meeting was short. No bull, just business. "It is here, amigo. Follow me," he commanded. I returned to my rig, turned up my scanner, took a deep breath, and rolled out behind the pickup.

Gomez led me on a zigzag route past faded brick buildings and dilapidated billboards through a Laredo neighborhood I wouldn't recommend to tourists after sundown. About a half hour later we pulled into the back of a large rundown warehouse, where we parked just beyond the reach of some dim floodlights on a far corner of the building. Immediately, out of the darkness, three old pickup trucks rolled slowly toward me. All three were piled high with big, TV-sized bundles of marijuana. I climbed out, swung the side doors of the trailer wide, and clamped them in place. Trying to look as casual as possible, I reached under my shirt and put a firm grip on my automatic. Six men scrambled out of the trucks and wasted no time hoisting the bales and loading them into my truck.

Keeping a loose grip on the pistol under my shirt, I walked through the shadows over to Gomez. With one leg propped up on the rear bumper of his truck, he watched like a hawk while his men formed a line and handed off bundle after bundle and heaved them into my trailer. The expression on his face was a combination of greed and arrogance. Without taking an eye off his merchandise, he gave me my instructions. "You will travel north on Interstate 35. We will follow. After you have completed your business at the checkpoint station, we will signal. You will stop and I will instruct you further. ¿Comprende?" I acknowledged him, then cautiously ambled over to my rig and climbed inside. In my rearview mirror, I watched Gomez's men slam and lock the side doors, then get into their vehicles. I geared up and took off.

I listened anxiously to the white noise of my scanner, checking the channel indicator and volume a couple times. Finally, the monotone static was broken by the crunch of the pilot's almost frantic transmission. "This is Alfa Tango Foxtrot to control. I have lost Outlaw! Repeat, have lost Outlaw! Please advise." There was a long silence. "Control! Do you copy?"

"Roger, Alfa Tango Foxtrot. We read you. Continue search. We're issuing an all-points bulletin. Special units are being dispatched to likely contact point. Control out." I took a deep breath, prayed, and drove.

As I reached the checkpoint station and approached the barricade, an armed border patrolman jogged toward my rig. The instant the big Mack shuttered to a complete stop, the patrolman jumped up the steps of my rig. "I'll need to see your license, sir." I took my ID out of my billfold and handed it to him. Holding the rail on the side of the cab with his right hand, he studied my license for a second and glanced down at the painted letters on my door. "I won't be but a minute—routine check."

The young officer jumped down, trotted over to his booth, made a quick phone call, and returned. He climbed back up and handed me my license. "Tex, I got a message from your guardian angel—keep on truckin', cavalry's on the way."

I grinned ear to ear and slapped the dash. "Thanks, pardner—thanks a whole bunch!"

Shortly after pulling out, as I rounded a curve on the

interstate, a pair of headlights flashed off and on behind me. Reluctantly, I pulled over and stopped on the shoulder. The night sky was crystal clear and in the midst of the twinkling points of starlight, I caught the red-and-white flashing beacon of a small plane. I heard the rasp of D channel. "Alpha Tango Foxtrot to control. Outlaw is stationary and being approached by another vehicle approximately ten miles north of Highway 44. Over."

"Roger, Foxtrot. Ground units have visual on Outlaw. Black-and-white will detain the second vehicle for positive ID. Control out."

I flipped the scanner off and tucked a .38 snubnose under my right thigh a few seconds before Gomez's wild eyes peered through the passenger-side window. While I leaned over to unlock the door, he rapped impatiently on the glass. He swung the door wide and hopped in. "Drive," he ordered.

I steered the Mack back onto the roadway. Gomez's truck pulled out in front and maintained a position about fifty yards ahead. As I drove, I kept one eye on the squirrelly dope dealer and one hand at the edge of my leg, inches from my gun. Hector made a sudden move toward the sleeper and my palm tensed around the grip of the .38. "Where the hell you goin'?" I yelled.

Quick to reassure me, he apologized. *Permiso,* amigo. I do not want to be seen when we pass through Cotulla." He forced his way into the sleeper compartment and, as he did, I caught the flash of an autoloader under his shirt. For the life of me, I couldn't figure out why he was going back there except maybe to bushwhack me. I booted the clutch and stomped on the accelerator. The engine roared and the cab shook as the needle on the speedometer climbed and then vibrated just under the century mark. In competition with the noise of the engine, Gomez hollered. "Wha . . . what are you doing?"

I hollered back. "Just tryin' to make better time is all!" I figured that with the scenery rushing past us as fast as it was, Gomez would be less likely to cancel my ticket.

The lead truck picked up speed, too, and all but disappeared ahead of us for a few seconds as it rounded a bend. I caught sight of him again as the road straightened. All of a sudden, about six car lengths ahead, a DPS cruiser fishtailed into my lane from the median. I cursed at the top of my lungs as I wrenched the wheel hard to the right and hung on for dear life. With a heavy thud, Gomez tumbled to the left side of the sleeper. I wrestled the steering wheel, geared down, and swerved back onto the pavement from the right-hand shoulder. Siren blaring and lights flashing, the black-and-white sped off.

Gomez emerged and leaned forward, rubbing his head. I smiled as his expression of pain changed to shock while he watched his man get pulled over by the patrol car. Gomez crawled forward, slowly strapped himself in his seat, turned to me, and mumbled weakly, "Stop at the next rest area."

As we slowed and passed the scene, Gomez stared blankly at the flashing lights. Several minutes later we drove into a rest stop. Finally, a set of headlights swerved and came toward us. As it approached, the vehicle's cluster of yellow running lights on the roof told us it was Hector's truck and his man, Juan. The pickup cruised up to my door and Gomez all but tore his door off getting out. He bolted over to Juan. Within earshot of their mile-a-minute Spanish, I heard that Juan was stopped for speeding. Gomez got back in the cab laughing, but he was visibly shaken by our contact with police.

As we rolled up the last stretch of highway into the city, the lights of San Antonio's skyline burned like the embers of a slowly dying campfire. When we reached the outskirts of town, Gomez directed my every turn. He led me in circles, trying to cover his ass.

I wanted to get on with it. I cursed in frustration. "Damn it, man! That must be the third time we passed that grocery store! We're wastin' diesel!" He checked the rearview and spotted his man, who was behind us now.

"*Sí*, amigo. Take the third left." I turned down an extremely narrow street that was barely wide enough for my truck. The scenery left a lot to be desired. It was a stockpile of broken-down cars and decaying plywood shacks. We wound our way through the seedy ghetto until we came to a small boarded-up adobe house set back from the road. It was almost buried in a field of high weeds. Massive piles of junked tires, scrap lumber, heaps of trashed auto parts and five flashy cars built low to the ground surrounded the place. I eased my truck through a tight, clear space and the Mack's hydraulic brakes let out a shrill screech as I stopped beside the house.

Instantly, eleven men poured out of the building and ran to meet us. Gomez jumped down and, in Spanish, barked out his orders. I stayed in the cab while the mob opened the trailer doors and transferred the bails to the shack. Hector watched their every move. About the time I figured the job was near done, I got out and cautiously approached Hector. Waiting for my payoff, my right hand rested lightly over the pistol in my belt. Seconds later, the thug who was inside handing bails off to the others popped his head out of the trailer and yelled, "*¡Finito!*"

Abruptly, Gomez turned and reached under his shirt. Every muscle in my body tightened. Instinctively, I lunged out and grabbed his wrist. Hector's face twisted in surprise as I yanked his arm out. He laughed like Lucifer at a lynching as a wrinkled yellow envelope fell to the ground.

Embarrassed and momentarily lost for an explanation, I relaxed my grip on his arm. "Man, I must have had too much coffee while I was waitin' for the haul."

He smiled, shook his head, bent over and picked up the envelope, then handed it to me. "Amigo, there is no need for explanation. We have much in common, you and I. To survive we must trust no one. Is this not so?"

"Amen," I said. Hector walked me back to my truck, we shook hands, and I hopped in.

Unable to turn around, I threw it in reverse and slowly backed all the way out by the same route I'd taken in. Once off the property, I flipped the scanner on. D channel blared and I caught the pilot in midsentence. ". . . and is leaving scene. Repeat, transfer complete. Outlaw is leaving the scene."

"Roger, Foxtrot. All units are mobilized to those coordinates. Maintain surveillance. Report suspect activity. Control out."

Winding backwards through the filthy, narrow alleyways, I finally reached the two-lane cross street at the edge of the slum, where I had to back out into traffic. My visibility was piss poor. In the rearview mirror I saw cars rush past in both directions. I knew I'd never live it down if I blocked the way for arresting officers and the bust went sour because my damn truck was caught in traffic. There was no time to screw around. I crossed my fingers and edged the rig back, gradually swinging the tail into the near lane. In every direction, tires squealed and smoked as cars swerved to keep from slamming into me. I kept right on going. As soon as I could, I threw her in first gear, wrestled the wheel, romped over the curb and part of a yard. Blaring horns and angry curses followed me as I tore off down the road.

I was two blocks away when the police showed. Lights flashing, nearly a dozen squad cars fishtailed around the corner. Tires screamed as the torque from the big engines sent the cruisers barreling past me. In the mirror I saw what I thought was one of Gomez's men tailing me. I pulled over and, sure enough, I caught sight of the driver's ugly mug as he passed. Before I could get back on the road, a cruiser pulled in front of me. Its flashing red and blue cherries were overpowered by the blinding searchlight that was trained on my rig.

I rolled down my window and stuck my head out. "What can I do for ya?" I asked the Weight and License officer who was approaching on foot.

He replied arrogantly, "I think you know you're running without tags. Y'all want to step out of the truck." I jumped down, he gave me the once-over, and said, "Let's open up the back."

The officer swung his flashlight over his shoulder and held it like a club. The beam hit me square in the eyes, temporarily blinding me. In spite of the fact that I could barely see, there was no mistaking what I heard—the click of a holster strap opening followed by the hollow scrape of a magnum clearing leather. "Move!" he shouted. I was damned near in shock. What I had expected was some news about how the bust was going down, maybe even a couple words of congratulations. Instead I felt like I'd been shot at and missed, shit at and hit. Disheartened, but more than that outraged, I damn near yanked the trailer's double doors off their hinges.

Scattered marijuana shake on the floor was enough to get me a pair of steel bracelets clamped on my wrists and an all-expense-paid trip to the gray-bar hotel. I spent the night on a cold slab and a blanket in a five-by-ten cell with nothing but a filthy sink and a filthier toilet. Next morning I finally got to make my phone call.

"McMann here," he boomed. It must have been my lousy night's sleep that made his voice sound like a gun just exploded next to my head.

I yanked the receiver from my ear, cringed in pain, then said, "Duke, this is Tex. I'm in a fix and I need some help."

"Jealous husband?" he joked. Somehow, I already knew he'd be giving me more than just a little shit about my predicament.

"Who's got time for messin' around? Besides, I could handle that one on my own. No, Duke, seems Weight and License stopped me for runnin' without tags—that and some shake in the bottom of my trailer. I got my ass hauled in last night."

Through a stifled laugh, he said, "Shoot, I ought to leave you in there for callin' me darlin' and sweetie last time you phoned me. I don't know if I'm safe with you out on the streets, Tex!"

A few minutes later, the desk sergeant handed me my

personal property and a receipt for the $3,500 that I was turning in as evidence. Apologizing all the way, the arresting officer drove me back to my rig. He shook my hand as I got out of his squad car.

"No hard feelings?" he asked.

"Hey, you're just doin' your job, man."

CHAPTER 5

A month later, I still felt that waking up in my own bed every morning was almost too good to be true. One day, after a late, leisurely breakfast with Becky, I ambled over to the barn and checked on my horses and made sure the covered wagon was oiled and ready to roll. The restored wagon was kind of a big kid's toy that helped me get away and forget the ugly filth of my everyday work. I made a few bucks on the side leasing the wagon out for promotional events. On weekends, when I wasn't on the road, Becky and me took the wagon and a team of horses over to a local orphanage. From the youngest to the oldest, all the children anxiously looked forward to hayrides and sing-a-longs in the covered wagon. After a day full of riding, we'd have a big cookout and tell tall tales around a campfire. Our covered-wagon adventures gave the youngsters some good clean fun while teaching them about horses and the Old West. They gave me even more—a chance to escape.

I left the barn as soon as I'd made sure everything was shipshape for the coming weekend's outing at the orphanage. After a short walk, I kicked back in my living room recliner with a tall glass of iced tea and watched a John Wayne Western on television. It was the first time in nearly two months that I really had a chance to relax. I'd almost forgotten what it was like not having to look over my shoulder. Watching actors get shot at instead of getting shot at myself was a welcome change. I was really getting wrapped up in the movie, sweating it out with the hero. Arrows whizzed past the Duke's head. Bloodthirsty Indians, in hot pursuit, were gaining on his stagecoach.

All at once, the thought hit me—a stagecoach! I jumped out of my chair, spilling iced tea all over myself. I could just see the kids at the orphanage going wild as I rolled through the front gate on Saturday in an authentic stagecoach with a full team and tack. I remembered that I'd seen a stage with horses for sale a few months back at a stable in Benbrook just outside Fort Worth. As I recalled, it needed a little paint but it was in fine shape. Getting it slicked up and looking good as new wouldn't take a whole lot.

I grabbed the phone and called information. I figured by leasing the stagecoach out for county fairs and store openings, it would pay for itself in a heartbeat. Then I realized that Colonel McCutchin, the old guy who owned the stable and had the stagecoach for sale, hated my guts. I had helped send one of his boys to the penitentiary for three to five years on a drug charge. I knew the old codger would never sell anything to me. I hated like hell sneaking around, having somebody else buy the buggy and horses for me, but I was determined to have them. Deceit seemed like the only way. A stagecoach for sale is a rare find—especially one that's safe to climb on and ride in. Once I got the idea of owning it in my head, I wasn't going to let the colonel's hatred stand in my way.

I dialed the number. "B and B Stables. This is Samuel, can I help ya?" I got right to the point.

"Yeah. I'd like to talk to somebody about the stage-coach y'all got for sale."

The voice on the other end obviously wasn't McCutchin's. "Okay, that'd be the colonel. I'll fetch him directly." I never thought I'd ever have any dealings with Colonel McCutchin after several officers had to hold him back to keep him from clobbering me with his cane outside court following his boy's trial. In a matter of seconds, the colonel was on the phone. Luckily, he didn't recognize my voice and we negotiated a deal for the stagecoach and four sorrel horses. Then I lied.

"I'll tell ya what—I busted myself up fallin' off my cuttin' horse day before last. I can't make it up there myself, but I'm gonna send one of my hired hands up with the cash to close the deal tomorrow."

It took a while but, with the help of the CB radio in my Blazer, I tracked down Bob, my hired hand. Bob met me at a cattle guard near an irrigation canal at the south end of my property and I told him the plan. He was darn near as excited about the stagecoach as I was and he welcomed the chance to get away from his regular chores for a day.

Early next morning, Bob and me took off in our pickups. I hauled the flatbed and he hauled the horse trailer. We headed up Interstate 35 through San Antonio and Austin. It was a long drive, but at least we could talk to each other on our CBs. We took Interstate 20 around the south end of Fort Worth, then caught U.S. 377 down toward Benbrook. I pulled off the highway about three miles from B and B Stables and Bob went on down to the colonel's spread. In two shakes Bob was back. Seeing the stagecoach winched and cinched on top of the flatbed made me happier than a pig in shit.

Waiting for Bob to go after the horses, I felt like a teenager hiding outside a liquor store while somebody else went in to buy me beer. I gave the stage a real good once-over. It was a little dusty and the paint was peeling, but the wood, steel, and brass fittings all had a nice solid feel. Bob was back in a flash and we headed for Laredo. Before we returned to my place, we stopped to have a veterinarian take a look at the four sorrels and verify their papers.

The next day I took the old stage to a friend, who sanded and repainted all the wood. After that, I had an upholsterer fit the interior with a nice tan belting leather. When all the work was completed, she was a mighty pretty sight. The steel rims of her bright yellow wood-spoked wheels crunched smoothly across the dirt drive as the workmen rolled her out of the upholstery shop. With the sun behind me, the fresh antique brown paint job absolutely glowed. I think I did, too. As I grabbed the polished rails and hoisted myself up into the driver's seat, I felt proud as all get out to own a piece of real western history. I laughed like a kid as I held the brand-new leather reins, bounced up and down on the driver's seat leaf springs, and hollered, "Giddy-up."

That Saturday at the orphanage, struggling all day at the reins behind the team at full speed was a real workout. It was also about the most fun I remember ever having. The laughter of the children, the wind in my hair, and the roar of the team in full gallop made me feel like John Wayne, the Lone Ranger, and Santa Claus all rolled into one. I honestly think I got a bigger kick out of that stagecoach than all those wide-eyed, excited kids. The next day, the general manager of a local country and western radio station who'd heard about my new stagecoach rushed out to have a look. He went wild when he saw it and damn near busted a blood vessel. When I took him for a ride, he made a deal with me to lease the stage for parades and special events.

Bright and early the following Monday, I threw a suitcase in my Blazer. I went out to the barn to have a quick look at the stagecoach before driving up to San Antonio Justice Court to give a deposition in the Hector Gomez case. I felt like a new man, but I was sore in muscles I didn't even know I had. Becky complained that she was starting to forget what I looked like and wanted to do some shopping in San Antone, so I took her along. We left Bob in charge of things back home for the three days we'd be gone.

My deposition lasted hours. It was the kind of routine law-enforcement task that you don't see in the movies. The assistant district attorney who took my sworn statement told me there were a total of eighteen defendants in custody and authorities had seized Hector's truck, his house, and five cars.

During the long drive home from San Antonio, all I could think about was getting back up on my new stage and taking her for a ride around the ranch. As Becky and me rolled down the last stretch of dirt road between the house and the barn, I noticed the barn doors were open. I parked the Blazer, got out, and stretched my legs. I was about to take our suitcases into the house when I noticed that the barn looked empty.

Just then, Bob walked out of the bunkhouse and stood there looking kind of fidgety. He shuffled his feet, scratched his head, and folded his arms anxiously. At first, I thought nothing of it, then I went numb. On a gut level I knew something was wrong—real wrong. I dropped the bags and raced to the barn. The horse stalls were empty. The stagecoach and the flatbed trailer were nowhere to be seen. My jaw dropped and I felt like I'd just been kicked in the gut by a mule. I just stood there frozen.

The next thing I knew, Bob was standing in the open barn doorway and I had to fight like hell to keep from grabbing a shovel and smashing something. I screamed at him. "Bob! What in the fuck happened here?"

With one hand in his side pocket and the other pulling at the back of his neck, Bob grimaced. He stammered a bit and then just blurted it all out. "Old . . . old man Hatfield and a couple of his boys come up here yesterday 'n' said y'all owed him some money."

I paced a few feet, rubbed my forehead, then kicked a barrel full of tools. "Damn it, man! This is my place and you ain't got no right to give up nothin' on it! I thought you was working for me, not Hatfield!"

Bob cringed and stuttered nervously. "But . . . but he said you owed him money and he . . ."

I cut him off and screamed again, "I don't owe that son of a bitch jack shit, and even if I did, you should have told him he'd have to take it up with me personally!"

With his head hanging low, Bob stood there in silence. I kicked one of the horse stalls and stormed off toward the house. Bob yelled, "I'm real sorry, Ray."

I was almost at the back door of the house when I stopped dead in my tracks, bowed my head, and stomped my foot. "Shit!" I turned around, looked at Bob, then slowly walked back to him. "Ah, shoot," I said. "I know you were outnumbered and probably scared out of your boots. It ain't you I should be taking this out on. It's Hatfield!" I paused, collected myself, then calmly said to him, "Why don't you get back to your chores."

With a troubled look, Bob smiled gratefully and nodded. He held his hat in his hands, nervously twisting it. Bob looked down for a second, then back up at me and said, "Thanks, Ray." He turned slowly and walked off toward his pickup.

I smashed open the screen door, went into the kitchen, filled the sink with water and ice cubes, then dunked my head. I was beside myself with rage. I just couldn't figure out why Felix Hatfield, one of the richest men in Webb County, Texas, would do a low-down thing like this to me. I'd heard word the DEA suspected him of dope smuggling, but I sure as hell didn't think he had any idea that I was anything but a cross-country trucker. I figured it had to be a mistake.

I looked up Hatfield's phone number and called. It rang a long time and I was about to give up when a man with a deep, nasal twang answered, "Hello."

Doing my best to stay cool and friendly, I asked, "Mr. Hatfield?"

"Yeah, this is Hatfield."

"My name is Ray Brown. I think there must be some kind of misunderstanding. Seems you and your men came over to my place and told my hired hand I owed you money . . . took my stagecoach and four three-year-old sorrels. Mr. Hatfield, I'd like to straighten out this mixup and get my property . . ."

Hatfield cut me off. "Why don't you just fuck off, narc!" Next thing I knew, he slammed the phone in my ear.

If his neck had been my receiver, I'd have snapped it in half with my bare hands. I stopped just short of throwing the damn phone against the wall and frantically dialed Joe Gutterson, a friend on the Laredo police force. As the phone rang, I could feel the blood rushing to my face. Even though Joe isn't a lawyer, he studied law in college. I didn't like what he had to say. He told me that since the stage and horses weren't taken by force, I didn't have much of a case. Joe said something about possession being nine-tenths of the law and that by the time I got through a court case, even if I won, the horses could be dead.

It seemed the police couldn't do a whole lot to help me. The rig wasn't purchased in my name. It was in the name of the man who let Hatfield take the stage and horses. The man they were purchased from wouldn't so much as toss me an anchor if I were drowning, let alone testify on my behalf.

I jumped in my pickup truck and tore off in a cloud of red dust. There was no way in hell I was going to sit back and let a bastard like Hatfield do me wrong like this. Speeding all the way, I drove over to my buddy J.D.'s Rivera spread, about ten miles southeast. I skidded to a stop next to the corrugated steel building where I knew I'd be most likely to find J.D. working on his helicopter.

As soon as he heard me, J.D. dropped what he was doing and rushed out. "Hey, Tex! Ain't you a sight for sore eyes! What in tarnation's your big rush? Ya got a problem?"

As we stood outside the hangar, I told J.D. about Hatfield and his men stealing my stage and team. "That man is a dope smuggler, sure as shit," J.D. said with a scowl. "My cousin David's a detective with the Laredo PD and he's been investigating Hatfield for a long time. I don't know the particulars, but there's no doubt that the man's into some heavy shit."

Things were starting to make a little more sense, but even J.D., one of my closest friends since high school, didn't know I was involved with the DEA. I had to maintain my cover.

"I still don't know what the hell I did to piss the son of

a bitch off." I turned away and blindly kicked a divot in the ground, raising a cloud of dirt.

"Who knows?" J.D. answered. "The important thing now is to get your property back from that lowlife. Let's take a ride in my chopper and get a bird's-eye view of his place and see if we can spot your stagecoach."

We rolled the helicopter out of the hangar, hopped inside, and strapped ourselves down. J.D. turned a key, flicked several switches, and the huge blades started to turn with a shrill, deafening roar. Once the blades were up to speed, J.D. gave a slight tug on the joystick and we were lifted effortlessly into the sky. We rocketed straight upward, then swung halfway around to the right as all the buildings below us appeared to rapidly shrink to the size of dollhouses.

We were flying about three times higher than the tallest oak tree as we neared Hatfield's compound. The damn place looked like somebody had plopped a gigantic resort hotel smack dab in the middle of nowhere. The main house was a monstrous, two-story Spanish villa that had a gigantic front courtyard with a circular driveway and a fountain as big as a good-sized catfish pond. Out back there was a long veranda that ran the entire width of the house. Over to one side was an outdoor kitchen and barbecue—on the other, two tennis courts and a guest house. Between all that was a body of water that looked, at first, like a small lake. The way the sun shimmered off the water and the angle J.D. and I were flying over, we couldn't make it out too clearly. As we headed out further from the house, we saw an eight-stall garage, a bunkhouse, and the biggest stable either of us had ever laid eyes on outside a racetrack. Just beyond that, there were three big barnlike buildings followed by a whole lot of wide-open space.

As J.D. took the chopper back over for another look, I couldn't believe my eyes. What we had thought was a small lake turned out to be an enormous swimming pool the shape of the state of Texas. After we got an overview,

J.D. circled the place several times at a distance while I scanned the property with his binoculars. Through the headphone intercom I hollered, "I don't see nobody!"

J.D. cringed and grabbed my arm. "Tex, you don't have to yell. I can hear ya just fine."

I just laughed and said, "No vehicles down there neither."

Just then, J.D. dropped down and went in a little closer. As we cleared the back side of the hacienda, I saw the glimmer of reddish brown through a row of shade trees. I couldn't contain myself. I yelled again. "Son of a bitch, there's my stagecoach! It's down there sure as hell, man!"

J.D. gave me a hand signal. "We're goin' in for a closer look." At that, we dropped down to just above the treetops. "Ya know, Tex, I ain't one for breakin' the law, but I am one for correctin' injustice. Goddamn it, man, I say we come back at night and reclaim what's rightfully yours. Wouldn't break my heart to do that bastard Hatfield some dirt. Look at the way that man lives off other folks' misery!"

I looked down at my stage, then back at J.D. "I tell you what, J.D., I'm gonna talk to a lawyer. There's got to be a way I can do this thing proper."

The following night I drove over to Hank's Rib House to meet J.D. and a few of our other friends. Feeling like I'd just shot a prize horse that had a broken leg, I shuffled in real slow and joined the fellows who were seated at a big picnic table toward the back. As usual, they were all telling lies, each one bigger than the next, and they were getting rowdy with the waitresses. One of the gals who was used to putting up with their guff came over and I ordered a rack of baby back ribs and a Coke. Just then, one of the boys across the table reached over and punched me lightly in the shoulder. "Tex, you look like you could use a beer."

I looked up and said, "Billy, the way I feel right now, this place ain't got enough beer to do me any good.

Besides," I continued while eyeballing his big belly that kept him a good foot from the table, "I best leave it all for a growin' boy like you." All the guys, including Billy, burst out laughing.

The laughter was short lived as Matt, who was sitting at the other end of the table, opened his mouth. "Say, Tex, I hear tell somebody hijacked your new stagecoach."

My smile died and the boys got real quiet. I pounded my fist on the table. "Man, I just come back from the lawyer's office. I just spent an hour and a half and a lotta hard-earned money just to find out that there's not a blessed thing I can do about it!" The guys all looked at each other, then turned to J.D. like he was the spokesman.

J.D. cleared his throat, then said, "Tex, I was talkin' to cousin Dave today—just in passin', mind ya. I asked how the Hatfield investigation was goin'—just makin' small talk, see—and cousin Dave told me that Hatfield's left for a couple days. Seems him and his hands took some horses over to a racetrack in Louisiana."

Barely able to contain himself, Matt cut in abruptly. "We got it all figured out, Tex! Before dawn we'll park a flatbed and a trailer just off Interstate Thirty-five near U.S. Eighty-three."

J.D. broke in, "Yea. What I'll do is put the chopper on the flatbed and we'll drive her out there to save fuel."

Matt continued, "J.D. will fly you and me into Hatfield's place one at a time."

I put my hands up and interrupted. "Now hold on just one minute, guys! You know what you're talkin' about here, don't ya?"

Matt's booming voice overpowered mine. "Tex, damn it! It ain't like we're stealin' nothin'! That stage and them horses—that's your property, man! The son of a bitch done stole 'em from you!"

Billy jumped in, "Yeah, Tex, we're all behind ya one hundred percent and we're all set to help make it right."

They obviously had had it all figured out way before I

had arrived at Hank's. After two of us were flown in, the plan was to grab the horses, hitch them to the stagecoach and drive as fast as we could off Hatfield's property. Without headlights on the stage, it all had to be timed so we'd hit I-35 at sunup. We'd cross the northbound lanes and race like hell straight up the middle of the median, run the team into the trailer, and secure the stage on the flatbed. While J.D. flew his chopper home, Matt and me would casually drive the trucks back to my place.

"Hot damn," shouted Matt, "this is gonna be fun! I always wondered what it would be like ridin' shotgun an' runnin' wide open in a stage like somebody was chasin' me."

I don't know whether it was all the enthusiasm, the fact that it sounded like a solid plan, or just my determination to get my stage and horses back that convinced me.

"We better be haulin' ass when we come up that interstate," I added. They all paused for just a second, then let out a roar as they realized I had agreed to give it a shot.

The next morning J.D. called. "Tex, I need your help installing the hay bale racks on my chopper." I was baffled. J.D. had been a professional helicopter pilot for a lot of years and sometimes in winter he'd be hired out to drop hay bales onto snowbound cattle ranches. This was the middle of summer and for the life of me I couldn't figure out what he was up to.

"You got a job somewhere in Siberia?" I asked.

He laughed. "No, not quite, but I sure could use your help. It's a little surprise for that son of a bitch Hatfield."

After breakfast, I drove down to J.D.'s. He had already started bolting one of the two steel-framed, plywood platforms to one side of the chopper. Each one had a spring-loaded arm that was controlled by a switch from inside the cockpit. The release lever had a long cable running to a mechanism that looked like the hand brake on a bicycle. The launchers' arms had about 175 pounds of spring-loaded pressure behind them and it took a lot of elbow grease to cock them.

We were almost finished mounting the second rack when I couldn't help commenting, "These things look like about the meanest skeet throwers I ever did see."

J.D. smiled and asked, "You ever see these things in action?"

I shook my head. "Nope, can't say I ever did."

"Well," he continued, "it's about the most damned fun a man can have with his pants on. When I was delivering hay to remote herds, I used to go on hay-bale bombing raids. Man, I could drop a bale right on a log or a rock or about any damned target I picked. . . ."

Laughing, I finally asked, "Well, what the hell are ya gonna do with these things tonight?"

J.D. gave me a wry grin. "You'll find out soon enough."

Just then, Billy and Matt pulled up and Billy yelled, "Hey, J.D., I got them sacks of cement like ya told me. Where do ya want 'em?"

Looking right into J.D.'s eyes, I stopped dead in my tracks. "The bastard's swimming pool?"

He never answered—just winked. The four of us then rolled the helicopter up onto J.D.'s flatbed trailer, anchored her down, and hitched the flatbed to his truck.

It was about three the next morning by the time we got to a gully near the intersection of Interstate 35 and U.S. 83. After we parked, the four of us carefully rolled the chopper off the trailer and into a clearing away from the trucks. J.D. cocked the arms of the bale throwers and we helped him secure two sixty-pound cement bags on each of the launchers. With his Bowie knife, J.D. slit the bags, then stuck a small strip of tape over each opening.

Billy stayed with the vehicles and Matt waited with him while J.D. flew me in first. With all the added weight, the helicopter seemed kind of sluggish during the twenty-mile flight to Hatfield's place. Coming in at treetop level, we dipped down into a meadow, veered to the right and headed straight for the enormous Texas-

shaped swimming pool. Letting loose with a bloodcurdling rebel yell as we approached the target, J.D. kept a
tight grip on one release lever. Not as enthusiastic, I was
hanging on for dear life. When J.D. squeezed the trigger,
the heavy bags on the right jolted from their cradle and
plunged into the water with explosive force.

The chopper lurched upward and banked to the left the
instant the load lightened. J.D. responded instinctively
and circled for another pass. On the second run, he
handed the release lever to me. The remaining bags were
on my side. We were moving in fast and close to the deck
as we approached the pool. J.D. coached me, "Steady,
boy . . . steady." The huge pool loomed up in front of us
and J.D. yelled out, "Now, Tex, now!"

I pulled the trigger and saw the bags roll off the side of
the bird. The ground was speeding past below us. It
seemed like slow motion. The water was pushed away in
all directions as the heavy sacks barreled into the pool
like freight trains. They nearly hit bottom before the
massive walls of churning water began to swallow them
up as we passed over the far side of the pool. J.D. swung
around, found a clearing near the stable, and hovered.
The big blades sent out whirlwinds and spiraling dust
devils as we gradually touched down. I jumped out, J.D.
took off, and I rushed to the stable, which I was surprised
to find unlocked.

I searched all the stalls, located my four sorrels and
verified their identities through the numbered tattoos
inside their lips. I was just about finished harnessing the
last beast when the near deafening roar signaled the
return of J.D.'s helicopter. An instant later, Matt ran
through the open stable door, chuckling and howling.
"Hot damn! That was one hell of a ride! I thought them
cement bags would damn near empty that pool!" I was
antsy. This was serious business and I was in no mood
for small talk. I just wanted to get in, get the job done,
and get out.

Together, Matt and me led the horses out to the clump

of trees where the stagecoach was stashed and hitched up the team. I double-checked every strap and we climbed aboard. I gave the reins a swift slap and off we flew across a rolling pasture toward a sparse row of shade trees. I yanked my Stetson down tight to keep the brisk wind from taking it. The light of the moon was enough to see by, but I didn't want to take the chance of winding up in a ditch in the middle of nowhere. I kept the team at a safe, steady clip.

As we got to the top of a tall grassy knoll, I yanked the reins. The horses threw their heads and we gradually slowed to a stop. In the distance the headlights on the highway looked like a long, lonely string of Christmas lights in the wilderness. We detoured around gullies and washes, then set out across a desolate stretch of pasture. I swatted the reins and the sorrels loped a little faster. As we neared the end of the field, I caught a glimpse of something dark stretching across the landscape just ahead of us.

In an instant I knew we were in trouble. "Fence!" I screamed.

"Oh, shit!" Matt yelled. Desperately, I pulled back on the reins, hit the foot break as hard as I could, then yanked the reins to the left, hoping to keep the momentum of the rig from hurling us into the rusty barbed wire. I felt my heart trying to leave my body through my throat as we finally came to a screeching stop alongside the fence.

"Damn, Tex. Better watch out y'all don't lose them horses before ya get 'em home." We scrounged through the toolbox I kept under the driver's seat and found a pair of wire cutters. Matt cut through the fence, pulled the old wires back, then I drove the team and stage on through. When we finally got to the edge of the interstate, where I expected more fence, I'd already slowed down enough for Matt to hop down and slice our way through.

It was still dark, but the eastern sky was purple, just beginning to show signs of first light. Highway traffic was sparse, but I wasn't taking any chances. Rather than risk getting out there with no lights and getting bulldozed by a semi doing ninety, we waited till dawn.

Once sunup came, I whipped the team into action and we hightailed straight across the northbound lanes, hit the median, then took off at full gallop. As we thundered down the grassy strip between the two roadways, the passing headlights cast an eerie glow through the misty morning air.

Cars slowed and some screeched to a halt when motorists saw the gloomy outline of the stagecoach and shadowy figures of the horses. We just kept flying like the wind straight down the middle of the interstate. As the sun rose, we could see the astonished faces in the passing cars. We couldn't help but laugh at all the attention we were getting.

Suddenly, a highway patrol car flashed his blue and reds alongside us. Then he sped up, pulled ahead, and swerved into our path, skidding to a halt in a cloud of dust. I pulled back on the reins and the team reluctantly trotted to a halt. The officer walked over to us with his ticket book ready. He had a big wad of chewing tobacco in his cheek. As he got close to my rig, he spat a stream of brown drool about fifteen feet, then turned to me and said, "What 'n the hell do you think you're doin'? Y'all tryin' to pull some kinda stunt here?"

I looked down at him from the driver's seat and gave him a real friendly smile. "No, sir, just out for a mornin' ride," I answered.

The patrolman scowled at me and said, "Y'all can't be drivin' this contraption on the interstate."

I smiled and told him, "Sir, I already done checked on that. Texas law clearly states that horses have the right of way on any thoroughfare."

His blank stare told me he was trying to figure out what he was going to say next. "How far did you plan on goin'?" he asked.

"Just about a mile or so. We got a pair of trailers waitin' for us down the road," I told him.

"I hope for your sake you do. If I see y'all out here

again, I'm gonna make your life real complicated."
Slapping his ticket book against his thigh, he spat and
mumbled to himself all the way back to his cruiser.

Matt stifled a laugh, I snapped the reins hard and we
tore off down the center of the interstate.

The clatter of the hooves, the creaking and squeaking
of the harnesses, and the grinding of the wheels in the
dirt woke Billy. He sat up wearily and rubbed his eyes,
then pulled himself out of the sleeping bag in the back of
his pickup. "Man, J.D.'s had time to fly home and get his
ol' lady in a family way twice by now," he jeered. We
loaded the horses first, then rolled the stage up on the
flatbed, tied her down, and were on our way.

The following Saturday my three buddies joined us
and a bunch of other friends for a celebration at the
orphanage. There must have been sixty or seventy people
in all and we spent the day riding around in the stage,
playing horseshoes, having wheelbarrow and three-
legged races. Before it was over, we had a tug of war and a
contest to see who could eat the most pie. Everybody
won.

Becky and me were dog tired by the time we got back
to the homestead with the horse trailer. I was surprised
to see the sheriff's car parked under the yellow bug lights
by my back doorstep. I drove past him to the front of the
barn just as Bob arrived with the flatbed and stagecoach.
I'd barely stepped out of my Blazer to unhitch the horse
trailer when the sheriff walked over. His hand hovered
close to his low-slung revolver and he yelled, "Ray
Brown, I got a warrant for your arrest."

My arms and legs tingled like I'd been mule kicked.
The idea of being taken away in front of my wife and
hired hand overpowered me with shame. I stood up real
slow and glared at the man. "What in the hell for?" I
demanded.

"Warrant says trespassing, horse theft, and breaking
and entering," he replied. In anger I whipped my hat to
the ground and the sheriff quickly drew his revolver and

leveled it at my chest. "Freeze! You move and I'll be takin' you off this land feet first." I assumed the position —spread-eagled across the hood of my Blazer.

A hundred forty miles later, after being cuffed and stuffed in the back of a squad car, I was booked into custody at the Bexar County Jail in San Antonio. The next day I made bail and Becky drove up to get me.

Several months later, I was in my Blazer shadowing a weapons dealer I had seen load a truck full of stolen M16's. We were passing through Del Rio, up north of Laredo, next to the Mexican border and a short distance from Laughlin Air Force Base, when I was stopped by a local cop. The officer was a rookie and didn't believe me when I showed him my credentials and told him about the suspect I was trailing. He ran a check on my license, walked back to my truck, pulled his revolver, and said, "You're under arrest, mister." I was taken in for failure to appear in San Antonio for trespassing, horse theft, and breaking and entering.

I wasted my breath trying to convince the greenhorn he was making a big mistake. I was held overnight in the Del Rio Jail and transferred to San Antonio the next morning. Again my wife met me at the Bexar County Courthouse, this time with the letter I'd received weeks earlier stating that charges had been dismissed. The judge took one look at the letter and threw the case out. Becky and me went home. I was pissed, but I figured it was over. I figured wrong.

Almost two years later, I was eating lunch at a coffee shop in downtown Laredo when a good friend, Stan Guffy of the Texas Rangers, walked in. Stan was tall and burly with short, clean-cut hair and a very distinguished appearance. I noticed he didn't seem to have the usual spring in his step as he walked over to my table. I held out my hand as I greeted him, "Stan, you old rascal. How the hell ya been?" He just stood there, several feet away, and looked down at the Stetson he was nervously tumbling through his fingers.

"I got some bad news for ya, Tex." I frowned in concern.

"Wha . . . what's the matter? Is my wife all right? Did somebody get hurt?" I asked.

Without so much as an upward glance, Stan began apologetically, "Tex . . . this is hard for me."

Dying to hear what the fuss was, I said, "Well, what in the hell is it, Stan?"

He lifted his head and looked me square in the eye. "Tex, you're under arrest!"

I laughed. "Shoot, Stan, I ain't so much as spit on a sidewalk since I don't know how long ago!"

The Texas Ranger looked down again for a second, then back at me. "Shit, Tex, this one goes back a couple years. It's about that damned stagecoach deal."

I sat back heavily in my seat, took a deep breath, then looked back up at my friend. "But that case was dismissed back then . . . twice!"

He frowned and slowly shook his head side to side. "I'm sorry. I got to do it, Tex. After you finish eating, follow me in your truck and we'll park it down at the DPS yard. It'll be safe there." Stan sat with me while I finished my meal and even offered to pay the check.

"Stan, there ain't no need to do that. This ain't your fault. How 'bout we go to lunch when this thing blows over . . . *then* you can buy." He just nodded and forced a smile.

On our way out, I stopped at the pay phone and called Duke McMann collect. This time I wasn't being arrested in the line of duty and I felt pretty low down about it. I explained what was going on, that it must be another mistake, that the charges had been dismissed twice before. What he had to say was not very encouraging. "Tex, I'll see what I can do, but I think you're pretty much on your own this time."

As he walked me out to my Blazer, Stan put a big hand on my shoulder and said, "I ain't supposed to tell you this, but you remember Billy Dee Truscott?"

I thought for a second, then answered, "As a matter of

fact, I do. Is he still with the Rangers? That S.O.B. almost got me killed when I was workin' with him."

Stan squinted into the bright afternoon sun and said, "Well, you must've done somethin' to get him riled, because he came across an old warrant with your name on it and decided to churn up the embers and feed the flames on your case."

I forced a laugh and said, "Well, he's doin' a right good job of puttin' me out, I'll tell ya."

We pulled into the back lot of the Webb County Jail in Laredo. As we approached the door to the jailhouse, Stan stopped, looked down with his hands on his hips. "Tex, man, this makes me feel like shit, but I got to cuff ya. I'll put 'em on real loose."

I half smiled and told him, "Don't worry yourself none, Stan. You got to do what you got to do."

The sound of those cuffs clamping down on my wrists sent a shiver up my backbone. When Stan and me reached the jail entrance, I stopped short. "Oh, shit, Stan! I plumb forgot about my damn guns! There's a .38 in my left boot and a .25 auto up inside the crown of my hat. It'd be a good idea if y'all took 'em from me, don't ya think?"

"I'll take good care of 'em for ya, Tex," he promised.

I could see the hurt in my wife Becky's eyes when she brought me a book to read and to say good-byes. About one thirty in the afternoon on the second day of my incarceration at Webb County, I was ushered out of my cell to take a call from Duke McMann. He was obviously concerned. "What I'm about to tell you may not help ya in court . . . but, do you recall that information you leaked to the San Antonio *Express* about a year and a half ago?"

"Sure," I said as my eyes widened remembering the incident. "I tipped 'em that the tomato-processing company was a front for the Mafia and they was buyin' up land in south Texas."

"Right," Duke continued calmly. "I found out there are some pretty powerful people behind all your troubles.

They want to shut you down, but there's no way we can prove it."

That night I was taken on another hundred-forty-mile ride with my hands shackled behind me. I believe that trip to San Antonio, twisting and turning to prevent the cuffs from biting into my wrist bones and keep my circulation going, was the most humiliating, degrading experience of my life. Being booked and standing for my mug shots didn't add one inch to my shrinking self-esteem. By the time the officer was rolling my fingers, one by one, in black ink, my dishonor had turned to rage. I felt my blood boiling while I was led down a series of drab corridors through several sets of locked, steel-barred doors. Every square foot of the place was painted battleship gray. Finally, I was directed into the musty holding cell where I spent the night.

The following morning's breakfast was a bowl of watery oatmeal and an eight-ounce carton of milk. Later, I was taken into court for arraignment. I entered a plea of not guilty and the judge refused to release me on bond. There was nothing that could be said to change his mind. The lady counselor who represented me until my attorney and old family friend, Joe Albertson, could get up to San Antone, requested a speedy trial. The judge set a date twenty-one days away. I was hauled out of the courtroom and off to a different cell. It was a large holding tank with four Mexicans and an immense, powerfully built Anglo guy whose sun-darkened, weathered skin was covered with a mass of tattoos and scars.

Disheartened, I slumped down on a bench close to a bare, yellowed light bulb shining in the hallway. I opened my book, but from the corner of my eye couldn't help noticing the massive Anglo prisoner watching me. The big guy stood up and took a step toward me. "I know you from somewhere," he grunted. I glanced up over the top of my book for a second, then turned my attention back to my reading. "Hey!" yelled the behemoth, "I'm talking to you!"

I put my book down slowly and looked straight up at him. "Pardner . . . it seems we're goin' to be here for a while, so we better learn to get along with each another or there's gonna be a problem." The huge man seemed lost for words as he stood silently frowning. He sat down and I went back to my book.

I'd read about three-quarters of a page when the big lummox jumped up and screamed, "You're the son of a bitch that put me away four years ago!" He lunged across the cell with his huge hands leveled at my throat. Just as he was about to throttle me, I planted the heel of my boot squarely into his gut. He doubled over with pain and, holding his midsection, took a couple steps backward. Now he was even angrier. Before he had a chance to come at me again, I leaped out of my seat and slammed my forehead into his nose as hard as I could. Then I grabbed both sides of his collar in a cross grip and tightened it around his neck like a tourniquet. The giant punched me in the eye and the rib cage while I held my choke grip on his shirt. He thrashed and gasped wildly for a couple seconds before slumping to the floor.

The four Mexicans sharing the cell sat in wide-eyed amazement. In whispered Spanish, they debated whether I'd killed the huge Anglo. I grabbed the unconscious man's feet and motioned my cell mates over to help. They approached reluctantly, stood over the man's motionless body, made the sign of the cross, then helped me lift the carcass up onto a bunk. I reassured them my attacker was still alive. I offered them each five dollars a day, which they happily accepted, to keep watch while I slept and see to it that I stayed healthy for the rest of my twenty-one-day stay.

If I got any sleep at all during the next six nights, it was with one eye open and my back to the wall. In the early hours of the seventh day I was awakened by one of my Mexican bodyguards. José, who had been sitting on the floor at the foot of my cot, was shaking my legs and hollering frantically. *"¡Cuidado! ¡Señor!* Wake up!"

Instinctively, I bolted out of bed just in time to see the faint outline of a hulking figure coming at me through the darkness. One of my other bodyguards, Juan, grabbed for the brute's legs but was brushed away by an enormous hand. As my attacker was damn near on top of me, I wound up and punched as hard as I could. My fist connected dead on with the man's collarbone, snapping it in two with a loud, gut-wrenching crack. He screamed in agony, staggered aimlessly, and finally slumped down onto one of the cots.

It was a good minute later when two guards rushed to our cell with flashlights. Once they were sure it wasn't a setup, they unlocked the door. One maintained his position outside while the other checked on the injured prisoner. "Must have fallen out of bed, officer," I said. Both guards gave me cold stares and the giant was helped off to the infirmary.

On my day in court, Joe Albertson arrived in San Antone early and sent for me. A guard ushered me into a visitors' room where my old friend sat on the far side of a long wooden bench shuffling papers in his dog-eared briefcase. Maybe it was my imagination, but for as long as I could recall, Joe stayed the same. He was a tall, white-haired, pink-cheeked, roly-poly Southern gentleman in his sixties. I'd been expecting him to retire for years and more than once was grateful he hadn't.

As I sat down, the foot-high strip of glass seemed to separate us more than physically. Joe appeared very formal, very serious, which didn't encourage me too much. He leaned forward. "Hello, Tex. How have you been?" Without waiting for my answer, he went on. "I spoke with the prosecuting attorney about your case and it doesn't look too promising for us." I just looked at Joe. I know there was a frown on my face as he continued. "I don't think you're going to the penitentiary over this thing but . . ."

That was about all I could stand. I cut him off and demanded, "What are you tellin' me, counselor? What the hell is going on?"

With a heavy sigh, Joe said, "Well, Tex, you have options. You might consider a plea agreement."

I clenched my teeth and shook my head sternly. "No. I won't do it."

Joe shrugged his shoulders and told me, "Tex, we don't have a case. Oh, sure, you might luck out and get a jury to side with you . . . but if you lose the case . . . well, these are serious charges."

Still shaking my head, I made it plain as the beard on my face. "I ain't copping no plea. I just want to tell my side of it, Joe."

The prosecutor finished presenting his case against me before the judge and it was Joe's turn to speak. He rose slowly, stepped away from the table where I sat before the bench, looked back at me, then solemnly turned to the judge. "Your honor, my client wishes to approach the bench." The judge scowled, looked at his watch, looked at me, then nodded in agreement. I stood before him and explained what I used the stagecoach for and how it was taken from me by a known drug smuggler. By his expression, it was real clear the judge didn't seem to give a tinker's damn about a word I was saying.

Ultimately, after I rambled on a bit longer, he asked just one question. "Did you, or did you not, go to the Hatfield ranch and take the property in question? Yes or no?" I felt cornered. There was no way out. I put my hands on my hips and just stared blankly at the judge. Unable to conceal my utter frustration, I all but screamed out my response.

"Your honor, I . . . I did do that, but . . ." The sharp crack of wood on wood right in front of my nose felt like a slap in the face. "Guilty," he pronounced as he slammed the gavel. "Mr. Brown, would you prefer I schedule a future date for sentencing or carry out sentencing forthwith?"

I glanced back in disgust at Joe, turned back to face the judge and said, "Today, your honor. Now, please." I held my breath.

"Mr. Brown, these are very serious charges. I see in

looking over your record, however, that this is your first offense. To your credit, a number of letters of reference have been submitted by respected members of various law-enforcement agencies. I have decided to sentence you to one year's probation. You are free to go, Mr. Brown."

CHAPTER 6

Free to go. Those words burned into my brain like they'd been stamped there with a branding iron. But I sure as hell wasn't going to lie down and take the guilty verdict without a fight. I knew it'd take time and money, but I was damn sure going to clear my name. As I walked away from the judge's bench, I shot a cold glance at Joe, who was trying to look busy stuffing his briefcase. He saw the look on my face and froze as I stormed past him. He shut and latched his case and hurried after me.

"Tex! Hold on a minute!" Joe said as he rushed through the swinging gate that divided the courtroom. Without giving Joe a second look, I tore through the courtroom at top speed, pounded the heavy oak door open with my fist, and bolted down the corridor. I stopped outside the courthouse and cooled my heels a little. Joe caught up with me and set his hand on my shoulder. I pulled away, wheeled around to face him with my fist drawn back, ready to throw a right cross. I caught myself and turned away, my fists still clenched.

I paced a couple steps, turned to him again, and said, "I'm real disappointed, Joe. There must've been somethin' you could have said to the judge, somethin' you could've done."

Joe looked me square in the eye and forced a smile.

"Tex, we're going to appeal this thing. You mark my words, we'll . . ."

"Damn it, Joe! That affidavit was phony and you know it! I got the bill of sale that Bob signed over to me. I figured you'd put up more of a fight than that!"

Joe kept his cool. He gave me a fatherly pat on the shoulder. "Now, Tex, I know you're riled up about this. Hell, I'd be surprised if you weren't. Why don't you go home and take a long hot bath, go fishing, or get on a horse and ride off somewhere. I'll take care of all this."

I shook his hand halfheartedly and nodded in agreement. Becky was waiting for me in the Blazer. After we got rolling, she grabbed my right hand from the steering wheel and held it tight with both her hands. I didn't talk much about the trial. There wasn't much to say. I wasn't very good company during the long haul back to the homestead.

I couldn't rightly work for the government with this conviction hanging over my head. I wasn't even supposed to carry a gun until my probation was up, but there was no way in hell I was going to set foot outside my door without a handgun to protect myself. There was no telling when or where I'd meet up with somebody I'd busted before—somebody set on revenge.

My court costs would bankrupt me pretty soon if I didn't find some work. I knew I could always go back to independent trucking, but just hauling lettuce wasn't going to pay all the bills.

By the time we got home I was tired and road weary, but the day wasn't over and I had to get my tail in gear. Becky went on to the store after I took her luggage into the house.

I pulled out a small leather address book and looked up some of the bail bondsmen I used to work for. The first place I called was Ace's Bail Bonds in Houston. No work for me there. Then I called Jake Roberts. Jake was surprised to hear about all the shit that had been shoveled at me after I repossessed my stagecoach. He said he felt real bad about not being able to hire me. Most of the bondsmen I'd ever worked for had at least some idea that I'd moved on up into law enforcement and it kind of hurt my pride having to come back to them looking for work.

I finally got hold of a good friend named Big Jack Bowlin up in Houston. I had worked for Jack quite a bit during my bounty-hunting days. He was exactly what his name implied, weighing in at about 475 pounds and standing six foot six. He had a flat-top crew cut and always wore neatly pressed, very businesslike pinstripe suits. Every morning like clockwork Jack sat down to a double stack of buttermilk pancakes with maple syrup and a pound of crisply fried bacon, all of which he washed down with four big glasses of milk.

To me the man was big-hearted Jack. He had taken care of me years earlier after I'd had a truck accident and was too busted up to work. I paid him back in full and he never charged me one red cent of interest. I didn't feel so bad about going to Jack for work because he was like family to me.

Jack answered the phone in his usual husky, jolly-sounding voice and was real happy to hear from me. We shot the breeze for a minute before I got to the point. "Sounds like you're gettin' a raw deal, Tex," he said in a serious tone. "I'll tell ya what—I got a guy that skipped out on a fifty-five-thousand-dollar bond. His record shows he was busted with six hundred forty-five pounds of marijuana and he's due back in court fourteen days from now. For you, Tex, I'll give fifteen percent to get him back."

"I really appreciate that, Jack."

"Shit, don't thank me yet, son. This guy's a real bad-ass—can't even use regular handcuffs on the son of a bitch, his damned wrists are so big. And, Tex, he's been known to carry a knife, so watch yourself."

"I'll tell ya, Jack, the son of a bitch would be a damned fool takin' a knife to a gunfight."

Jack broke up in his deep baritone laugh, then went on with the briefing. "The guy's name is Robert Bloomfield. His last known residence was in Lubbock at Thirty-three Thirteen East Ninety-eighth Street, apartment number fourteen. Now if he ain't there, his wife'll know where he's at for sure. I'm gonna send ya some photos of Bloomfield along with his rap sheet. Want me to send it all to your place?"

"I figure I'd better get a head start on this deal, Jack. Tell ya what. There's a truck stop on Interstate Twenty up by Big Spring—it's called the Mustang Truck Stop."

Jack paused, mumbled slightly, and asked me to hold on while he wrote down the address. I waited till he was done writing before I continued. "Jack, I'm sort of in a bind. With all the lawyer's fees, fines, mortgage, and the like, I'm a little strapped. I wonder if you'd advance me some runnin' money? I hate askin' ya like this, but . . ."

"Don't give it another thought, Tex. I'll have it wired to ya as quick as I can."

I told Jack to send the money to a Western Union office about two blocks from the Segovia Truck Stop in Junction. It was on Interstate 10, about 260 miles away—which would put me about halfway to Lubbock. The people at the Segovia knew me, so there'd be no problem cashing the Western Union check. Since Junction was on the way to Big Spring and the money would be wired right away, I figured I'd pick it up, refuel, and visit with friends for a day. That would give the photos plenty of time to reach the Mustang Truck Stop ahead of me.

I wandered out to my empty barn and stood silent just inside the door, watching thin wisps of dust whirl through shafts of sunlight that poured between the old boards. It was almost like looking at a ghost town. The old gray wood posts and rails of the horse stalls were bowed and gnawed down in spots. The emptiness of that barn gave me an eerie feeling I couldn't shake. I'd arranged for a friend to board all my horses and take the stagecoach in case the state had any notions about confiscating them. I knew I would have to sell the lot of them to keep my head above water. I tried not to think too hard about what might have been or about the kids at the orphanage.

I went back inside the house and started packing for the trip. Becky finally came through the front door with an armload of groceries and I grabbed one of the bags from her and set it on the counter. She saw the suitcase standing near the door. She also spotted my shotgun and .45 laid out on a piece of newspaper with cleaning rods, solvent, and cotton gun-cleaning patches. She stared at them for a second, then turned to me as her eyes welled up with tears and asked, "When do you have to go?"

"Look, darlin'," I told her in a reassuring tone, "this deal'd like to bankrupt us. I'm gonna go out and make me some money like I used to."

"Man hunting?" she said with a worried frown.

"Now, hon, don't you worry. Big Jack's sendin' me on a milk run—a real easy job—and I'll be back before ya know it."

With a sniffle, Becky wiped a tear from her eye. Doing her best to hide her fear, she said, "Raymond Brown! If you go off and get yourself killed, I swear I'll never speak to you again!"

I gave her a big hug and lightly stroked her long, brown hair. "I'm leavin' tonight. Tell ya what. Why don't we go out to a restaurant for supper? Would ya like that?" Becky smiled and nodded.

As we drove home from the restaurant, I could tell that Becky wanted to know where I was going, but she was fighting the urge to ask. She knew the rules. I felt it was better she didn't know where I went when I was bounty hunting. As we got to the road leading to our house, I broke the silence. "If anybody asks where I'm at, tell 'em I'm haulin' a load of onions to Florida, okay?"

She squeezed my hand. "You know I don't like stretching the truth to our friends . . ."

I shook my head and firmly told her, "It's not our

friends I'm worried about, but I can't have the wrong people knowin' about my business. It's just to protect the both of us."

After we got home, I threw my suitcase into the sleeper cab of the Mack, gave Becky a long hug and a kiss, and was on my way.

Traveling long stretches of road gives a man a lot of time to think—maybe too much time. I just had to pray and to believe that my name would be cleared, the bills would get paid, and we'd all live happily ever after. I took Highway 83 north, directly to Junction, Texas, at Interstate 10. I went to the Western Union office just off the interstate and, sure enough, the check was waiting for me. Next I stopped in at the Segovia Truck Stop. Cathy, the manager, knew me as a regular customer from years back. She didn't think twice about cashing the check for me.

I fueled up, checked the oil and tires, then got on the phone and made a social call to DPS Sergeant Al San Angelo. Al told me to come on by, have dinner with him and his wife that night, and visit awhile. Al's wife, Doris, insisted I stay overnight in their guest room. The next morning—after Doris fixed us a nice big breakfast—Al went to work and I was back on the road.

I continued north on 83, then took 87 northwest into Big Spring. As I climbed into higher country, it did my heart good to get a change of scenery. The low rolling hills and valleys were covered in a blanket of green and dotted with wildflowers. The sky was clear and bright overhead, but in the distance far ahead of me there were ominous storm clouds, and every once in a while I saw the flash of lightning.

Before I reached Interstate 20, I pulled into the parking lot of a hardware store. Since this fugitive I was after was so damned big, I bought eight feet of heavy steel chain and six good-sized padlocks.

It was around lunchtime when I arrived at the Mustang Truck Stop. I went to the fuel desk, picked up the big brown envelope that was waiting for me, sat down at a booth in the busy coffee shop, and ordered lunch. I tuned out the loud voices and the clatter of plates and silver-ware as I studied the contents of the package. The black-and-white mug shots showed Bloomfield to be six foot eight with cold, dark eyes set close together and sunk into an overhanging brow. His nose was wide at the bridge and bent to one side. He had no neck to speak of, just a big, pudgy head sitting right on top of a pair of muscular shoulders. Bloomfield's rap sheet listed arrests for assault with a deadly weapon and armed robbery, along with various drug charges and pages full of minor offenses.

After I finished lunch, the waitress filled my thermos bottle with coffee. I tipped her, paid the cashier, then went to a pay phone. I needed a car or a pickup truck to hunt Bloomfield, so I called a man named Don Jameson up in Lubbock.

About seven years earlier, a leaky radiator hose had brought me and Don together. It was early evening and my old black Mack's engine started to overheat as I rolled into Lubbock on my way to Amarillo. I pulled into a truck stop to see what the trouble was. As I drove toward the back of the lot and started to swing the rig around before backing into a slot, I caught sight of a scuffle behind a building about seventy-five yards to my left. I geared up and drove toward the commotion, getting as close as I could, then jumped down out of the cab and ran over to the ruckus.

There were five men. One was being held by two others while getting whomped on by another. I was about thirty feet away when I caught the flash of a knife in the hand of one of the attackers. I drew my .45 autoloader and fired a shot into the air. Three of the assailants bolted away and turned a corner, but the one with the knife wound up like he was fixing to throw the blade at me. Quick as I could, I crouched, aimed, and fired two quick shots at the man. The impact from the quarter-ounce chunks of lead hitting his right thigh picked him up off his feet, spun him face forward, and dropped him like a rag doll on his left shoulder at the feet of Don Jameson, the man who would become one of my best friends. Don was bleeding and busted up pretty bad. The other three men got away with his wallet, but his life was the important thing and he still had that.

Don was a wildcat trucker, and since the job takes him on the road most of the time, I was lucky to catch him at home when I called. "Hey, Don! How the hell are ya, son?"

"Tex Brown, you old dog! Where are you?"

"I'm at the Mustang Truck Stop in Big Spring and I'm on my way up into your neck of the woods."

"Shoot, man, stop on by and I'll have Connie fix us up a big supper. Whad'ya say?"

"Well, sure Don. Ah, yeah, I'll be in Lubbock by this evenin'. Say, listen, I need to ask a favor. I'm comin' into town to find a bail jumper and I wonder if I can rent your pickup truck?"

"Hell, no, you can't rent my pickup, but I'll damn sure let ya borrow it. Just come on over as quick as ya can."

Once I hit Lubbock, I wound my way through the narrow streets till finally I saw the house and geared down. The brakes whistled and screeched, bringing me to a stop in front of Don's place. The shadow cast by my Mack damn near covered the entire block as the sun began to set. From the cab of my rig I could look over just about all the rooftops in Don's quiet little neighborhood.

His house was a modest, one-story, red-brick, three-bedroom job with sun-bleached, gray wooden roof shingles and a small screened-in front porch. The front yard was small with short dry grass, neatly trimmed shrubs, and a short silver chain-link fence along the sidewalk.

As I got out of the truck, Don; his wife, Connie; and their son Mike came out to greet me. "You sure are looking good for an old man, Tex."

I shook Don's hand. "Old! Shoot, Don, I done run outa' birthdays at thirty-five."

He slapped me on the shoulder, laughed, and said,

"Hey, don't try'n con a con man, now. Come on inside, Tex."

Connie and Mike said hello and headed toward the porch in front of us. Don put his hand on my shoulder, stopped short, and in a low voice said, "Say, speakin' of birthdays . . . Mike just turned fourteen and I was wonderin' . . . he's heard a whole lot about ya, Tex, and with him bein' on his way to manhood'n all . . . could Mike go with ya on this bounty hunt? He knows his way around town."

"I don't see why not. I could use the company. But I ain't gonna have him there when I take the man down. I can't be responsible for Mike's safety."

Don smiled and patted me on the back. "Don't let him get in your way," he said as we walked inside.

The house smelled like pine trees and home cooking. The rooms were small and the ceilings were low. A lamp in the corner cast a yellow glow through the tidy living room. The wood floor was covered in the center by a brown spiral throw rug and the furniture had an antique look to it. The walls were covered with old family pictures and some of Don's trophies—a stuffed bass on a plaque and the mounted head of a four-point deer.

As we sat down, the table was filled with steaming hot fried chicken, mashed potatoes, gravy, and green peas with carrots. We said grace and I ate like there was no tomorrow. After supper Don and I played a few games of pool on the table he had set up in his basement. Finally, I excused myself, explaining that I wanted to get an early start the next morning, and Don showed me to the guest room Connie had fixed for me.

After breakfast the following day, Don gave me the keys to his pickup, then young Mike led the way to the truck.

"Take good care of my boy now, Tex, hear?" yelled Don from the porch as I fired up the engine.

I waved to him as I backed out of the drive and we were on our way.

When we got to the end of the street, Mike turned and asked, "What are you gonna do when you find this man? You gonna kill him?" I scowled at him for a second, then shook my head.

"Son, I'm bringin' a fugitive to justice. The man was arrested and he ran away. I'm just trying to get him back so our criminal justice system can give him the fair and speedy trial he deserves."

Mike frowned thoughtfully. I truly believed the words I was telling the boy, but I realized that what I had just described was about the opposite of what I'd just gone through in my own court case.

"Why did you save my daddy from those robbers?" Mike asked curiously.

I looked over at him and said with a smile, "Because the man was in trouble."

"But you didn't even know him then. Why did you risk your own life?" he persisted.

I thought hard for a second. "Ya know, that's somethin' that a man just don't think about when it happens. I did it because . . . well . . . because it was the right thing to do . . . and because I'd want somebody to do the same for me if I was in that situation." Mike smiled and nodded in agreement.

The address listed on Bloomfield's rap sheet was on the south side of town. Mike showed me some shortcuts and back ways through the city streets. We got to the building, but there was a vacancy sign on the apartment. I saw an old woman sitting on a lawn chair next door, so I walked over to talk to her.

"Howdy, ma'am. I'm tryin' to find Robert Bloomfield . . . looks like he's moved. You wouldn't know where he went, would ya?"

The woman squinted and shielded her eyes against the sun as she looked up. "They done moved out nearly three weeks ago. They was having a real fight . . . not that I was tryin' to listen in, mind ya. It's these walls—they're paper thin."

"That's fine, ma'am, but . . ."

"I think he done hit them kids . . . and I know he's been beatin' his poor wife. Say, are you a cop or somethin'?"

"Ah, no, ma'am. I'm just a concerned citizen like yourself and I just wanted to try'n talk some sense into the man is all."

"Thank the Lord. That woman can surely use all the help she can get."

Trying to muster all the patience I could, I asked again, "Well, do ya know where they went, ma'am?"

The old woman shook her finger as if to convince me. "Now I ain't one to eavesdrop, mind ya, but I do recall them talkin' about Levelland, Texas. He said he had a pipe-layin' job waitin' for him and somethin' about nobody knowin' him up there."

"Much obliged, ma'am," I said as I tipped my hat and walked back to the pickup.

I opened the driver's side and was about to hop in when I turned and hollered, "Ma'am, you wouldn't by chance know what Bloomfield was drivin', would ya?"

The lines in her face deepened and she was silent for a few seconds before snapping her gnarled fingers. "Why, yes! It was an old black pickup truck—a Ford, I think. Oh, and the license plate was AB-one-three-two. I remember because my old phone number was very . . ."

"Much obliged, ma'am," I yelled as I cut her off and quickly jumped in the pickup.

We headed out on State Highway 114, west about forty miles, past Reese Air Force Base to Levelland. It was a sunny day and Mike was good company. We both got a kick out of watching fighter planes zoom across the sky.

Levelland wasn't a bustling metropolis, but searching every street and alleyway would take more time than I had. It was getting close to noontime. Connie had packed us a big lunch of roast beef sandwiches, apples, and pecan pie. I pulled into a convenience store and Mike went inside to buy us a couple of sodas. After we ate, I went to the pay phone and dialed information. The operator showed no listing for a Robert Bloomfield, so I called three major credit card offices to see what I could find out. He didn't have an account with any of them.

I was about to dial the power company when the loud grumbling of a 454 engine caught my attention. Glancing up, I saw an old black Ford step-side pickup truck. It pulled up right next to the loaner I was driving. I might have turned my attention back to the phone if I hadn't been distracted by Mike's excitement. Watching the tall, powerfully built man step out of the truck next to him, Mike all but fell out the passenger-side window. As the big guy crossed the sidewalk and made his way toward the front door of the market, Mike yelled to me. "Tex! Hey, Tex, it's . . ."

Before Mike could get one more word out, I ran toward him and outshouted him. "I told ya, boy, no Twinkies before supper! You're gonna get a whippin' if ya keep up this infernal hollerin'!"

As soon as the man entered the store, I checked his license plate, then jumped in Don's pickup and backed out. "Yeah, I know," I said to Mike, "I know that's him, but ya can't go yellin' like that, Mike. I got to surprise him."

I drove about eighty yards down the street and parked facing away from the store. I left the engine running and kept an eye on Bloomfield's vehicle in the rearview mirror. When he pulled out and headed in the opposite direction, I swung the truck around and took off after him. He accelerated quicker than I expected and I had to step on it to catch him. The narrow road was filled with oncoming traffic and cars parked along both curbs. We were going north and I was tailing about fifty yards behind. Suddenly, a van pulled into my lane from a side street. It was so damned big and moved so slow I lost sight of the Ford pickup. I couldn't pass. I couldn't do a damn thing but honk the horn and pray.

I thought I had lost him until Mike jumped up and down in his seat, pointed out his window, and hollered. "Tex! He's turnin' right! He's turnin' right!"

We finally reached the street Mike saw Bloomfield take

and I barreled around the corner. The black Ford was about two hundred yards away when he turned left at a traffic light. I laid a patch of rubber as I stepped on the gas and brought the truck up to about sixty-five miles an hour. The light was red when we got to it and I was tempted to run it. If I'd been alone, I probably would have. With young Mike in the truck, it would not only set a bad example, I'd be risking the boy's life to boot.

After what seemed like an eternity, the light changed, then I had to wait for oncoming traffic to clear the intersection. I turned left, but there was no need to hurry. The Ford was nowhere in sight. I drove the area for hours while Mike and me looked up and down every street. I hoped Bloomfield hadn't parked inside a garage or backyard.

By late afternoon the sun was blocked by clouds in the west. The sky was blue, but there were no shadows below and everything looked gray. We had wound our way back and forth through ten-plus miles of neighborhood streets. Tired and bored, Mike was leaning against the passenger door when I looked over and smiled. "Still wanna be a bounty hunter? Ain't like ya see it in the movies, is it?" He frowned wearily. "I'll take ya home pretty soon . . . I just wanna cover a little more ground before dark."

Fifteen minutes later, the sky was dark blue with a streak of blood red across the horizon. As I started to pull out of the subdivision, Mike bounced back to life. "I think I see him! Stop!"

I stomped my foot to the floor, jammed the truck in reverse, backed up, pulled to the right, and slowly cruised up the street. "I'll be darned, Mike," I said with a laugh. "You got a good eye."

It was a small house, not more than forty feet across, with a dirt driveway on the right-hand side and a small bare tree on the left. There were two little orange plastic tricycles on the barren front lawn. The black Ford pickup was in the drive and there was still enough daylight left to read the license plate.

I continued driving up the street. "Ya gonna go get'm now?" Mike asked.

I glanced at him and grinned. "When the time is right, boy. I got a plan."

I stopped the truck about six houses away and shut the engine down. Through the rearview mirror, I kept an eye on the place. While we waited, Mike tried to keep us both entertained by telling jokes. I told him every clean one I knew along with a few that were just this side of an R rating. It got late and I noticed there were no lights at the house where Bloomfield's truck was parked. Slowly, I drove around the block, finally passing the house.

"I'm takin' ya home, son."

Mike looked surprised. "Ain't ya gonna catch him?" he asked.

"I'm sorry, boy. Like I told your daddy, it's too dangerous for ya. I'd be responsible if anything happened to ya, so I'll get him tomorrow." Mike was quiet during the ride home. I felt bad that the boy was disappointed, but I'd rather have him mad at me for the rest of his life than to have my conscience gnaw at me for the rest of mine if anything happened to him.

I parked Don's pickup in his driveway. "I'll tell ya what, Mike," I said as we got out, "when ya get bigger, maybe I'll take ya along for the capture. Would ya like that?" Mike just looked at me, slammed the truck door, and ran inside. Slowly, I followed.

Relaxing in the living room, I told Don and Connie how our day had gone and explained that I was going to spend the night in the sleeper cab in Levelland so I'd have an early start. I was back on the road within an hour.

I've always said I'd rather count on the sun than an alarm clock to wake me. When I got into Levelland and found a diner, I maneuvered my rig into a slot facing east, had a bite to eat, then I crawled up into the sleeper and turned in for the night. Next morning, the warm golden rays of sunrise nudged me into consciousness. I grabbed a tall coffee to go at the diner, drove up

Bloomfield's street, and slowly rolled my noisy old semi past his house.

The black Ford was still in the driveway. After circling the block once, I stopped in front of the house and left the engine running. I grabbed a clipboard and the brown paper bag that held the chain and padlocks. I tucked my Colt .45 in the back of my belt and climbed out of the cab.

I heard the sound of children's voices inside as I reached the door. I knocked, then stepped ten feet back and waited. The door opened about six inches and a woman peered out at me past a thin brass door chain. She was dressed in a tattered robe and fuzzy slippers. With a cigarette dangling from her mouth, she blinked and squinted through the bright sunlight.

"Yeah, whad'ya want?" she said.

"Good morning, ma'am. I'm sorry to disturb y'all at this hour." I took a hard look at the clipboard in my hand. "I got a load of furniture for a mister . . . ah, looks like Albertson or maybe Alverez. I can't even read this derned writing. Anyway, I'm lost and my pride would suffer somethin' fierce if I was to call in to my employer. Can y'all tell me where . . ."

The woman took a long drag on her cigarette. "Look," she said, "hold on just a minute." She backed away and shut the door.

Thirty seconds later, the door burst open and out stepped Robert Bloomfield, ducking as he dragged his bulky frame through the threshold. He wore a black T-shirt and old jeans. He was barefoot. "What'n the hell do you want, mister?"

I held my clipboard at arm's length like I was studying it and scratched my neck. "As I explained to your wife, sir, I'm lost and I can't even read this damned writing. I'm looking for Whitlow or Whitman street . . . could even be Wichita, I don't know." I offered the clipboard to him and shook my head in frustration.

Bloomfield came a few steps closer, then I looked over at his truck and said, "I'll be damned! Ya don't see too many of those beauties on the road nowadays." As I turned and walked over to his truck, I carefully pulled the autoloader out of my belt and covered it with the clipboard.

Bloomfield followed, grinning ear to ear at my supposed interest in his truck. "Yeah, I got a four-fifty-four hemi-head engine in her and . . ."

He stopped dead in his tracks as I spun around and leveled the bore of my .45 at his nose. "We can do this easy or hard—your choice, but I'm takin' ya back to Houston. Up against the truck! Move!"

Bloomfield stood frozen, his eyes wild and glazed. I flicked the thumb safety off with a crisp snap. "They don't care which parts of ya I bring in, just so long as you're breathin'." Slowly, he moved over to the truck and spread his oversized palms on the hood. I patted him down, checking for weapons. "All right, face down on the ground! Do it!" Reluctantly, he stretched his enormous body out in the dirt. "Hands together, out in front of your head!" I whipped the chain out, looped one end tightly around his left wrist and snapped one huge padlock through the links, then locked another around his right wrist. "Roll over!" I ordered as I held the length of chain in one hand and my Colt in the other. He complied, I pulled the chain tight, yanked his hands down toward his feet, shackled his ankles together, and left just enough slack so he could walk.

I ordered Bloomfield to his feet. The chain connecting his hands and feet forced him to shuffle his way along, bent over, as I ushered him to the cab of my Mack.

"I ain't gettin' up in that truck," he protested loudly.

"Suit yourself," I said. With that, I grabbed the padlock that secured an excess length of chain, unlocked it, fastened it to the handrail on the side of my rig, ran around, and climbed into the cab. "It's a long way to Houston, boy!" I yelled as I clutched in, threw her in first, and crept forward about thirty feet.

Bloomfield hollered like a stuck pig and pounded wildly on the passenger door.

I jammed on the brakes, leaned out the window, and laughed. "Did you say you'd rather ride up front with me?" Out of breath, Bloomfield nodded in agreement. I jumped down, walked over, and fished in my pocket for the key.

I was about to open the lock when I heard the woman's voice behind me. "Hold it right there, mister!" I froze solid and cautiously turned my head till I saw Mrs. Bloomfield holding a twelve-gauge shotgun on me. My pistol was under the seat of my truck.

"Ma'am," I said calmly, "I'm an officer of the court and I've got a warrant for your husband's arrest."

"Yeah?" she said as her angry look softened a little. "Let me see it."

Carefully, I reached for the court papers. "Please, ma'am, point that thing away. You're liable to scatter both me and your husband."

I handed her the document and watched her lips move slightly as she read. All at once, she flew off the handle. "So that's why we moved!" she shouted as she threw the papers at me, lowered the shotgun, and stormed back into the house. I took a deep breath, shook my head, released my prisoner from the handrail, and, because of the way he was chained, damn near broke my back helping hoist him up into the cab. Finally, he was settled in on the passenger side and I locked the trailing length of chain to the post under the seat.

Once I powered up and got moving, Bloomfield started thrashing around in his chains and cursing. "You low-down, sorry son of a bitch! This is fuckin' chicken shit!"

I reached over, grabbed the length of chain connecting his hands and feet, and gave it one swift shake. "Pipe down, asshole! We got five hundred forty miles to Houston. If ya don't shut the fuck up, I'm gonna slap duct tape across your mouth, toss ya back in my refrigerated trailer, and keep ya chilled out at forty-five degrees for a spell. If you think I'm bluffin', you just try me, man."

Bloomfield sat quiet, but he gave me one mean, dirty

sneer. I took Highway 84 south to Interstate 20 and went east. About five hours of steady driving got us to Fort Worth, where I pulled into a truck stop for fuel, food, and a fresh supply of hot coffee. I took a burger to Bloomfield, who wolfed it down and hollered for more. I guess I felt generous since I had him all chained up and hunched over. I brought him a sack full of sandwiches and hit the road again.

I drove on through the night till sunup, when I reached a Houston police station. I unlocked Bloomfield from the seat post but left him bound hand and foot. It took a little doing to get the prisoner down from the cab, but I managed without breaking his neck or mine. Hobbling into the station, hunched over like an ape bound inside the chains, the hulking figure looked like a freak from a circus sideshow. Inside, I turned Bloomfield over to an officer who howled hysterically while he opened all the padlocks, then secured him in a cell. Before I left, the desk sergeant handed me a receipt for the prisoner and about ten pounds of steel chain and padlocks.

CHAPTER 7

The pay phone caught my eye as I turned and headed for the door and I figured I'd let Big Jack know that I'd delivered the prisoner without a hitch. He knew to expect me since I'd called him from Fort Worth, but I thought he'd appreciate it if I kept in close contact with him. I also wanted to make sure he had his checkbook ready when I got there. I grabbed a handful of coins from my pocket, dropped a dime in the slot, and dialed Big Jack's number. It must have been earlier than I'd expected, because I got his answering service. I left a message, then went for breakfast at a diner not far from Jack's office.

In downtown Houston finding a place to park a car is tough enough, but parking my Mack was next to impossible. I wasn't about to go looking for a half-dozen empty parking meters to pull up next to. It took a few minutes, but I finally found a wide alleyway a couple blocks from Jack's office.

Walking down the quiet streets in the crisp morning air did me a world of good, even though I'd been awake for more than twenty-four hours; it got my blood flowing. I finished breakfast, grabbed my usual tall coffee to go, then took a brisk walk over to Big Jack's Bail Bonds. By the time I got to the office, the sun had risen full over the horizon. Big Jack hadn't arrived yet, but it wasn't long before his white Cadillac Brougham with gold grill and trim silently rolled to a stop right in front of me. Big Jack hefted himself out of the driver's side, came over to me with a big grin, and gave me a bone-crushing handshake. Then the passenger door opened and out stepped an attractive woman in her early thirties. She had fiery red shoulder-length hair and a figure that could stop a freight train. Her dark, sensuous eyes seemed to be studying me as she walked toward us.

"I thought Jack was putting me on about you," she said to me with a playful smile, "but you look like you'll do." Her deep sultry voice made my eyes widen for just an instant.

I took Jack to one side and whispered, "Man, I don't know what kind of service you told her I perform . . . but I'm a happily married man and . . ."

Jack started howling. "Tex, let me introduce you to Mary Kern."

Laughing slightly, Mary held out her dainty hand and I shook it. Looking into my eyes, she said, "I like him, Jack."

It's not often that I blush, but with her sweetly refined Texas accent ringing in my ear and the way she was looking at me, I could swear I felt my temperature rise. I smiled at her, then glared at Jack.

"Let me explain somethin' to ya, Tex," Jack said with a laugh. "Mary needs some horses delivered. Come on in and we'll talk it over."

Jack unlocked the door and we all went inside and sat down. I handed him the receipt for Bloomfield, and he smiled as he took out his checkbook and pen.

"Mary just got divorced," Jack said as he scribbled out my check, "and her ex-husband has her four thoroughbred racehorses at his ranch in Colorado Springs. She needs somebody to pick up the horses and take them to her new place in Florida." Big Jack then handed me a check for $8,250.

"I ain't gonna sneak onto no place to steal horses," I

120

said sternly. "That's what got me back to bounty huntin' in the first place." Jack rummaged through some papers in his briefcase, then handed me a folder. "Here's a court order that says the horses are hers, Tex, and there's gonna be a U.S. marshal goin' with ya . . . that is, if ya can use five thousand dollars, with half in advance, plus three hundred and seventy-five dollars a day. I ain't even takin' a cut on this one—it's a favor to Mary."

"Now that ya mention it," I said, grinning from ear to ear and fighting to keep from busting out with excitement, "I think I can find the time to do this for the little lady . . . but why do we need the U.S. marshal in on this?"

Jack got real serious and leaned forward in his chair.

"Mary's ex-husband, Jim, ain't in his right mind. These horses are worth a heap of money, and Jim has threatened to have the horses killed just to spite her, so there's no tellin' what the man's capable of. You still want in on the deal?"

I glanced at Mary, then turned to look Jack square in the eye. "I'm your man."

The three of us discussed the details; then I went into another office and got on the phone to make some arrangements. I called a man named Ron Pryor in Laredo who had done some driving for me in the past. I wanted to go nonstop from Colorado to Florida and needed the help of another driver. I figured we could drive in shifts, but I also had a job for a second man, so Ron agreed to bring a friend along. After giving all the details to Ron, I called my wife, Becky. I could have wired money to her and gone on my way, but I missed her. I asked her to meet me in San Antonio so we could spend a couple of nights together before I went on up to Colorado. I hung up the phone and returned to Mary and Big Jack.

"I'm gonna need somebody with a CB radio to keep surveillance on the ranch after we get the horses, so we know who's followin' us," I said as I leaned forward in my chair. "We just gotta expect that the man's gonna have us followed to find out where you're movin' to, Mary."

Big Jack was taking a few notes on some of the things I needed, and Mary was listening intently.

"I think we can get my mother's chauffeur to watch the place," Mary said calmly.

"I got two drivers coming to meet me," I said as I stood up and paced the floor. "I'm gonna need a one-ton pickup and two four-horse trailers.

Jack stopped his scribbling in midstroke and looked up. "Maybe you didn't hear correctly, Tex," Jack said, with his head tilted and his eyes blinking in disbelief. "There's only four horses to be picked up, so we don't need to rent a whole other rig to . . ."

I held up my hand and smiled. "No, I heard ya right the first time, Jack. Lemme tell ya what I got in mind."

After they heard my plan, Jack made all the arrangements with the U.S. marshal's office, then called a rental agency for the trucks and trailers. We decided to rent the vehicles out of San Antonio, where I'd meet my wife and the drivers. Big Jack offered to give me a lift to my truck when I told him where I'd parked, but I said I needed the exercise. I went directly to Big Jack's bank to cash the check, then I pulled up in front of his office, ran in with the engine still running, and paid back the money he'd advanced me. I shook his hand, then paused to look him eyeball to eyeball. Big Jack curled his lip, winked, and swatted his hand through the air.

"Now go on," he said with a laugh, "and check in with me as ya go."

I waved back as I headed out and the bar-covered glass door swung shut behind me.

As I rolled down the last stretch of Interstate 10, westbound, the red rays of sunset were dipping just under my sun visor, hitting me square in the eyes. I finally got to the Howard Johnson Motor Lodge in San Antonio, where I had made reservations. I swung around the back of the building and parked the Mack where it would stay while we fetched the horses.

Me and my wife had a great time. It was like a second honeymoon. We had a nice dinner and spent the rest of the evening slow-dancing to soft music in the lounge. After breakfast the next morning, we went for a swim and relaxed for the rest of the day. The following morning, Ron called our room from the lobby. He and his friend Joe were all set to get on the road. I told him to give me a few minutes, then hung up. I threw on some clothes and brushed my teeth. I gave Becky some money to pay bills and buy groceries. Then I gave her a hug and a kiss, grabbed my duffel bag, and went out the door.

A blanket of gray clouds covered the sky for as far as the eye could see. The pavement was nearly dry, but the trees and grass were covered with beads of rainwater and the air was crisp and fresh.

Ron and Joe were standing outside the lobby, dressed like they'd just come from the range after a cattle roundup. Ron introduced me to Joe and I filled both of them in on the game plan as we walked over to Ron's one-ton GMC pickup. I tossed my duffel in the truck bed; then we piled in the truck with me by the window.

Fifteen minutes later we pulled into the rental lot, and I went into the office to get the paperwork squared away. An attendant directed Ron as he slowly backed his truck toward the hitch coupling of the four-horse trailer. Another man parked the rental truck and second trailer in front of the office, then got out and handed me the keys. I slid behind the wheel and waited till Ron was all set; then we got on our way. We drove for three days, crossed two state lines, and passed into another time zone as we traveled north on U.S. 287. The sun was gone by the time we made our third and final motel stopover in Springfield, Colorado, on our way to Colorado Springs.

I woke before dawn, took a hot shower, then threw on some clothes and stepped outside. The cool morning air filled my lungs as I wandered over to a field at the edge of the parking lot. The stars were still bright and the eastern sky was showing just a trace of red, announcing the approach of the sun. As I stretched my legs I could hear the birds and crickets still chirping and the hollow, melodious hooting of an owl.

I grabbed a tall coffee to go from the diner, went back to my room, and got on the horn to the U.S. marshal's office up in Big Spring, Texas. We arranged to meet at a café on the outskirts of Colorado Springs, about a two-hour drive from the motel in Springfield. I hung up and dialed Big Jack's number. I let him know where we were and told him how long I figured I'd be.

Then, almost as an afterthought, Jack said, "By the way, that man ya asked for—the one who works for Mary's ma—he'll be parked near the entrance to the ranch with his hood open. His name's Albert. His handle is Mudflap, and he'll be talkin' to ya on channel thirty-two." I could hear him take a deep breath and sigh. "And you be careful, now, y'hear?"

I just laughed and said, "I hear ya."

The three of us grabbed a quick bite and got on the road. A couple hours later, we came to a rest area off Highway 25, just outside Colorado Springs, where we drove both vehicles off the pavement and parked them behind some dense scrub brush. We all got out and stretched our legs. I walked around, carefully checking out the terrain and the vegetation that blocked the view of the road and parking lot. I made a few calculations in my head, then turned my attention to the men.

"What I'm gonna do is take Ron's truck with the trailer on it, and pick up the horses. I want y'all to stay here till I get back. Just leave the rig where it sits." I went over the details of my plan with them one more time and then took off for Colorado Springs.

The marshal was waiting in his vehicle outside the diner when I got there. I parked two spots away from him, got out, and walked over to his window.

"Marshal," I said as I offered him my hand. "Name's Brown, Tex Brown."

We shook hands through the window; then he opened the door and got out. He wasn't what I'd consider short, but he wasn't as tall as I expected him to be. Stocky and solid-looking, the marshal looked like he might have been a football player. He had short hair, a neatly trimmed handlebar mustache, and pilot's glasses.

"Name's Adams . . . call me Bill," he said. "You had lunch yet?"

"As a matter of fact, I ain't," I said as I slapped my belly. "Let's grab us a bite."

After lunch I checked the trailer hitch, got in Ron's GMC one-ton and followed the marshal. The air was filled with the scent of pine and the trees that lined the road formed a dense canopy overhead. The road climbed steadily, winding its way past jagged cliff faces and boulder piles. Every once in a while the land to the right of the road would fall away, revealing a vast, rolling carpet of treetops. At the crest of the hill I could see the sunlight gleaming off buildings and car windows below. The bustling grid of roadways was alive with movement, like a giant anthill. We wound our way down into the valley through the forested countryside till we finally came to the entrance of the Horse Shoe Ranch.

The marshal's car slowed and turned left, dipping slightly as his tires left the pavement. I followed him through a thin cloud of dust, down the well-worn dirt road. As we cleared the trees that lined the property, a wide pasture opened ahead of us. The road was straight, and it took us past three wood-railed riding arenas to the left and a wide expanse of grazing land on the right, all bordered by a steel pipe fence. In the distance there were several ranch-style buildings, a barn, and a huge steel-roofed indoor arena that looked to be the size of a battleship. I could see the faint shadows of people scattered throughout the place.

As we approached the compound, a handful of men

stopped dead in their tracks and fixed their eyes on us. We rolled to a stop in the dirt outside a long wood building. The doors at both ends were open and the stalls, hay, and familiar smell of horse shit told me this was the stable. I got out of the truck and leaned against the left front fender with my arms folded while the marshal approached three of the hands.

"Where's the foreman?" he asked, like a drill sergeant addressing recruits.

One man stepped forward holding a large pitchfork, its four spikes polished by endless lunging and stabbing into piles of hay. A greasy baseball cap shaded his dark beady eyes. He casually cocked his head. "I'm it," he said in a slow, deliberate voice. "Wha'd'ya want?"

"I've got a court order here," the marshal said as he held up the paper, "for the release of four horses: one sorrel stud, and three bay mares."

The man shifted his weight and leaned on the pitchfork. "Well, Mr. Kern ain't gonna be back for about a week, so I ain't gonna give up no horses to nobody."

Marshal Adams rested his hand on the grip of his revolver. "Then you'd better call your wife and tell her you'll be a couple years late for supper," Adams said coldly, "because if you don't cooperate, you're going to federal prison."

The foreman paused for a moment, then threw the fork down, swearing under his breath as he led me and the marshal to a barn behind the stable. The ranch hands brought out four sleek, handsome horses. Each animal had a lustrous brown coat, bright eyes, and a stern, proud gait as it was led to the horse trailer. I reached into the cab of the pickup and grabbed a clipboard with the horses' papers, then walked to the back of the trailer as the men were opening the doors. "Hold up a minute," I yelled, as I trotted to the back of the vehicle, "we ain't through here by a long shot."

I went up to one of the mares and rubbed its neck as I carefully gave it the once-over. I looked inside the animal's mouth to see if the number tattooed inside its lip matched the number on the sheet. The stud was next in line. After examining the stud I walked over to the marshal.

"This ain't the stud that I came for," I said calmly.

"What'n the hell makes ya think that?" said the foreman, his arms folded and feet planted firmly.

"Well, first off," I said with a laugh, "the horse I came for is a thoroughbred racehorse, and this here ain't no racehorse."

"You can't prove that," the foreman said angrily.

I stood there for a second and stared at the man, then I went back to the stud, grabbed its hoof, and pushed its knee. The beast obligingly shifted its weight, allowing me to lift its leg and hold it under my arm.

"You see this?" I yelled. "This horse has steel plates on its hooves." The marshal walked over to see.

"You mean horseshoes? What's that mean, Tex?" Adams said as he squatted down to take a closer look.

"Ask your boy here," I said as I let go of the leg and stood up. "He knows damn well what I'm talkin' about."

The foreman frowned and looked down. "You're crazy."

I rested my arm on the horse and paused a second, looking at the foreman as he stood uneasily.

"Racehorses have aluminum plates on their hooves, not steel . . . but that's just for starters." I crouched next to the animal and motioned for the marshal to come closer. "These hooves are finished outside like a show horse. You won't see a racehorse with hooves lookin' like this." I got up, took hold of the horse's bridle, and pulled its lower lip down to expose the tattooed numbers. "Now, these look like they could be legitimate numbers, but they're too new . . ."

The foreman stomped over and cut in sharply. "What'n the hell makes you say that?"

I glared at him for a second, then went on. "This tattoo's too dark. After a couple of years they get lighter—and besides, you can still see the scar tissue from when the tattoo was put on."

While I held the horse, the marshal took a closer look in the full light of the sun. Marshal Adams looked at me, then grabbed the butt of his revolver and took a pair of handcuffs out of his belt.

"Son, you ain't gonna like it in Leavenworth penitentiary . . . lot of bad motherfuckers in there, I hear. Turn around, hands on the vehicle!" he ordered.

The foreman stepped back and raised his hands in panic.

"Okay! Okay! Hey, look, I just work here . . . I'll get the horses for ya."

"Yeah, you do that," said the marshal as he turned to me and winked.

We loaded up the mares while the men brought out the real sorrel stud. I checked the markings with the ones on the sheet and everything checked out. The animals were secured inside the trailer and the doors locked tight. I pulled a canvas cover down over the back so the horses couldn't be seen from behind. I walked over to Marshal Adams and we shook hands.

"I'll follow you till we get to Highway 16 . . . I think you can handle it from there," Adams said as he got in his car. Then he stuck his head out the window and yelled, "It was good to meet ya, Tex." I nodded and waved as I drove off.

Before I was even halfway down the road leading off the property, I grabbed the microphone of my citizen's band.

"Breaker three two, this here's the Texas Outlaw callin' Mudflap. Come back." I listened to the white noise of the radio and glanced over my shoulder to see how the trailer was taking the bumps of the dirt road.

As I approached the dense row of trees at the edge of the property, the radio squawked, "Read you loud and clear, Outlaw. This is Mudflap. I am in position and will notify you of any activity. Over."

"Ten four on that, Mudflap. I'll keep my ears on."

We reached the pavement, then took the service road

to the foot of the hill and started winding our way upward.

"Breaker thrcc two, this is Mudflap, come in, Outlaw."

"I got a copy on ya, Mudflap. Whatcha got?"

"There's a brown pickup coming your way. It pulled out of the ranch about fifteen seconds ago and is burning rubber."

"I copy that . . . I'm layin' the hammer down. Thanks, pardner."

As I pulled into traffic on Interstate 25 southbound, I gradually put the pedal to the metal and edged into the fast lane. The highway gently wound its way through the green forest of high country, but I had no time for sight-seeing. I started slowing down and edging back over to the right-hand lane when I saw the blue rest area road sign. With a load of horses hitched to the one-ton, I had to take the turn into the rest area a little slower than I would have liked. I drove to the far end of the lot, then went off the pavement behind the thick brush and trees to where Ron and Joe were waiting. I pulled up next to Ron's rig and jumped out with a pair of binoculars. Ron and Joe already had the doors to both trailers open and were leading the horses from one trailer to the other. I positioned myself between a gap in the underbrush and kept an eye on the entrance to the rest area.

I barely got a chance to focus before I saw the brown pickup Mudflap had described pull in and roll slowly toward us from the left. The two men inside seemed like they were studying all the vehicles in the lot. It was hard to focus on the moving truck, but I caught a glimpse of two rifles in a rack across its back window. The two men parked the pickup about fifty yards to my right and waited. I took my eyes away and stepped out of the brush to check on the progress of the transfer.

"How's it comin', boys?"

"We just about got her licked, Tex," Ron said as he emerged from the near trailer.

"Okay, we got company, so we ain't got time to waste."

I pushed my way back through the bushes and focused the field glasses on the brown pickup. I saw one of the men standing next to the driver's side, but I'd lost the passenger. I leaned forward a little and peered over the binoculars. Out of the corner of my eye I saw something moving. I had to lean out a little farther to see past the foliage to the right. A shadow fell on the pavement in front of me, and the bright sunlight reflecting off the car windows made it tough for my eyes to adjust. Forty feet away, I saw the outline of a rifle barrel and a Stetson hat coming closer. I jumped back and ran over to the men as they were coaxing the last horse out of the first trailer.

"Ron, grab onto that horse!" I said as I quickly pulled the canvas cover down over the back of the empty trailer.

"Joe, here are the keys . . . and take my hat. Now get goin'!"

Joe bolted off and jumped into the pickup. He turned the engine over, spun the tires slightly in the dirt and rolled away with the empty trailer in a cloud of dust. The rig jostled and bounced over the edge of the pavement, then disappeared behind the trees. I drew my .45 and ran into the bushes at the edge of the parking lot.

Joe tore through the rest area, heading straight for the exit. The cowboy with the rifle dashed back to his pickup while the other gorilla revved up the engine, pulled out, and swung around to pick him up. Kern's men followed the decoy like a bat out of hell.

Ron shut the back of the trailer and hopped into the cab with me. He was laughing like a madman and I was grinning, but it was a close call and it could have turned ugly real fast. I rolled the horse trailer slowly through the dirt, then eased her gently up onto the pavement so as not to spook the horses. I took my time leaving the rest area and getting back on Highway 25.

The rest area was just on the near side of the exit I'd planned on taking. We followed U.S. 50 eastbound, then got onto Highway 83 and headed south. Joe was leading Kern's men west. I figured it'd be safe if we stopped to feed and walk the horses, so I drove into another rest area.

Nearly twenty-four hours of steady driving finally got us to Fort Worth, Texas. Ron and I drove in shifts, with frequent stops to feed and exercise the horses. One of us would sleep while the other drove. We came to a truck stop, stretched our legs, fed the horses, and went in for supper. After we ate, both of us went to the pay phones. Ron called home while I phoned Big Jack to give him a progress report. I made the call short, hung up, and went back to the table to finish my coffee.

About ten minutes later, Ron joined me. He was trembling slightly, his eyes were bloodshot and watery, and his lower lip trembled as he spoke. "My wife and son . . . they were in a wreck on the highway . . . they ain't sure if my son's gonna make it."

I looked at him, unable to find words that would say what I felt. I'd seen my share of hardship and I knew that nothing anybody could say would change things or make me feel better at a time like this. I put my hand on Ron's arm. "I'm taking you to the airport."

I called and made plane reservations for Ron, then drove him to the terminal. As he got out of the pickup with his duffel bag, I suddenly remembered something.

"Hey, Ron, I don't think they'd take too kindly to you waltzin' through the airport with that hogleg strapped on your side."

Ron seemed to be in a trance. He looked down at the revolver on his hip and shook his head at the sudden realization. He handed me his sidearm, and I shook his hand. "I'm gonna be prayin' extra hard for them, Ron . . . you keep your chin up, ya hear?"

As Ron went inside to the ticket counter, I got out to make sure the trailer hitch was secure and the doors in back were fastened down tight, then fought my way back into city traffic. The sky was pale blue but the sun was dropping fast. As they inched their way forward in the rush-hour traffic, cars formed an endless sea around me.

By nightfall I got through Dallas and picked up Interstate 20 eastbound. As I was barreling down the road forty miles outside Dallas, a torrential rainstorm came upon me out of nowhere. It was like hitting a brick wall. The water pelting the hood, windshield, and roof sounded more like bullets than rain. The tires seemed to dig in as they hit the pool of water covering the pavement. Gusts of wind drove sheets of rain at right angles to the road and buffeted my rig. I slowed way down and looked for a place to stop.

Through the darkness I saw a blue and red neon sign that read BINGO TRUCK STOP and I pulled in to wait out the storm. I reached behind the seat, pulled out a long, heavy raincoat, and put it on. I was regretting having lent my Stetson to Joe, but if I hadn't, Kern's men might have suspected the switch.

The rain was coming down like hail. I pulled my collar tight against my neck as I trudged around back to open the trailer. I put feed bags on the horses and made sure they were all right, then dashed over to the door of the truck stop. When I got under the overhang outside the door, I shook my head and stomped my feet to avoid tracking in too much water.

Inside, I hung my coat up, then dabbed my face and neck with a large red bandanna. I took a booth right by the door and politely called my order to the waitress. At this time of night it was pretty slow. In the booth next to mine sat a burly man with his back to me. He wore a greasy, damp checkered shirt and a dirty baseball cap. The back of his neck was weathered and hairy.

"I didn't know they'd let your kind in a fine place like this one," he said as he swung his muscular arm onto the seat back and turned to me. I was cold, tired, and hungry, and in no mood to deal with any hard-asses with a bad attitude. I stared out the window and paid him no mind. Out of the corner of my eye I saw the hulking figure stand up and move toward me. I was getting ready to bash a sugar jar over his head when I heard the harsh voice again.

"Tex, you old sidewinder, how the hell ya been?"

I turned and looked up at the man blankly, relaxing my grip on the glass sugar dispenser. I paused for a second to collect my thoughts, then suddenly recognition hit me like a stampede of cattle.

"Homer, you old buffalo chip!" I said as I shook his hand. "You are one hell of a sight for these sore eyes. Whatcha been doin' with yourself?"

Homer sat down and we talked for a while, catching up on experiences we'd had since the days when we'd regularly bumped into each other in truck stops across the country.

The rain finally slowed to a drizzle and we both had to get back on the road. I scrawled my phone number on a napkin, we paid the cashier and left. Homer was dying to see the prizewinning racehorses I was hauling, but with the weather as bad as it was, I told him he'd just have to look in through the side window. Then we went our separate ways with a promise to keep in touch.

It was slow going on Interstate 20 due to heavy fog. I crossed the Texas-Louisiana border and saw the welcome sight of a rest area, so I drove in. A blanket of mist covered the road, making it hard to see the parked cars and the terrain. Dim lights scattered throughout the lot cast gloomy shadows in the trees that lined the edge of the crumbling pavement. I parked toward the back of the place, alongside a curb, taking up nearly ten spaces. There was a small restroom building about thirty yards to my left. One by one, I backed the horses out of the trailer, walked them around in a dirt clearing, then tied the reins to a nearby tree. I strapped a feed bag on each animal, then stretched my legs. The air was heavy and moist. The smell of parched, withered grasses, brought back to life by rain, filled my lungs. Droplets of water fell from the trees as I wandered. The moon was a bright round blur overhead. It cast thin shadows and glistened faintly on the moist foliage. The sound of horses snorting and whinnying barely broke the silence of the still night air.

A distant voice caught my attention. As I moved toward the sound, I could hear urgency in the high-pitched cries. I ran back to the truck and got my pistol. I figured it could've been a trick to lure me away from the horses, but I had to take that chance. I racked the slide of my Colt halfway back to reveal the live round in the chamber, dropped the slide, flicked the safety back on, then tucked the weapon into my belt. I left the horses tied where they were and made my way toward the commotion.

The cries were louder now—the frantic screams of a woman and child muffled behind the glass of a wood-paneled station wagon. I crouched down and moved slowly toward the driver's side window. A young girl, no more than ten years old, was tied to the steering wheel, twisting her arms against the ropes. In the back I saw the outline of bodies thrashing and struggling. A chill raced through my body. I didn't dare shoot through the glass, but I had to move fast. Doing my best to stagger like a drunk, I moved in and slammed my hand on the hood of the car.

"Hey, anybody got a cigarette?" I said in a heavy slur, teetering from side to side.

"Hey!" I banged on the hood again. "I'm talking to y'all."

"Fuck off!" a voice rasped from the rear driver's side window as it opened halfway, "or I'll cut your fuckin' heart out and make ya' eat it!"

"Well, if y'all ain't got no smokes," I said as I stumbled closer to the open window, "how 'bout a drink? I'm partial to bourbon myself and . . ."

The sudden crunch of metal caused me to instinctively brace myself and wrap my hand tightly around the grip of my .45. The car's back door burst open and out flew a wiry, long-haired guy. He was barely dressed and struggled to get his pants on as he approached me.

As he swung at me with lightning speed, I saw the flash of a blade in his hand. I felt a sharp tug on the left sleeve of my denim jacket as I jumped to the side. Instantly, I drew my pistol and fired two shots at point-blank range. The bullets smashed into his left arm and tore the flesh away from his bare shoulder.

A dark red mist sprayed in all directions, covering his face, his white tank-top shirt, and the windshield of the station wagon. The impact of the bullets knocked him off his feet and threw him backwards. He bounced against the car on his way to the pavement and the knife flew from his hand.

As the knife landed, I stepped toward it and kicked it away from the reach of the wounded man. Hearing a noise behind me, I turned my head and saw another man winding up with a machete. I bolted toward the back of the vehicle. The blade made a shrill whipping sound as it cut through the air inches from my neck. Sparks flew as it hit the car's side mirror.

With no time to think, I wheeled around and brought my pistol up, firing as I raised it. The first round hit him in the foot and the second slug struck him square in the thigh. The impact yanked his leg out from under him, spinning him forward and toppling him headfirst onto the blacktop.

I picked up the machete and threw it over the vehicle, then took a good look inside the station wagon to make sure there were no more attackers. I put my gun away as I ran to the other side of the car, opened the door, and found a nude woman, battered and bloody, laid out the full length of the seat with her hands tied to the headrest of the front seat. She cowered in fear, curling her legs up close, her feet toward me, to protect herself from further abuse.

"Easy, now . . . I won't hurt ya," I said in what I hoped was a reassuring voice, "and those men ain't gonna hurt ya either."

I took off my jacket and draped it over the woman, then went to the front seat, pulled out my pocketknife, and cut her ropes. A man came running over to me as I was cutting the ropes that bound the young girl to the steering wheel.

"I seen the whole thing," he said with great concern and eagerness. "Anything I can do?"

I stood up and pointed to my truck. "See that one-ton with the horse trailer on it? Get on the radio and send for help. Channel nine, okay? The police monitor channel nine." As the man started off toward my vehicle I added, "And behind the seat there's some blankets . . . bring 'em."

CHAPTER 8

As I cut the ropes, freeing the terrified child, she scurried over the seat back to the arms of her mother, who lay trembling and sobbing breathlessly. When I stood up, I saw people staring from cars parked within spitting distance, their eyes wide and their mouths agape. They quickly looked away as I caught their glances. I just couldn't believe that this many people could sit idly by in the face of such a brutal attack.

The woman struggled to cover herself with her tattered clothing as she feebly inched her way toward the open door. Her face was swollen and bloody; her hair was matted and greasy. The little girl got out first, clenching her mother's hand. The woman's bare feet touched the pavement and she carefully pulled herself out of the vehicle. Just as the child went to hug her mother, the woman's knees buckled and she slumped to the pavement. The girl screamed in terror. I rushed to the woman's side and cradled her head in my hands. I checked her pulse and breathing, wrapped her in a blanket, then picked her up and carefully set her back in the car.

The distant siren, a welcome sound, quickly grew to a shrill roar as several emergency vehicles whipped around the corner. Solid beams of colored light cut through the fog, spinning wildly as the cruisers and ambulances barreled toward us.

The paramedics took great care in transferring the injured woman to the stretcher. The young girl rode with her mother to the hospital. An officer came over and seemed about to ask me something, but stopped short.

"You're bleedin', son," he said as he leaned closer.

I looked down and saw my left arm covered with dried blood.

There was a long, shallow gash just above my elbow. One of the medics cleaned me up some, then bandaged the wound. He told me I'd be all right, and he didn't think I needed stitches, but that I should probably have it looked at.

The two wounded kidnappers were both placed under arrest, strapped to gurneys, and taken away in another ambulance.

I showed one of the officers where the two weapons were. As I started to make my statement, I heard something.

"Excuse me, officer," I said, looking toward my truck, "would you mind if we talked while I put these horses up? They're gettin' spooked by all this commotion."

As we walked to the horses I told the man what happened. The officer wrote down my statement, while I led the animals into the trailer. He left for a minute to compare notes with the officers who talked to other witnesses. As I got the last of the horses into the trailer, the young officer walked over to me.

"Mr. Brown, I'm goin' to have to have you go downtown with me," he said dryly. "Need ya to fill out a report."

"I ain't gonna leave these horses here all night," I told him firmly.

"It's okay," he said, as he laid his hand on my shoulder, "you can follow us in your truck."

Two detectives led me through a heavy steel door framing a narrow window covered with steel mesh and a two-way mirror. The room was small and bare. I was seated at a solid wood table in a metal folding chair. I went over every detail at least three or four times, and I must have had twice as many cups of coffee.

"One of the men you shot," said one detective, "is an escaped convict from Georgia, and we're gonna need you to testify at an informal extradition hearing within the week."

I gave them Big Jack's number and agreed to appear at the hearing on my way back home.

It was four o'clock in the morning by the time I left police headquarters in Shreveport, Louisiana, and got back onto eastbound Interstate 20.

Night gradually lifted to reveal a bleak sunless day. Fog covered the ground. The trees and houses were mere shadows along the roadside. Thin wisps of vapor rushed past me on all sides, as though I were flying through a cloud bank. Out of curiosity, I tuned in to a news channel on the CB radio. I'll admit I was kind of proud to hear reports of the incident, but I was happier to hear that the young girl was uninjured and that her mother was listed in good condition, with only a few broken bones.

I called Big Jack from a friend's farm outside Jackson, Mississippi, where I spent the rest of the day and got a good night's sleep.

"Jack, it's Tex. I ran into some people in trouble off Interstate 20 and . . ."

"I know all about it," he cut in. "The Louisiana State Police called me first thing. I'm glad it turned out okay."

"Is somethin' wrong, Jack?"

"Your friend Ron . . . his boy died last night," Jack said somberly. I was stunned and speechless as Jack continued. "His wife has regained consciousness, and the doctors say she's gonna pull through. She wants to thank you for gettin' her husband on the plane so quick."

A day and a half later, I pulled into Mary Kern's new place in Wildwood, Florida. She was waiting for me to arrive and had people ready to unload the horses and put them in their stalls. She hugged my neck to thank me for bringing 'em from Colorado and handed me an envelope with a bonus in it. I didn't want to take it, but she insisted, so I jumped back in my one-ton and headed back to Texas. Down the road a piece, I opened the envelope and found an expensive gold necklace. I knew Becky would be delighted.

I testified at the hearing in Shreveport, picked up my truck and my paycheck from Big Jack in Houston, then returned home to Laredo for the boy's funeral. I think everyone in the whole town came to pay their respects. Mrs. Pryor had to stay in the hospital during the service, but Ron told me that it might have made her more upset than she already was anyway.

I was brushing down one of my horses in the barn when Becky called me to the phone. I took the mare back to her stall, hung up the curry comb, and ran over to the house. Becky was standing outside the front door and said, "It's Dave Moore."

Last I'd heard, Dave was working with one of the Federal Task Forces on Organized Crime.

"Hello, Dave. How the hell ya been?"

"Real good, Tex, and yourself?"

I didn't feel like going into detail about any of my troubles, and I'm sure Dave didn't really want to hear them anyway.

"Oh, pretty good," I said flatly.

"I'm sure glad I caught you at home. Say, listen, Tex, we got us a major problem up here," he said with a hint of anger in his voice. "Our office is investigating a ring of truck thieves. They're stealing tractor-trailer rigs from independent truckers and the vehicles vanish."

"You found any of the rigs yet?" I asked.

"So far not one of them has been recovered. Our sources tell us the trucks are being dismantled and sold as parts, but we haven't been able to locate the chop shop. They hit at random, and since they're targeting independent truckers rather than major outfits, it's tougher for us to get men on the inside. Will you help us on this one?"

I sure as hell didn't have to think about it too long. "I'm your man, Dave. If it's one thing I can't stand it's a goddamned thief. When do y'all need me on this?"

"As soon as possible, Tex. My boss wants to move on this thing right away."

"I got some people comin' out to the house to look at some horses I got for sale, so I'm tied up for the next two days. I'd cancel it if I could, but they're on their way over."

"That's fine, Tex. Take your time . . . but be quick about it," Dave said with a laugh.

I wrote down his number, address, some directions and instructions, then got off the phone and went back out to finish preparing the horses for their prospective buyers. The next morning, the buyers showed up as scheduled and, after a little dickering, drove off the proud new owners of three horses.

Having finished my business, I hurried over to the house to grab my duffel bag and a large paper sack that Becky had filled with some sandwiches, apples, and a large thermos full of coffee. I gave her a big hug and kiss and was out the door.

The sun was hanging just above the barn, bathing the front porch in its warm golden light. I walked over to my old pickup truck, threw my stuff on the seat, then popped the hood. The old Chevy half-ton step-side looked real rough on the outside, but she had a heart of gold and an engine that could burn the doors off damn nearly every vehicle in the county. With a four-hundred-thirty-mile trip ahead of me, I thought I'd better make sure she was one hundred percent. I checked the water, oil, belts, and hoses, then closed her up and was on my way.

With the Chevy up to speed I eased the pedal back off the floor. The needle was buried. The guardrails were rushing past me and the broken yellow lines on the surface of Interstate 35 northbound seemed a solid, continuous blur. The sun had just dropped below sight, filling the sky to my left with a bright orange glow. The thin clouds hanging motionless to the west looked like vast sheets of flame falling from the heavens.

The radio was playing a Willie Nelson song, and I reached over to tune the station in better. Then I caught the tiny pinpoints of blue and red light flashing in my rearview mirror. As I eased over into the right-hand lane, I pumped the brake pedal and brought her back down to the speed limit. The police cruiser came up on my bumper fast and I knew it was me he was after, so I pulled off to the side and slowed to a final stop.

I kept my hands locked high on the steering wheel because I knew that if it were me stopping a vehicle at night, miles from civilization, I'd feel a whole lot safer knowing what the driver was holding on to.

"License and registration please," the officer said briskly.

I reached for the information he wanted and handed it to him along with a piece of paper.

"You may not believe this, officer," I said firmly, staring him straight in the eyes, "but the DPS Task Force on Organized Crime has engaged me to assist in an investigation, and I'm on my way to the briefing in Dallas."

The officer smiled as he listened and looked at my license and credentials.

"Of all the excuses I've heard for gettin' out of a ticket," he said with a laugh, "this one's got to be the most original."

"I figured you might not believe me," I said with a smile. "Wouldn't it be a kick in the ass if I was tellin' the truth?"

The officer came closer and aimed his flashlight into the cab of my pickup and he paused.

"I expect it surely would," he said with a frown.

"I'd be beholden to ya if you'd have your dispatcher call the number on that piece of paper you got in your hand."

The officer paused and scratched his head as he looked at the slip of paper. He looked back at me and laughed under his breath.

"All right, I'll do that," he said as he walked back to his cruiser. Dave had told me to break the sound barrier if I had to, and I told him the last thing I needed was a black mark on my license. Dave assured me that if I got stopped his office would fix it, so the two of us entered into a kind of gentleman's bet—and my hand was being called.

The officer returned and promptly handed back my papers. "Real sorry for the delay, Mr. Brown, but I had no way of knowin' that you were . . ."

"That's why I'm still alive, son," I said with a smile. "Nobody knows." The patrolman smiled back and shook his head as I threw her in gear and eased my pickup back onto the road.

The early morning skyline looked cold and quiet as I took the I-45 exit and rolled into downtown Dallas. I parked in front of the Federal Building just off Ross Avenue and reached behind the seat for my pillow. Dave was to meet me at 8:00 A.M., which would give me about four hours' sleep, so I cracked the windows, locked the doors, put my gun under my pillow, and sacked out on the bench seat of my Chevy half-ton.

I was startled out of a sound sleep by a thump on the side of my truck and I jumped up pointing my pistol toward the noise. All I saw was a man in a suit stiffen up and raise his arms in shock.

"Tex!" yelled the man, his voice muffled by the glass. "Good morning to you, too."

My eyes focused and I lowered my automatic upon seeing the familiar face of Special Investigator Dave Moore.

I tucked the weapon away, unlatched and opened the door, then dragged myself out of the vehicle.

"Good morning, Dave," I said as I rubbed the sand out of my eyes and shook his hand. "Sorry about the hardware."

"Hey, no problem," Dave said, taking a deep breath. "Good to see you've got quick reflexes. Let's grab us some breakfast."

Amid the clatter of dishes and the low rumble of voices, Dave briefed me on the assignment.

"Out in the storage yard we've got a semi that we impounded in a raid about a year and a half ago. We've been using it now and again to haul equipment. We want you to drive down to San Antonio and talk to people, poke around a few places that we know are . . ."

"Now hold on just one minute," I said, frowning with amazement, "don't y'all have anything solid for me to go on?"

Dave lowered his head for a second, then looked up with a frown.

"Actually . . . no. We know the general vicinity where the thefts occur, but there hasn't been any real pattern in the . . ."

"Shit, Dave," I said with a laugh, "I'm supposed to just go out there and hope somebody's gonna steal the truck?"

"Now just hear me out," he urged. "Our sources tell us that these poor ol' independent truckers who've been gettin' ripped off are actually being approached by the thieves, who agree to pay them to report their truck stolen after the thief has a good head start . . . and the trucker gets paid by the insurance company on top of it all."

We finished breakfast and went back to Dave's office. After we passed security, we walked down a series of long, busy corridors lined with doors, bulletin boards, and fire extinguishers. The building was carpeted wall to wall and brightly lit throughout by fluorescent ceiling fixtures. Dave took me to a lab at the end of the hall and introduced me to one of the men.

"This is Officer Jones," Dave said as we approached a table with an ink roller and large sheets of paper. "He'll take your prints and pictures."

This was one part of the job I didn't like—it brought

back bad memories—but the photo and fingerprints were necessary both for the surveillance teams to recognize me and for the crime lab to differentiate between my prints and those of the suspects' on any piece of evidence taken in. Officer Jones then asked to see the serial numbers on all the weapons I carried, but I knew them by heart and he took my word for it.

With all the formalities out of the way, I jumped into my old Chevy pickup and followed Dave to the department's security lot. Dave showed his ID to the guard, who immediately let us through. Ripples of heat rose from the pavement as we walked past hundreds of vehicles of all types. We finally came to a Peterbilt cab-over—a real beauty with a 400-horsepower Cummins engine, thirteen-speed transmission, and a four-eleven rear end.

"I just don't like the idea of me givin' this beauty to a goddamn thief," I said as I shook my head.

"Relax, Tex, we'll have a surveillance van following every move you make. And besides, if we lose it, it's our baby—you won't catch any shit for it."

Dave handed me the keys and a thousand dollars for expenses. "Follow me back to headquarters," Dave said, "and the lab boys'll put the tracer beacon on the truck."

"Hey, Dave, gimme a hand a minute," I said with a wave of my hand. Dave followed me over to the trailer coupling.

"What in the world are you doin'?" he said as I handed him some cables I'd unhooked.

"I'm leaving this trailer behind," I told him as I torqued on a lever with all my might.

"What'n the hell for?" Dave asked.

With the work finished, I grabbed the cables from him. "If I'm playin' it like I'm down on my luck, I'm playin' it to the hilt." I started to climb up to the cab, then stopped short. "Oh, yeah," I said, snapping my fingers, "we're gonna need some signs on this side."

"You think that's necessary?" he said impatiently.

"Look, Dave," I said sternly, "I've been runnin' my

own truck cross country since I was eighteen years old, and I been drivin' longer than that. These people know what they're doin', and to do this thing right we can't take shortcuts. If we don't have signs on the doors, people are gonna wonder."

"Okay, okay!" He put his hand up with a smile. "I'll tell'm when we get back," Dave said as he headed toward the gate.

I fueled up and drove the Peterbilt to the Federal Building, where a handful of men climbed all over the vehicle, engraving identification marks on different parts and attaching the homing device to a secure place.

While I waited for the men to finish, Dave gave me a few last-minute instructions.

"You see that light brown van over there?" Dave asked as he pointed across the parking lot. "I'll be riding in that van along with your surveillance team. We've got tracking monitors, night-vision equipment, and we'll stay on you the whole way. Oh, yeah—when you make contact, call me immediately."

Dave scribbled something on a piece of paper and handed it to me. "This is the number of the van's mobile phone."

My shadow stuck with me as I drove through the city streets of Dallas, and the freeway interchanges, then onto Interstate 35 southbound for the long trip ahead. I picked up the CB mike and started chattering like a ratchet jaw.

"Breaker, breaker, all you northbounds out there. This here's the Texas Outlaw, southbound on thirty-five. Come on back."

After talking to several truckers, one old boy's voice cracked the airwaves.

"I gotcha, Outlaw. You got Melonhead, northbound, talkin' atcha. Is that your purple Peterbilt headin' for San Antone?"

"That's a big ten-four, Melonhead." I laughed under my breath.

"What'n the wide, wide world o' sports happened to your trailer?" the trucker asked with concern.

"Ahh, the damned finance company's got it," I replied.

"That's a durn shame."

"Man, I'll tell ya—I got two payments behind and they jerked her right out from under me," I said angrily. "You know where I might find a load?"

There was dead air for a second, then the radio crackled. "Tell ya what. If you're stoppin' over in San Antone, go to the San Antonio Motel and talk to a security guard named Ranson. He maybe can help ya out with your money trouble. Tell 'em I sent ya."

I came to the San Antonio Motel and parked in a back lot with extra-large spaces for eighteen-wheelers. I checked into the motel, called Dave and told him what I knew, then had lunch in the coffee shop. As the waitress wrote me out a bill, I said, "A buddy of mine told me to look up a friend of his here at the motel. A security guard named Ranson. You wouldn't know where I could find him, would ya?"

She continued scribbling and said, "Ahh, I think he's workin' nights."

She handed me the check. I paid the cashier, then went to the lounge where they had a pool table and played a few games. Most of the guys there were long-haul truckers taking a breather between loads.

"I hate to admit this," I said as I lined up for a shot. "The goddamn finance company yanked my refer trailer out from under me. Now I ain't got no trailer to make a livin' with. Anybody know where I might find a load?"

"Not without a trailer, I don't," said one of the men watching the game.

I shot the cue ball hard, sending it the length of the table, till it crashed into another ball, dropping it in the corner pocket.

"A fella I talked to told me to look up a security guard named Ranson," I said as I chalked my cue. "Anybody know where he's at?"

A man in the far corner holding a cue in one hand and a can of suds in the other stepped forward.

"Who's askin'?" he queried dryly.

"Name's Brown—everybody calls me Tex."

The man took a hard look at me, then said, "You stayin' in the motel?"

I put the chalk down, then looked up at him and said, "Who's askin'?"

The man chuckled and walked over to me with his hand extended.

"Fullerton," he said as we shook hands, "Bill Fullerton. I'll tell ya what, Tex. I'll have Ranson get in touch with ya."

I went to a pay phone and called Dave.

"Dave, this's Tex. I made contact with a man who knows Ranson. He says he'll put Ranson in touch with me."

"When?" Dave asked.

"Could be tonight, but I don't know for sure."

Dave paused for a second, then said, "I'm gonna come to your room and tap a wire to you."

"All right," I said. "But I really hate like hell havin' those things torn off my flesh after the deal's done."

I could hear Dave howling in the background.

"Okay, Tex, I'll meet you at your room."

Five minutes later Dave came to my room carrying a small case. I took my shirt off and he fastened an electronic listening device to my body with white medical tape. Dave talked to the men in the van through a small hand-held radio, making sure the wire I was wearing functioned properly.

After Dave went back to his post, I sat by the phone and caught up on some reading. It was hard to find a comfortable position to sit in with the tape tugging at the hair on my body whenever I moved.

The phone shook the table and I tore my eyes away from my book at the sudden noise.

"Brown here," I bellowed into the receiver.

"Mr. Brown?" the voice asked in a heavy Texas accent. "My name is Ranson. I heard ya got some money troubles."

"You heard right," I said sternly, "but I ain't gonna talk about my business over the phone with somebody I ain't ever seen before."

"Words to live by, my friend, words to live by," he drawled. "Why don't you meet me out by your truck?"

I paused for a second, then said, "All right, I'll do that. It's parked . . ."

"I know where your rig's parked at," he cut in with a slight laugh. "It's my job to know these things."

"What time you gonna be there?" I asked.

"Son," he said, smugly, "as we speak, I am sittin' in my vehicle in front of your vehicle."

"I'll be out," I said, and hung up the phone.

I went to the door and said into the microphone, "Okay, guys, it's show time."

It was a warm, moonless night. Clouds of flying insects swarmed around the light posts in the parking lot as I walked toward the Peterbilt. In front of the rig was a two-tone Japanese pickup truck with a rack of yellow lights on the roof. As I got closer, a voice said, "Brown?"

"That's me," I replied.

Dull white light from a distant pole illuminated the small truck and revealed the face of the driver as he leaned out his window.

"Get in," he ordered.

I got into the truck and we slowly drove around the property. "These are the damndest things," he said as he held up his car phone; then he laughed. "Ya wanna order a pizza?"

I just looked at him without so much as a smile, and he continued. "Well . . . gettin' down to business, it appears you'll be losin' your vehicle to the bank pretty soon if ya don't do somethin' fast—am I right?"

I lowered my head, then looked back over at him. "Yeah," I mumbled.

He took his eyes from the road and squinted at me. "How much would a down payment on a new truck set ya back?" he asked.

I thought for a second before replying. "Ah . . . five or six thousand."

"How would you like to have your cake and eat it too, so to speak?" he asked with a smirk. "I can arrange for you to get that five thousand dollars and get paid off by the insurance company. You do have insurance, don't you?"

"For about another month," I told him.

"Well, that's good," he said with a smile. "Are you in?"

"Sounds like a plan to me," I said eagerly. "When can you get me the money and what do I have to do?"

"Settle up your bill at the front desk, go back to your room, get your bags together, and I'll bring your money to ya directly," Ranson said as we stopped in front of my door.

Twenty minutes later, Ranson came to the door. "I ain't gonna get into trouble, am I?" I asked nervously. "You ain't no cop, are ya?"

"Relax," he said in a casual tone, "I ain't no cop, and you ain't gonna get into no trouble . . . if ya do exactly what I say."

He handed me an envelope. I opened it and leafed through the bills. Satisfied the money was all there, I handed him the keys.

"Now, that man over there," Ranson said, pointing to a white Ford Thunderbird double-parked with the engine running, "is gonna drive you to a motel in Edinburg, down south. You check in, go to sleep, wake up tomorrow morning, and, to your surprise, your eighteen-wheeler has been stolen." He sarcastically slapped his cheek with false amazement and continued, "Then you report the vehicle stolen and contact your insurance company—simple as that. Shoot, it's so close to the border, they'll think it went to Mexico."

I got in the car and took a five-hour drive to the Rio

Grande Valley. The driver of the T-bird let me out toward the back of a motel and I got the license number as he drove off.

I went to the motel office and found the night clerk asleep in front of a television broadcasting test pattern. I rented a room and sacked out for the night.

Next morning I called Dave's office and they put me on hold. Finally Dave got on the horn.

"Hello, Tex," Dave said with distress in his voice.

"Hey, Dave, you don't sound too good. Somethin' wrong?" There was a long silence.

"Get on a bus to Falfurrias. I'll meet you there and debrief you over lunch."

Dave was parked and waiting for me at the bus station. I climbed out of the bus and slung my duffel bag over my shoulder. I walked up to Dave's Chrysler as he started the engine.

"Hey, Dave," I said as I tossed my bag in the back seat and jumped in the front.

Dave just sat quietly, gave me a feeble smile, and rolled away from the curb. I handed Dave the envelope containing five thousand dollars as we drove away from the bus station.

We stopped at a local diner for lunch, where we took a booth at the window, facing the road.

"So what happened?" I asked, anxiously leaning forward.

Dave stared out the window with a dour expression, then turned to me and said, "We fucked it up."

I leaned back in my seat and took a deep breath. "Y'all lost the truck?" I asked, frowning in disbelief, "with a homing device on the damned thing?"

Dave nodded sorrowfully. "How'n the hell did that happen?" I asked.

Shaking his head, Dave took out a small notepad.

"Okay. Let's see. Yeah. We followed the vehicle north on Interstate Thirty-five, through Austin, Waco, etcetera, etcetera . . . then north at Thirty-five west, through Fort

Worth, north on U.S. Two-eighty-seven, where the vehicle stopped for approximately forty minutes. The vehicle then proceeded northeast on State Fifty-nine for approximately twelve miles, where the beacon signal ceased to register."

Dave looked up from his notes. "And it wasn't an equipment failure—at least not the receiver. The lab boys made certain of that. They also said that it's very doubtful the tracking device was discovered. We don't know what the fuck happened."

"So what happens now?" I asked.

Dave shook his head in disgust. "Well, we've got a man on the security guard, Ranson, in San Antonio, and we suspect the chop shop is up in Bowie, where the truck stopped last night, but we can't take the risk of raiding the place because we can't be sure we'll find any evidence."

After lunch, Dave called his office, then we began the long journey back to Dallas. We arrived at the basement garage of the Federal Building just after dark. As we rode the elevator to his office, Dave leaned against the wall and shook his head with a sigh.

"My boss is tearin' his hair out over this one," Dave said with a forced laugh.

We entered the office of Mike Patton, Dave's superior, and the secretary instructed us to go right in. Chief Investigator Patton was staring out the window at the city lights as we entered. We stood silently for a minute. I was about to speak up when Dave shook his head and frowned at me with his finger to his lips. Without moving, Patton spoke in a deep, grinding voice, "What the hell happened out there, Moore?"

Dave reluctantly answered, "As I stated in the report, sir . . ."

Patton whirled around and slapped his hand on the desk. "Damn it, man, I saw the report! I want you to tell me personally what actually happened out there."

"It was a bad judgment call," Dave said firmly. "We

152

had followed the vehicle to a location in Bowie, where we set up a command post. When all my men had assembled, I sent two agents in on foot for reconnaissance and was about to have all units converge on the premises, when the signal from the tracking beacon began registering movement. We pursued the vehicle, maintaining a safe distance . . ."

"You did not have visual contact?" Patton interjected sharply.

"Well, sir," Dave said, "we did make visual contact initially, but we relied on the tracking signal for the surveillance."

Patton eased himself into his chair, rested his elbows on the desk, and rubbed his temples.

"You lost a thirty-thousand-dollar truck," Patton slowly remarked, "and came away with only five thousand dollars and no arrests?"

"Excuse me, sir," I said. "I think that if I bring another truck up to Bowie, I can gain the confidence of the people on the inside."

They both looked at me like I had two heads, then Patton broke the silence. "Shoot, you ended up two hundred and fifty miles from the point of contact, for Pete's sake," he said, jumping out of his seat, "and you want to go out there with . . ."

"Hey, look," I shouted, "I made contact from leads I dug up myself. I was workin' blind. I did what I was hired to do, and I did what I had to do to get results—and I got results. I can do it again if y'all give me the chance."

As Patton sat back in his chair, his angry expression softened. I rubbed my neck and paced around the room a little to cool off. After what seemed like a long silence, Patton said, "Okay, Brown, you got your chance." He turned to Dave. "File the requisition forms for another vehicle. That'll be all."

I went to a phone and called Becky to let her know I'd be home later that evening, then I caught up with Dave. As we waited for the elevator, Dave said, "It might take a couple of weeks for the paperwork on that truck to clear, but it could take longer. I'll call you and let you know when everything's set."

Dave dropped me off at the security lot, where I picked up my Chevy and started the eight-hour trip home.

Two months after I left Dallas, I was out mending fences about three miles from the house. It was scorching hot, but the morning sun was still low in the east when I heard Becky's voice over my CB radio.

"Breaker one nine, breaker one nine. Tex, can you hear me?"

I grabbed the mike from the dashboard.

"Go ahead, Becky."

"Tex, Dave Moore is callin' from Dallas."

"Tell him I'll call him right back," I replied.

I threw the tools into the bed of my pickup and drove on back to the house. I called Dave's office and was put on hold, then Dave came to the phone. "Hello, Tex. How y'all doin' in this heat?"

"Oh, pretty good," I said, as I wiped the sweat from my brow. "Whatcha got, Dave?"

"Tex, you are not going to believe this," he said with an ironic laugh. "We found the truck. In fact, we found about forty trucks that have been stolen in recent years."

"Well, that's good," I said with a laugh.

Dave paused a second, then said, "No, that's bad—we found them at the bottom of a lake outside of Bowie that dried up recently. They've all been stripped down to nothin'."

"Damn," I said.

"They used cutting torches," Dave said. "They cut the motor mounts . . . they got the transmissions and rear ends. They took everything out of 'em. They had to've hauled them with a flat-bed, eighteen-wheel wrecker."

"Well, I'll be sheep-dipped," I said. "So, have y'all got the new truck yet?"

"As a matter of fact, we have," said Dave. "Can we expect you within the next few days?"

"I'll be there before dark. See ya then," I said as I hung up the phone.

By the time my destination was in sight, the sun was just off the horizon; its orange rays flashed off the tall glass buildings of Dallas in the distance. When I reached the city I went straight to the Federal Building, left my truck in the parking garage, then went up to Dave's office. Dave had nothing new to tell me, so he gave me another thousand dollars for expenses and instructed me to meet him at the security storage lot the next day. I checked into a nearby motel and got a good night's rest.

After an early breakfast the next morning, I picked up the semi and headed north on State Highway 287 with Dave following in the surveillance van. The truck I was using for bait was a brand-new Mack, and it handled real nice. Of course, any truck handles well without a trailer hitched to it.

I arrived in Bowie, Texas, and stopped at the first diner that had enough room for me to park the beast. It was too early for lunch, so I sat at the counter and had coffee. I started jaw-jacking with some good ol' boys. "Say, any you fellers know anybody's got a trailer needs hauled?"

They all shook their heads, then the leather-skinned trucker sitting next to me wearing a dirty baseball cap and a shirt with white rings of dried sweat under the arms and on the back spoke up. "You ain't got no trailer? Why not?"

"The damn bank repo'd it. I couldn't believe it. I unhitch it to bring my rig in for service, come back, and it's gone. I figured it mighta got stolen, but my wife got a call from the bank, and if I can't raise enough for my past two payments—well, I don't even wanna think about it."

The men at the counter were all cursing and shaking their heads. Then the man sitting next to me spoke.

"Listen, I know a feller who might help ya out of this bind," he said as he wrote a name and address on a paper napkin. "You got insurance on your rig?" he asked.

"Yeah," I said. "It's due to run out in about a month and a half."

He looked around, leaned real close to me, and whispered. "Now, what they'll do is buy your truck for about six grand and then you report it stolen in another town. That way, you get paid by the insurance company plus you get a pocketful of tax-free cash. You just tell 'em Whitey Albertson sent ya."

I slapped two bits onto the counter, paid the cashier, and went to a pay phone.

"Lemme talk to Dave Moore. . . . Hello, Dave? Tex. It's a go. An old trucker gave me the name of somebody at the chop shop east of town, out by State Fifty-nine."

"Good work," Dave said with a note of happiness. "We've got a visual on your truck. I want you to start driving east, and we'll signal you to pull over."

"I gotcha," I said as I hung up and left. I pulled onto the main road and saw the large brown step van pull out of a parking lot across from the diner. They eased out into traffic and followed me about six car lengths back. As the buildings thinned out toward the edge of town, the van pulled out in front of my truck and turned off the road. I followed them to a clearing behind a row of buildings, climbed out of the cab, went over and banged on the side of the van. Dave opened the door, I stepped inside, and he quickly closed the doors behind me.

Dave sat me in a cushioned swivel seat with safety belts hanging to the side that was anchored to the floorboard in front of a panel full of switches, dials, buttons, and blinking lights. The other two agents with Dave were seated in front of a bank of video monitors and a huge tape recorder. They had stereo earphones hanging loose around their necks, and they started turning on several pieces of equipment as Dave reached for the box with the electronic listening device.

As I took off my shirt, Dave was pulling foot-long strips of cloth tape from a two-inch roll. The loud tearing sound was like fingernails on a chalkboard, and I could almost feel that tape pulling thousands of tiny hairs from my body. With the wire in place I put my shirt back on, went back to the Mack, and drove on over to the shop at the edge of town.

I parked to the side of a large cinderblock building with chipped, peeling paint and a weathered sign above the huge rollaway doors that read LONE STAR WELDING. As I swung the door open, stepped out on the rungs, and climbed down the side of the cab, a scrawny guy wearing a greasy, brimless, cloth welder's cap and dirty blue coveralls burned at the edges came over to me.

"Somethin' I can do for ya?" he asked, lisping through a gap where teeth used to be.

"Ah, yeah," I said, as I pulled my hat back and scratched my head, "I'm here to see Matt. Whitey Albertson sent me."

His expression hardened, and he paused for a second.

"You a cop?" he said with a frown.

I chuckled and shook my head. "No, I sure ain't."

After a brief moment, he turned and waved his arm, motioning for me to follow. He led me through a front office, a huge shop with a roof three stories high, past machinery and large steel bottles of flammable gas to a storage room in the back where a man with wire-rimmed glasses holding a clipboard was taking inventory.

"Hey, Matt," yelled the welder, "this here guy says ol' Whitey Albertson sent him over."

"You a cop?" he asked sternly.

"Like I told your man here, I ain't no cop. I'm a long-haul trucker what got hisself into a bind."

"How do you know Whitey?" he asked.

"Just met the man this morning at the Day Long Diner. I've been so dad-blamed worked up about the bank repo-in' my trailer, I just had to tell somebody . . . and Whitey steered me to y'all."

The man thought a second, then turned to the welder. "Frisk him, Bill."

I took a step back and put my hands out as the man approached me.

"I'll be goddamned if I'm gonna have some greasy son

of a bitch lay a finger on my person," I said as I slammed my hand onto a box of welding rods. "Man, the bank has already put the fuck to me without so much as a kiss or flowers, and if this is the way it's gonna be, you can just eat shit."

I'd started walking out the door when the man called after me. "Whoa, hold up a minute, pardner. I didn't mean to git ya all riled up about this. Tell ya what. Bring your rig back this evenin' at nine and we'll do business."

After I climbed up in the Mack and started the engine, I talked into the microphone I was wearing. "That was a close one, guys. They might tail me, so keep your distance."

Sure enough, as I drove away down the long flat stretch of road back into Bowie, I watched the rearview and saw a vehicle leave the place about two hundred yards behind me. I went directly to a truck stop, grabbed a nice big lunch, and played some pool in the lounge for the rest of the day.

At eight thirty I got back in the truck, secured an ankle holster to my leg, checked the cylinder of my Colt .38 snubnose, and slid it in the scabbard under my pant leg. I arrived at the shop and lined my front fender up with the massive door. I caught sight of a face looking out the front window, then a few seconds later the door began to slide to the left.

I slowly rolled the Mack into the building, shut her down, and got out. The door rolled back and was securely latched. Eight men stood by with cutting torches, motorized overhead cranes, motor mounts on rollers, and industrial-sized air ratchets. I walked over to the man in charge. "Talk to me," I said firmly.

"Six thousand," he said as he handed me a thick yellow envelope, "and we take ya to another town where you check into a motel and report the rig stolen the next day. Whitey tells me ya got insurance—they'll pay it off."

"Six thousand dollars. . . . This sure looks pretty," I said with a laugh.

At that point I heard tires screech, rapid footsteps

outside, and thunderous pounding on doors at either side of the building. I ducked down, reached under my pant leg, and pulled out my .38 as all hell broke loose. The steel doors came crashing down from the force of five-pound sledgehammers, while agents in three-piece suits rushed in with pump shotguns and Magnums.

As the leader started to bolt, I grabbed his shirt and pressed the muzzle of my revolver firmly under his chin. I saw terror in his eyes as he stared at me, then he looked over my shoulder and I turned to see one of the criminals about to throw a pipe wrench at me, so I pushed away from the leader as the weapon flew past my face and crashed into a nearby window.

"Hold it, slime dog!" I yelled, taking aim with my revolver as the man started to run to the other side of the truck. The felon stopped short when he saw the muzzle of a twelve-bore shotgun leveled at his head from the far side of the diesel rig.

Dave walked up to me as the suspects were being taken away in chains. "C'mon," he said, shaking my hand with a smile, "let's get outta here."

CHAPTER 9

I was at the tail of a convoy headed south to Dallas. It wasn't really what I'd call a convoy. I followed a paddywagon, the surveillance van, and four plain blue-wrapper sedans south on U.S. 287. We arrived in Fort Worth at about 10:45 P.M. and got on Airport Freeway 183 eastbound. When we reached Dallas proper, I followed Dave to the security lot, where I dropped off the Mack, then we rode back to headquarters. I was glad to see happy faces for a change in that office, and I'll admit there's a huge feeling of accomplishment that goes along with it. I found a vacant desk, stuck a piece of paper in the typewriter, and started to wrestle with the keyboard, when one of the agents hollered over to me.

"Hey, Brown. You got a message here to call home."

"Is it urgent?" I asked impatiently.

"It doesn't say," he replied.

I wanted like hell to get this report finished before sunup, but I was also a little concerned that there might be trouble, so I dialed home.

"Hello, hon. I got your message. Is somethin' the matter?" I asked with concern.

"No, nothin's wrong," Becky replied. "I got a message for ya to call a Mr. Jack Tyler up in Midland."

I scribbled down the number she gave me and said,

"I'm spendin' the night up here in Dallas. I'll be down tomorrow afternoon. You need me to bring ya anything?"

"Can't think of anything." she said.

"Okay, see ya tomorrow. Love ya. 'Bye," I said as I hung up and continued pecking at the keys.

By the time I finished the report I was starting to get saddle sores. The muscles in my forearms were stiff and the knuckles on my typing fingers (both of 'em) were aching a little. I stood up and stretched, then I gathered up the pages, handed them in, and left. I checked into a motel south of Dallas off Interstate 35 and got a good night's rest. Bright and early the next morning I dialed the number that Becky'd given me.

"Drug Enforcement Agency, hold, please," the receptionist answered.

Before I had the chance to tell her whether or not I wanted to, I heard a sharp click followed by easy-listening music. She finally got back to me.

"Hello, this is Ray Brown. I got a message to call Jack Tyler. Is he there?"

The girl put me on hold again, then Jack answered.

"Tex, how've ya been?" he said with a laugh.

"Oh, pretty good," I said. "Just finished up an investigation when I got your message. What's up, Jack?"

"There's a meeting scheduled two weeks from today. I'd like for you to be there," Jack said.

"Tell me a little about it," I said.

"Hold on a second," he said with the sound of shuffling papers in the background. "The meeting is in Fort Stockton, at the Stockton Inn. Now, without going into too much detail on this, several law enforcement agencies are going to be there, and basically what they're looking for is a recon of the Big Bend National Park on horseback."

"I thought Customs patrols that area," I told him, "and they ain't exactly Cub Scouts."

"Yeah, I know. They've got night-vision equipment

and the whole nine yards, but it seems like the dopers stay three steps ahead of them. We're hoping to form a game plan for an interagency operation in the area, and I figured you'd be right for the job."

"Well, I appreciate ya callin' me, Jack. I'd be glad to go."

Jack gave me the location, the time, and the date of the meeting, then I got off the phone and went for breakfast. After I finished my steak and eggs I called the waitress over to the booth.

"Darlin', I'm facin' an eight-hour drive to Laredo, and I'd sure appreciate it if you'd fill this up with coffee for me." I pulled out my tall metal thermos bottle with half the green paint chipped off and dents in the side. She picked it up and looked around hesitantly, then smiled and said, "Okay."

I left the girl a big tip, paid the tab, then jumped in my Chevy pickup and got back onto Interstate 35, southbound for the trek homeward. It was good to see the familiar features of the land I owned. As I drove, I saw a lot of things I needed to get done around the place, and I smiled as I thought of how good it was to be back home. For the next two weeks I spent nearly every daylight hour catching up on most of the heavy chores I'd been putting off. It was hard work, but I considered it a vacation.

The day before the meeting, I packed a few things in my duffel and headed for Fort Stockton. I figured I'd save time by avoiding the interstates, so I got on U.S. 83 northbound, to U.S. 277, through Eagle Pass to Del Rio, then along the Rio Grande on U.S. 90 past the Judge Roy Bean Saloon and Museum. The sky was clear and blue, and the sun was getting low in the west by the time I reached U.S. 285, the last stretch of road before Fort Stockton.

Jack had a room reserved for me at the Stockton Inn. I checked in, then went to my room and changed into my swimsuit. The motel had a real nice pool, so I thought I'd relax awhile and go for a swim. At seven the next morning Jack met me in the coffee shop. We had no trouble at all getting a booth.

"At the first meeting," Jack said as he stirred his coffee, "they decided to send someone into the park on horseback to scout around and report back. What they're not sure of is how to proceed after that. We've got some hotheads on the committee who just want to send a man in cold to make a buy with twenty sharpshooters hiding in the bushes."

"Are you serious?" I said in disgust.

"See, it's these budget cuts. They need results right away, because the paper pushers in Washington are getting ready to decide how to divvy up the pie. Everyone's worried about how big their piece is going to be."

As soon as we finished breakfast, me and Jack headed straight to the motel conference room where the meeting would be held. The tables were arranged in a horseshoe, and each one was covered with a white tablecloth. Waiters busied themselves setting out pitchers of water, pots of coffee, mugs, and glasses.

As we walked toward the meeting room, Jack introduced me to some of the people in the lobby. There were about thirty people from different federal agencies seated or standing around the table. One of the men at the head of the table started banging his spoon against a water glass to get everybody's attention. Every head turned and the man told us all to have a seat. He introduced himself as Thomas Miller from the United States Customs Service. He had silver hair, broad shoulders, and a beet-red complexion. Miller started the meeting by having each of us introduce ourselves, then he spoke his mind.

"Gentlemen, as most of you well know, the U.S. Customs Service patrols Big Bend National Park, primarily with four-wheel-drive trucks. Most of the time these patrols are carried out at night and the vehicles run with lights out and the agents wear night-vision equipment. We know there is illegal activity in the park, but by the time the vehicles get out there . . . nothing. In short, gentlemen, it has gotten to the point where we might as well stay home."

Miller took a big drink of water and continued. "This gentleman on my left, Jack Tyler with the Drug Enforcement Agency, has brought with him a man with whom he has worked before on several cases, Ray Brown, or 'Tex,' as he is known. Mr. Brown is not officially attached to any government agency and therefore is able to be a little more flexible in his methods. As we discussed in our last meeting, it is essential to have accurate intelligence reports on nighttime as well as daytime activity in the area. Jack recommended Mr. Brown because, among other qualifications, he is familiar with the area, is an accomplished rider, and he owns his own horses."

Miller turned to me and said, "Mr. Brown, I . . ."

"Call me Tex." I offered, loudly.

The man smiled and continued with a slight laugh. "All right, Tex, I know Jack has briefed you on this. We'd like to know, first of all, if you will conduct the survey of the park on horseback. Will you do it?"

I looked around the room and all eyes were on me. "Yes, sir, I'll do it, but I'd kinda like to know what y'all are plannin' to do afterwards."

"That's fair enough. We're not exactly sure of the particulars on the course of action we've decided to take. We have confirmed reports that there's a place on the Rio Grande, inaccessible by vehicle, where someone can walk up to the edge of the river and place an order, even for large quantities of marijuana, and they'll just bring it across the river. I know that sounds pretty farfetched, but it's true.

"Therefore, the plan we're seriously considering is to have upwards of twenty men take up strategic positions around the clearing at Santa Elena Canyon on the Rio Grande and send an operative in to make a buy."

I held my hand out and cut in. "With all due respect,

sir, I think you could build a better case and maybe even capture more suspects if you went slow and got a man on the inside. Find out where the stuff's comin' from. The plan you're talking about might put a crimp in their evenin', but y'all can't go in there every night. At best you'll get a few of 'em and maybe some bundles of weed, but you ain't gonna stop the flow of drugs that way, and it might get some of our people killed."

Miller sat there shuffling papers and looking around at the other men, then he turned back to me and said, "Your point is duly noted Mr. Br . . . I mean, Tex. Unfortunately, the matter is not open for debate at this time. If you have no further questions, Jack will brief you on your way out."

Jack stood up, gave me a light swat on my arm, and we left the room while they continued the meeting. As we walked down the hall Jack shook his head.

"Like I told ya before," he said with a laugh, "they've got a real hard-on for a big bust. I guess your suggestion just makes too much sense. Don't let Miller get to ya—he's just a pompous ass."

"That don't bother me," I said, "but what he's fixin' to do does. Man, I'm tellin' ya, it's . . ."

"I know, I know," Jack said, "I don't like it any better than you do. But anyway, you let me know when you're on your way back, and I'll set the meeting for the following day."

"I'll do that," I said as I walked away. "Talk to ya later."

Jack turned around and snapped his fingers. "Hey, Tex," he said as he walked back over to me, "I've got a pair of Star-Tron night goggles in the trunk of my car if you wanna use them. They're a hell of a lot better than infrared and . . ."

"I'll tell ya what, Jack," I said flatly, "on the off chance I get shook down by any of these dopers and they find somethin' like that on my person, you know what they'd do?"

Jack held up his hand and nodded. "I get your point," he said as he went back to the meeting.

I went to my room, packed up my things, and called Duke McMann. I told Duke a little bit about the meeting and the plan they were likely to go with. He thought it was a bunch of shit, but he realized that the threat of budget cuts can push some people to drastic measures.

I checked out of the hotel and drove home the same way I came. By the time I got there, Becky was already at her job as a medical secretary. I wasted no time gathering up the gear I needed. I grabbed a bedroll, a skillet, heavy jacket, gloves, socks, flashlight, and a few other odds and ends. I went to my gun vault and took out an old Winchester model 94, in 30-30 caliber, and a Colt single-action Army Buntline revolver in .45 long Colt caliber. I strapped on my gunbelt, then picked out some boxes of shells.

I always take my Colt Buntline model with me when I go riding because with a twelve-inch barrel you can really put the hurt on somebody from a long ways away. With my two-horse trailer hitched up to the Chevy, I bridled one of my Appaloosa mares and coaxed her into the trailer. I took an old saddle and blanket from the tack room and put them in the trailer stall next to the horse. Finally, I loaded the truck with plenty of water and feed, then got back on the road. With the trailer in tow, I figured it'd be best if I got on Interstate 35 northbound; it took about another hour, but it was smooth driving.

When I got to San Antonio I rolled in at a truck stop and had dinner. I sat at a booth next to the window and kept an eye on my rig as I ate. The sun was falling fast, so I finished up and got back on the road. I continued on through the center of San Antonio on Interstate 35, then I hit Interstate 10 westbound. As I approached Fort Stockton, I pulled over at a rest area to feed and walk the horse.

The last leg of the day's trip was U.S. 67 southbound, and by the time I reached Presidio at the Rio Grande I was ready to sack out. I parked in a lot just outside Fort Leaton State Park, chained up the doors to the trailer, then locked myself in the cab of the pickup and fell asleep with my six-shooter close at hand.

I woke with the sun the next morning and dragged myself out of the truck. I checked on the horse and walked around a little to get my circulation going, then hopped back in my rig and got moving. I came to a small general store at the east end of town. It looked more like an old house than a business and probably served both purposes. The overhang covering the front porch was supported by heavy beams, cracked and sun bleached, with faded signs advertising companies that probably had gone under decades ago.

The wood flooring creaked and sagged a little as I walked through the building. The place smelled of burnt mesquite, fresh cut firewood, and fresh brewed coffee. I went back out to my truck and got my thermos, came back, and filled it with almost a whole pot of the hot brew. I grabbed an armload of canned meat, beans, and peaches, and set them on the counter. An old man with a week's growth of white whiskers shuffled over to the cash register.

"Well, young man, looks like you're goin' campin'," he said. Then he asked with a toothless grin, "Will that be it for ya?"

"Yeah," I said, looking through my billfold. "Actually, I would like to ask a favor of ya. I'm headin' into the park on horseback, and I wonder if I could leave my rig parked on your property for a few days?"

As he carefully looked at each item and rung it up, he said, "Well, I got a storage area out back. It's fenced in. I'll charge ya . . ." He turned and looked at me, squinting for lack of light. ". . . two dollars a day."

"That's a bargain if I ever did come across one," I said as I paid him for the food. He walked out with me and told me to drive around back. I eased the Chevy down a little dirt road that was actually two side-by-side trenches left by the countless grinding of vehicles through the soft earth. The old man stood by, holding the gate open as I rolled my pickup through the opening in the chain-link fence. I got out, opened the trailer, and brought the mare out.

As I saddled my horse the storekeeper asked, "What ya gonna be doin' in there, if I might be so bold in askin'?"

"Sight-seein'," I said coldly.

"You plan on doin' any shootin'?" he said, taking a step closer.

"I don't expect to," I said as I cinched the saddle down tight, "but ya never know."

"Yessir, this is God's own country," he said, looking out at the mountains to the east. "But just a word of advice . . . you watch your ass in there, son. Them dopers from across the river'd cut your throat as soon as look at ya."

"I appreciate your concern, mister," I told him as I swung myself into the saddle, "but I figure I can take care of myself."

I reined the Appaloosa to the east, lightly kicked my heels, and slapped the reins. The mare started loping, but I slowed her to a trot and circled back to the storekeeper.

"Tell ya what," I said to the man as I scribbled on my notepad. "If you don't hear from me in three days, you call this number." I tore the sheet of paper out of my pad and handed it to him. "That's my wife. You tell her to call Jack Tyler. I'll write the name down for ya. Tell him . . . shoot, I don't know what'n the hell to tell him. Just have her tell him I ain't got back. Okay?"

He looked up at me to ask something, thought better of it, and nodded.

I wheeled the mare around and bolted off toward the mountains. After about one hundred yards, I eased back on the reins and slowed the animal to a light canter for the rest of the ride into the park. I rode thirty miles south, down a dirt road called 170 that skirts the Rio Grande and goes on through Big Bend National Park. By the time the sun was directly overhead, I found a good campsite under a tall mesquite tree by the river southwest of Lajitas, just outside the westernmost edge of the park. I secured the end of the reins to a branch where my horse had all the grass she could eat, then took an old beat-up pair of binoculars out of my pack and climbed up the tree to have a look around.

The Rio Grande snaked its way through the lowlands to my right. Dotted with clumps of sagebrush and greenery, the dry, rocky plains ahead spread out and rose gradually to meet the foothills and mountains of this untouched, west Texas wilderness. I climbed down from the tree, unsaddled the mare, laid out my bedroll, then me and the horse rested up for the evening's ride. As I rode along the river the clear night sky showed the stars burning brighter than I think I'd ever seen them. They looked like sparks from some ancient explosion frozen in time. Just thinking about the size and distance of those tiny pinpoints of light or the depth of space kind of makes me think how small and fragile this earth really is.

The half moon started to show itself just above the mountains to the east. I did a double take at first, not knowing what to make of the bright beacon of light, but as it quickly rose between two peaks of the Chisos Mountains, I could clearly see the craters and features on the surface and even a crisp outline of the dark side on that cold ball of rock.

Suddenly, the mare reared as I heard the roar of an engine from behind me. I pulled the reins to the left and kicked as the animal bolted over some bushes at the side of the trail. I stopped the horse, patting her neck to calm her down. I looked up and saw the dark outline of a truck with no headlights bouncing along the trail, tires spinning through the sand and clattering over river rock. As it quickly passed by I could barely make out the white lettering on the side of the vehicle. It read: U.S. CUSTOMS.

I walked the horse back onto the trail and kept going eastward into the park. The sound of the truck had just about died down, letting the quiet stillness return to the chill night air. From a mountain on the Mexican side of the river about two or three miles away, I saw a light flashing. Another beacon flashed as if to answer the first. I quickly got out my binoculars to catch a glimpse of the source, but the lights didn't flash again. With my compass I took bearings of my position relative to the locations of the signal lights and wrote them down on my notepad.

I figured that if those were dopers signaling the approach of the Customs vehicle from so far away, they must have the same technology as our agents. I rode to Santa Elena Canyon on the Rio Grande river, about ten miles as the crow flies from Lajitas. The river was shallow and you could easily throw a rock across without getting it wet.

Sheer cliff faces towered over the river on both sides, and in the silver light of the moon and stars I could almost swear the walls had tremendous faces carved into them. Huge rock piles and tufts of scrub brush lined the water's edge. The sandbars seemed to float like small boats endlessly fighting the current.

As I rounded a bend to the left I saw movement on the river. I immediately doubled back about a hundred yards and hid my horse behind some trees. I pulled out my Buntline Special .45, walked back to the bend, and climbed up the rocks to the edge of the cliff face. I watched through my binoculars as a man walked back and forth through the waist-deep water about one hundred and fifty yards away. He seemed to be crossing about every twenty to thirty minutes, and when he came back to the U.S. side he'd carry a small bundle over his head.

The Mexican side of the canyon had dense vegetation and a wide cleft in the rock that must have had a trail leading to the interior. As I carefully watched the far side of the river I saw dark figures moving and reflections of steel in the shadows.

I noticed several cigarette embers burning. Like fireflies, they'd continuously fly up and get bright, then drop back down and disappear. Having seen enough, I went back to my horse and left the way I came in. I got off the river and traveled another ten miles east, over to Mule Ears Spring just west of the Chisos Mountains. I unsaddled my horse, unpacked my bedroll, and made camp.

It was beginning to get downright cold with the light winds rolling down out of the hills, but I didn't dare make a campfire for fear of being seen by the wrong people. I woke before the sun had a chance to show itself. The eastern sky was a muddy orange; the morning air was cool and still, and birds of all sorts were chirping to beat the band.

I stood up, stomped my feet, and stretched my whole body to get myself in gear, then reached into my pack for breakfast. I took out a can of beef, a can of peaches, opened them, and ate right out of the tins. My thermos was empty, so I had to settle for a can of Dr Pepper. I watched the horse gnawing at the clumps of green grass at the edge of the clearing and laughed in envy as I washed down my cold food with warm soda pop.

I buried my cans, saddled up the mare, and headed northeast, picking up Dodson Trail toward Juniper Canyon and then going down through Glen Spring to Boquillas Canyon. The sun had climbed about half its full morning height, when I spotted fresh hoofprints on a deeply worn trail that crossed my path. Even from a distance I could tell they weren't made by tourists sightseeing on horseback.

I got off my horse and took a closer look at the tracks. The side trail was rugged and narrow, walled in by tall brush on either side. The ground was hard in places and soft at the flood washes. Most of the imprints were made by heavily loaded mules and on either side I saw the clear impressions of horse hooves. One thing that stood out was the fact that the shoes were poorly made; the shape, markings, and style told me they were from Mexico.

The tracks led north, so I followed them south for about a mile. As I came up over a rise, I saw something on the trail under a low canopy of dead branches that hung across the path. I got off my horse and ran closer, leading the animal by the reins. In the shadow of dense brush I found a package about a foot square wrapped in Mexican newspaper. The wrapping was torn open, revealing tightly packed marijuana. I saw small shreds of paper on the tip of an overhanging branch above the fallen bundle.

I stowed the evidence in my pack, marked the trail, then doubled back to the main trail and marked it. I took compass bearings and notes and then headed northwest. At nightfall I made camp under a tree about five miles north of Dugout Wells on Tornillo Creek. I unsaddled my horse and brought her to the creek to let her drink her fill. I splashed water on my face and filled my canteen, then brought the mare over and secured the reins to a tree branch.

With my binoculars around my neck, I climbed the tree and bundled up in a blanket. The leaves were sparse and I had a good view of the land for miles around. I can't say as I really expected to see anything, but I figured my only other choice was to sleep and that wasn't what I was sent there to do. Moonlight reflected off the creek and cast crisp shadows on the ground below me. The bright silver light almost looked a little like snow covering the rocks, scrub brush, and hills all around.

I was getting ready to climb back down and call it a night when I saw a cluster of lights less than a mile east of me. Through my binoculars I saw two pickups with their headlights on, side by side, facing north. About eight men on horseback carried torches and rode away from the vehicles in single file. I couldn't for the life of me figure out what in the hell they were doing, but as the horsemen took up their positions, I noticed that they were pairing off about forty to fifty yards apart in a straight line along a flat stretch of ground.

When I heard the high-pitched whine of a single-engine aircraft coming in from the north I knew for sure what they were doing. Without using the field glasses I watched in the direction of the noise and finally caught the metallic glint of moonlight reflecting off the wing of the aircraft. Through the binoculars I followed the plane as it landed on the makeshift strip. All the lights went out and the men gathered around the bird. I saw them load the plane with bundles taken from a total of nine pack animals.

In less than fifteen minutes the lights along the runway were lit and the plane's engine roared to life, pulling it slowly down the runway. The bird gradually picked up speed and by the last set of torches it seemed to leap from the runway. The moon flashed full off the tops of the wings as the craft banked toward the west, and in less than a minute it was gone.

I climbed back down, gratefully folded myself into the bedroll, and laid my head on my thin, hard pillow for some much needed shut-eye. The ground shook just slightly and I wasn't sure if I was waking up or still dreaming. I blinked my eyes in the pale light, took a deep breath of the crisp morning air, and shook myself out of a sound sleep. I heard the clatter of hooves nearby and carefully looked up to see a caravan of pack mules and men on horseback just across the creek about thirty yards from me.

They were traveling south and the packs harnessed to the backs of the animals were empty. They didn't seem to notice me until my mare snorted and whinnied and stomped her hooves. One of the horsemen looked over at me, pulled hard on his reins, kicked his horses, and galloped toward me. His horse splashed through the shallow creek and bounded up the bank to the entrance of my camp. The man jumped off his horse and stood cautiously holding his reins. The mule train stopped and all eyes were on me.

He was a Mexican with long, straight, jet-black hair,

wearing well-scuffed boots, brand-new blue jeans, a flannel shirt, and a denim jacket. I saw the butt end of a Smith & Wesson revolver sticking out of his belt as he walked closer. I stood with my left side toward him and my right hand rested on the grip of my Colt.

"What are you doing here?" he asked in a heavy accent.

"Well, the ranch I was workin' for went under," I said, kicking the dirt a little. "So I'm takin' a break for a while. Give me some time to relax and think things through."

He looked at me in silence for a few seconds and then walked over to my horse.

"I like your horse, gringo," he said with a smile. "How much you sell to me for?"

"She's not for sale," I said grimly.

The man's smile died and he stared at me long and hard, then he looked down at my belt and must have seen the cartridges in loops along the back. He started laughing and walking back to his horse. "Gringo," he said, shaking his head as he mounted his horse and took off.

I quickly packed up, threw the saddle on my mount and cinched it, then got out of there as quick as I could. I headed due west for twenty-five miles and came to a place called Study Butte at the west entrance to the park.

I rode into a small campground. It was a dirt clearing about the size of a football field, with recreation vehicles of all different kinds scattered across it. I walked my Appaloosa slowly through the grounds, casually looking around at the tourists.

About two hundred feet away I saw three people standing next to a half-ton pickup with a cab-over camper on top parked at the edge of the lot some distance away from everybody. They looked just a little suspicious, so I rode over to within earshot of them, got off my horse and let her graze. I sat down on a log, opened a tin of meat, and started eating out of the can.

A young Mexican boy with a backpack was talking to a young Anglo couple. Out of the corner of my eye I saw the woman motioning in my direction and talking fearfully in low tones to the man she was with. Then I heard him quietly say, "Oh, he ain't gonna do nothin'."

The boy handed the backpack to the man, who reached inside and seemed to study the contents, then stuck his face into the bag as if to smell it. I heard dollar figures argued back and forth till they finally agreed on $475. I tossed my empty can in a barrel, then got on my horse and started on my way. As I slowly rode past the vehicle, I twisted my neck and pretended I had an itch I had to scratch. I got a good hard look at the license plate and I wrote it down in my notepad as I rode off.

I can't say as I was getting sick of riding, but for the next eighty miles I sure looked forward to getting back behind the wheel of my pickup truck. I kept the mare going at a pretty fast pace and we made good time. I got back to Presidio just after dark and had the storekeeper unlock the gate for me.

"I was about ready to call that number ya gave me," he said as I backed my rig out, then unsaddled the horse and put her and her gear away. By this time I was bone tired but my day wasn't over yet. I paid the old man and asked to use his phone and I promised him it'd be collect.

"Hello, Jack, it's Tex, I just wanted to let ya know I'm outta the park and I'm on my way up to Fort Stockton."

"Good, good. What'd you find out?" Jack said anxiously.

"Look, I can't talk about it right now," I said, glancing over at the storekeeper, "but I'll tell ya all about it when I see ya. Oh, by the way, Jack, I'm on this man's phone. Can you do me a favor and call the . . ."

"I'm one step ahead of ya, Tex," Jack said with a laugh. "I'm gonna call the motel and reserve a room for ya as soon as you hang up."

"Thanks, Jack," I said with a smile.

I hung up the phone, then dialed the operator. "Operator, I'd like to charge a long-distance call to my home phone." The operator put me through to a friend of mine who had a spread just south of Fort Stockton.

"Hello, Bert, this is Tex. How ya been?"

"Good, Tex, how 'bout yourself?" he asked.

"Oh, fine, keepin' busy," I said, doing my best to keep from yawning. "Say, listen, Bert. I'm on my way up from Presidio and I wonder if I can board my horse at your stable for a day or so?"

"You're more than welcome, Tex," said Bert.

"I took my Appaloosa mare through the Big Bend for the last three days," I said, "and we covered some pretty rough ground. You think I can have her shod, too?"

"Just come on by," said Bert.

It was getting late and I had about one hundred and twenty miles of road between me and Fort Stockton, so I slept in the truck out in front of the General Store. In the morning I filled my thermos full of black coffee as always, then followed the dirt road over to State Highway 67 northbound up to Fort Stockton.

I dropped my horse off at Bert's place and visited with him awhile, then I told him I had business to attend to in town. After I checked into the motel, I filled the bathtub with steaming hot water and I must have soaked for an hour or more. I was lying on the bed just barely on the edge of consciousness when the phone rang.

"Hello," I growled.

"Tex," said the voice. "Did I wake ya, buddy?"

"Jack?" I said as I sat up and took a deep breath.

"The one and only," Jack said. "The meeting's on for tomorrow at eight A.M. sharp. I'll meet ya for breakfast in the coffee shop, okay?"

"Yeah," I said gruffly.

I lay in bed a while longer, then got dressed and went down to the restaurant for a big steak dinner. After I ate, I went back to my room and watched a Burt Reynolds movie on cable television.

The next morning I was reading the morning paper and having a cup of coffee in a booth at the motel coffee shop when in walked Jack and one of the other members of the committee.

"Tex Brown, you remember Mac Jefers," Jack said.

"I sure do," I said, as I stood up slightly and shook his hand.

"So, Tex, what've you got for us?" Jack said with a smile as the two men sat opposite me.

"I got a little surprise for the boys at the meeting," I said with a smug grin. I reached under the table, pulled out a brown paper shopping bag, and handed it to Jack. He had a puzzled frown on his face as he unrolled the top and looked inside. When he smelled the contents, saw it, and realized what was inside, he laughed out loud and showed it to Mac.

"That's it, Tex, possession of a controlled substance. I'm gonna have to take you in. You have the right to remain . . ."

We all started laughing, then with both a frown and a smile, Jack said, "Where did you get the money for this? We didn't authorize you to . . ."

"Hey, I found it, bud," I said with a straight face. "I even got compass bearings of the location and I marked the spot to boot."

"No shit!" said Jack, grinning from ear to ear.

"I ain't shittin' ya," I said firmly. "I found a trail the sons of bitches been bringin' it up on. But not only that, after I found that I took up a position in a treetop, and I saw the motherfuckers—at least, I think it was the same ones—I saw them set a runway in the middle of the night."

The two men listened intently as they stirred their coffee.

"What they did was, they had two pickup trucks side by side with their headlights pointin' north and eight horsemen paired off with torches along the strip."

Jack looked at his watch and said, "Shit, we'd better get in there."

I gave the committee a verbal report of my findings, which raised a few eyebrows. Some of the members saw it coming, and two of them were real impatient, even angry, because they wanted fast results.

"Look," I said angrily, "you hired me to survey the

park and report back to you. Well, I did that. Now you're askin me if I'm wantin' to go in there to make a cold buy. Under normal circumstances I'd do it in a heartbeat, but I'm tellin' ya, it ain't one or two Mexican college students out there. There were bunches of 'em along the river."

"Did you actually see these men?" Miller said coldly.

"I saw movement, I saw reflections of metal, I saw cigars burning, and . . ."

"Excuse me, Mr. Brown," Miller cut in sharply, "but we'd like to get on with the issue at hand. Will you go in?"

I took a deep breath, then laughed and shook my head. "Bottom line is, sir," I said as I stood up from the table, "you're askin' me to commit suicide."

I put my hat on and walked through the double doors and into the hall. I heard the rumble of loud voices from behind the doors as I paced the floor. After about a minute, one of the doors swung open. It was Jack, and he didn't look too happy.

"Tex, you've been on some pretty hairy ops before," Jack said with concern, "why are you so skittish about this one?"

My fists were clenched and my teeth were grinding. "Jack, lemme explain somethin' to ya," I said. "These men are professionals, and they know how to do their job, but they're tossin' everythin' they know about procedure and tactics out the window. They're treatin' this thing like they're goin' into a bad neighborhood. Shit!" I exclaimed, and turned away.

"Here's your money," Dave said, handing me a check. "Some other time maybe," he said as he went back to the conference room.

I went back to my room and called Bert to let him know I'd be there within the hour, then I gathered up my stuff and checked out. Bert could tell I was pissed off when I got to his stables.

"What's eatin' ya, Tex?" Bert said as he helped me hitch the trailer.

I shook my head. "Oh, nothin' much—it's just them truckin' unions makin' it hard to do business is all."

Bert just nodded. "That's a damn shame," he said as I paid him for shoeing and boarding my horse. "Keep in touch now, ya hear?" he said as I got in my pickup.

I waved back to him as I started rolling through the dirt. I drove up to Interstate 10 eastbound and I figured I'd stop off in San Antonio to look at some horses, since it was on my way and I had the trailer with me. I went to a stable just west of town, where I saw a few animals I liked, but I guess I wasn't in a bargaining mood just then, so I left and headed back home to Laredo on Interstate 35 southbound.

By the time I got back to the ranch, all the lights in my house were out. I put the horse up in her stall and stowed the gear, then I quietly went into the house and did my best not to wake Becky as I got into bed. I figured I'd allow myself to sleep in the next morning, so I set the alarm for 9:00 A.M.

Becky had already left for the office by the time I woke up. I dragged myself out of bed when the buzzer rang and went straight to the kitchen and started the percolator. After breakfast, I showered, brushed my teeth, got dressed, and went out to the horse barn to mend some wall panels.

That night, me and Becky went out for dinner and had a real nice time. With my job keeping me away from home as much as it did, I liked to spend time getting reacquainted with my bride whenever I could.

The next day, I finished up the work on the barn and decided to take lunch at a restaurant in town. I drove my Chevy Blazer on into Laredo and parked behind Ralph's Rib House near the convention center. As I walked to the door, I stopped to get a newspaper out of the machine. I knew everybody there by their first name, and without my having to ask, the waitress brought me a tall glass of iced tea.

After she took my order, I picked up the paper, unfolded it—and the headline hit me like a sledgehammer: AGENT KILLED IN WILD SHOOT-OUT. The article identified the dead man as Charles Plenger, age twenty-two, a police administration major at Sul Ross State University at Alpine, Texas. I quickly finished the article and stormed over to the pay phone.

"Drug Enforcement Agency, hold, please," the woman's voice said as I tried to cut in and tell her not to put me on hold. I was tapping my fist against the wall to keep from screaming. She finally got back to me and I told her to put me through to Jack Tyler's office.

"Tyler," said Jack.

"It's Tex, Jack," I said coldly. "Your guys just wouldn't take my word for it, would they? What the hell happened?"

"Ah . . . Tex." There was a long pause. "Ten of our guys were down at the riverbed where you saw the dope being unloaded. They were planning to catch 'em in the act, so to speak. But before our guys could make a move, the Mexicans came across the river on horseback like Pancho Villa's army, blasting away with rifles, pistols, and shotguns. Our guys fired back, of course, but when the smoke cleared Plenger was dead. Look, I know what you're going to say, and I don't blame you . . ."

I cut in angrily, "Do ya? Do ya really? That's good, 'cause I ain't got the slightest fuckin' idea what to say to you."

Jack sounded nervous. "It wasn't my party, Tex, it was . . ."

"Hey, I don't wanna hear it, Jack." I told him, "Man, that was just a kid y'all sent in there. I just can't . . . man, I'm beside myself, Jack. Was that thirty-five hundred pounds y'all got worth the life of a college kid?"

Jack was quiet for a few seconds and I heard him take a

deep breath. "Just don't talk to the press about this, okay?" he said nervously.

I laughed and said, "Shit, I wouldn't admit to bein' part of a deal like that one."

"Call me back when ya cool down, all right?" said Jack.

Grimly, I just slammed the phone back on the hook.

CHAPTER 10

What little I ate of my lunch didn't sit too well, so I had Alison, my waitress, put it in a doggie bag for me.

"You ain't feelin' too well, are ya, Tex?" she asked as I started to leave.

"Oh . . . I just got news of somebody dyin'," I said with a sigh.

"Somebody real close?" she asked.

"No, but it hit real close to home just the same," I said as I walked out the door.

On the way home I stopped off at a local sporting goods store and picked up a couple hundred rounds for my .45 auto, some targets, and a pair of earplugs. Then I went back to my ranch and did some target practice. At the time it was the only way I could think of to get away from people for a while and try to take my mind off the kid who took a bullet for me.

By the time the sun went down I'd finished firing the last of the shells, so I collected the targets, picked up most of the brass, then got in my Blazer and drove home. As I slowly rolled to a stop in the dirt by the front porch, I could smell supper cooking.

When I walked in Becky was busy at the stove, stirring, sampling, adding spices, and checking the oven. She turned suddenly when she heard the door close.

"Hi, hon," I said, as I came over to see what she had cooking. "Smells good."

"Thanks," she said with a smile. "Hey, somebody called up earlier for you, but he wouldn't leave a name. Said he'd call back."

"Well, what'd he say?" I asked with a frown.

"The man said, 'Is Tex there?'" she said, taking off her oven mitt. "He sounded strange, too, almost like he was scared or worried or somethin'."

"Well, that's damned strange," I said, sitting down at the kitchen table. "You ain't been givin' our number out, have ya?"

Becky looked over with a frown and shook her head. "Of course not. I realize how important it is to keep the number unlisted."

"Yeah," I said blankly, "well, if he wants to reach me I guess he'll call back."

I went in and washed the dirt and burnt gunpowder soot off my hands and face, then I watched the evening news until suppertime. Becky had fixed a meal fit for a Thanksgiving feast, except we had fried chicken, and no cranberries or stuffing. My appetite came back to me in full force as she laid the platters full of home cooking out in front of me.

I was close to being finished with my meal when the phone rang. I wiped off my fingers and went over to the phone on the wall.

"Hello," I said sternly.

"Are you Tex?" the man asked with a note of uncertainty.

"I am," I said. "Who am I talkin' to?"

I heard the man take a deep breath. Then he said, "You've worked with Edward D. Long, am I right?"

"Listen, pardner," I said, "I'm through playin' games. You tell me who'n the hell you are or we have nothin' further to say to each other."

"Damn it, man!" he said. "Ed's been killed . . . shot in the face with a twelve gauge yesterday."

A numbness swept over me and I leaned heavily on the kitchen wall. "My god," I said as I dragged a chair closer and sat down. "What was he . . ."

"Okay, let me start at the beginning," the man said. "My name's Jones, Doug Jones, and I'm with Drug Enforcement out of Kansas City. I've been working with Ed for the last six months from our office in Little Rock on a lead furnished by a snitch who was lookin' at hard time. The snitch gave us a major crank lab about forty miles northeast of Little Rock. To make a long story short, the lab is completely walled in and they've got armed guards on the roof and the perimeter. Ed took up a position in the trees at the edge of the property. I waited with two other agents back at our vehicles a few blocks away. After he'd been gone for a while we heard a shot. By the time we got there, he was dead."

"Well," I said, my voice cracking with anger, "why'n the hell haven't y'all nailed the sons of bitches?"

"Don't you think I wanna nail the fuckers? We've got no witnesses, but we can get warrants to go in for probable cause on the manufacture of narcotics and . . ."

"Look," I said in a troubled voice, "I don't mean to be rude. I appreciate ya callin', but I'd rather not talk to ya right now . . . nothin' personal."

"It's all right," he said. "Ed told me you two were pretty close. I'll give you my phone number. Call me when you get a chance, okay?"

I wrote down his name and number, then hung up and started to walk outside.

"What's wrong, Tex?" asked Becky. "You haven't even finished supper."

I slowly turned, staring blankly at the floor, then looked up at her and said, "A man I used to work with . . . you remember Ed Long?"

"Yeah," she said.

"He's been killed," I said as I turned and walked out the door.

Feeling sick and angry, I went out to the barn, turned on the light, and blindly walked around. I picked up a four-foot length of green pine two-by-four and went outside. At the side of the barn there was a fence made out of railroad ties and steel mesh. As I came closer to the corner post I started running and winding up with the two-by-four; then with both hands, I smashed it as hard as I could against the foot-thick piece of timber. The top half of the board I swung flew across the corral in a shower of splinters and my hands felt like they had been zapped by a cattle prod, but I hardly gave a damn about the pain. I tossed the chunk of wood aside, walked over to the horse trough, and dunked my head in the ice-cold water.

Back inside the house I grabbed a towel and dried myself off, then sat down in the den, picked up the phone, and dialed the number Jones gave me.

"Hello, Jones? This is Tex . . ."

"Call me Doug," he said.

"Yeah, ah, I hope ya didn't take offense before when I cut ya off," I said, "but I just had to get my head straight."

"Think nothing of it," said Doug. "Shit, I won't even tell you how I reacted when I found him."

I paused in silence.

"I'm wonderin', how'd ya get my number anyway?" I asked.

"Well," he said, "I got it from the Rolodex on Ed's desk. Ed talked about you from time to time. He talked about your unique cover and the advantages of using an operative who doesn't have a badge, things like that."

I just smiled and said, "Shoot, I'm just being myself is all."

"He even tried to get our boss to consider allocating funds to bring you in on this operation," Doug said, "but the boss wouldn't go for it."

"I want in on this one," I said flatly. "I want to see the sons of bitches sent to the penitentiary."

"Well, to be honest with you, Tex," said Doug, "I'd be happy to have you along on this operation, but like I said, our budget is frozen—we just can't pay you."

"Lemme explain somethin' to ya, Doug," I said. "I ain't concerned about the money. I wanna do it for Ed."

"I'm glad to hear that, Tex," he said. "I look forward to meeting you. You, ah, coming to the funeral?"

I hung my head down. "Yeah," I said sadly, "I'll be there. When is it?" I wrote down all the details, then hung up and turned to my wife.

"The funeral is gonna be in Little Rock four days from now," I told her, "and it'll take me a couple days to get up there, so I'm gonna turn in now and get an early start."

I grabbed my brown suit and matching Stetson out of my closet, then packed up some extra blue jeans, shirts, and socks. I took along a pair of dress boots and an extra pair of shit-kickers for every day, then I got my guns and ammunition together and stowed everything in the sleeper cab of my Mack so I didn't have to spend any time getting ready in the morning.

It was still dark when I got up the next morning. I threw on some clothes, went out, and fired up the engine of my old Mack diesel. I let her warm up for a few minutes since it'd been sitting for some months. After I filled my thermos full of coffee I went out and climbed into the rig, poured myself a cup, then threw the beast in gear and rolled down the long stretch of dirt road toward the interstate. With the windows rolled down the cool morning air whistled through the cab and brought me back to life.

As I headed northbound on Interstate 35 the stars began to fade and the sky to the east gradually changed from dark purple to a red that got brighter and brighter. I switched the radio to a country music station and tried to put my mind in neutral for the long haul, but all I could think about was Ed, the times we'd had, and what his family must be going through.

By midmorning I reached San Antonio, where I pulled in at a truck stop to fuel up and check on the fluids, then got back on the road to finish up the last two-thirds of the trip.

The sun was on its way back down toward the horizon by the time I reached Fort Worth. I looked up an old friend of mine named Darryl Hopkins, and his wife, Jeannie, fixed us supper. Darryl didn't know Ed but he and Jeannie were real sympathetic when I told them about his death.

"Listen, Tex," said Darryl. "We'd be glad to have you stay the night. Jeannie'll fix up the spare room for ya."

"Well, I really appreciate the offer," I told him, "but the way I feel right now, I'd rather be by myself."

We talked for a while about old times, then I told him I wanted to get an early start. I drove my Mack B61 over to the parking lot of a supermarket south of the airport and spent the night in the sleeper.

The next morning, bright and early, I went to a truck stop just off Highway 183 and had breakfast. Then I got back on the road. I followed 183 eastbound till I hit Interstate 30 eastbound through Dallas.

I decided to get on Interstate 20 eastbound through Shreveport, Louisiana, then take State Highway 79 northbound to avoid the Arkansas weights-and-measures scales. After driving nearly every daylight hour I arrived in Little Rock. I found another parking lot where I could leave my rig for the night, crawled back into the sleeper cab, and got unconscious.

After breakfast the next morning, I called Doug's office. He wasn't there, but the girl put me through to his car phone.

"Good morning, Doug," I said.

"Good morning, Tex," he shouted to compete with the loud country music on his radio. "How was your trip up here?" he asked as the sound of music died down.

"Shoot," I said with a laugh, "by now I'm used to drivin' the long haul."

He chuckled and said, "Tell you what, Tex, I'm going to call in a reservation for you at the Ozark Motel, on us. Why don't you go over there and get settled? I'll call you in about an hour, okay?"

"Real good, Doug," I said. "Talk to ya later."

After I checked into the motel, I hung up my suit, stowed my gear, then ran the water in the tub and took a nice hot bath. I left my watch on the counter facing me and checked it from time to time so I could finish up before Doug got there.

I dried off, got dressed, and sat down to put on my dress boots just as there was a knock at the door. I walked over in my sock feet and opened it. The man had long curly hair and a mustache. He wore sharp city clothes, with a thin alligator belt fastened by a gold buckle. His socks were gray with red stripes and he wore pointy Italian shoes with little gold doodads on the side.

"Tex?" he said, offering me his hand.

"And you must be Doug," I said with a smile.

We shook hands and I told him to have a seat while I finished getting ready.

"So tell me about you and that truck of yours," Doug asked. "How'd you ever decide to use it as a cover?"

I looked up at him as I was pulling my boot on and said, "There ain't much to tell. I've been in trucking since I was a kid, and I've had my own rig since I turned voting age. There ain't no play-actin' to it. Well, not much, anyway. I just gotta act like a doper, but you know what I mean."

Doug just smiled and nodded. "We'll swing by the crank lab," he said, "to take a look and . . ."

I cut him off in midsentence. "I'd like to go visit with Ed's widow first if ya don't mind," I said.

"No problem," Doug said. "In fact, I told her you'd be coming in for the funeral."

We took Doug's car and drove to a quiet neighborhood, past houses with well-kept yards and two-car garages. As we rounded the corner of the street I remembered as being Ed's, I saw cars of all description parked along the curbs on both sides of the street and people walking over to the house where I'd visited many times before. Doug pulled into the driveway, and as we got out of the car Ed's son, Mark, came out to greet us.

The struggle to hide his pain showed in his furrowed brow as I walked over to him and shook his hand.

"I'm real sorry, Mark," I said as I put my hand on his shoulder and walked with him toward the front door of the house.

"Thanks, Tex," he said sadly.

Inside the house, the rooms and hallways were filled with people wearing long faces paying their respects and recalling the times they'd had with the friend and associate they'd lost. Ed's widow, Joyce, was sitting in the parlor with her daughter. As I walked over to her she stood up and we hugged. Her body trembled and she sobbed quietly as I held her. Then she looked up at me through her tears and said, "Thank you, Tex, thank you for coming."

"Glad to, Joyce," I said. "Listen, if there's anything I can do at all, you just let me know, ya hear?"

She nodded and smiled. I walked around and talked with some of the men who'd worked with Ed. Some of them I knew and some Doug introduced me to. One of Joyce's girl friends was pouring coffee for the guests and I had a cup. I was heading back to the parlor from the kitchen when Joyce found me.

"Tex, I'm worried about Mark," she said with a frown. "He doesn't seem to be, but he's taking this real hard. He was away at college when he heard the news—it's his first year. You two used to get on real well on those hunting trips y'all used to go on . . . will you talk to him?"

"I sure will," I said, gently resting my hands on her shoulders. "Where's he at, d'ya know?"

"I don't," she said, craning her neck to see past the crowd, "and that's partly what's worrying me."

"Don't you worry now," I said. "I'll talk to him."

I wandered through the house and knocked on some closed doors. I finally went outside through the patio door and there was Mark sitting on the diving board of a good-sized kidney-shaped pool.

"You okay?" I asked as I sat down next to him.

"Oh, I'll be all right," he said as he stared down at the

clear blue water. Then he looked up. "What was the point in this, Tex?" Mark asked, his voice cracking slightly. "What good did it do for my dad to die? Huh?"

I looked him square in the eye. "Your dad was a fine man. He died doin' a job he loved and was proud of. He strongly believed he could make a difference and I know for a fact there are people alive today who wouldn't be if it weren't for your father. Some of 'em are back there in that house right now."

Mark's face brightened just a little. "Y'know, I was thinking seriously about becoming a cop . . . but now . . ."

"Look," I said, "a man's got to do what he feels is right deep down inside. Ya can't try and be somethin' because ya think it's expected of ya, and it'd be a damn shame to do it with vengeance in your heart. That kinda thing'll eat a man up from his insides out. I do know this, though. It's people like your dad that make this country a decent place to live in . . . and if ya do decide to follow in his shoes, I'm sure that this agency or any other would take you in a heartbeat."

As I stood up and walked toward the house Mark said coldly, "Tex, help get the sons of bitches that killed my dad."

I stopped, turned to look at him eyeball to eyeball, and just gave him a sharp nod and went inside. I went up to Doug and gave him a light backhand on his arm.

"You ready to go to work?" Doug asked.

I nodded to him and headed for the door. "You go on out and get the engine going," I told him. "I'm gonna tell Joyce I'm leavin'."

I told Joyce about the talk I'd had with her son, then said good-bye for the time bein' and left. As I got into Doug's car he said, "We'll be working with the sheriff's department on this one."

We arrived at the sheriff's office, where Doug introduced me to a man named Will Hodges. The three of us went to the motor pool and got in a small van. As we got out onto the road, Will looked back at me from the driver's seat and said, "You men had lunch yet?"

"No, we haven't, as a matter of fact," said Doug.

"I know a diner with some of the best lunch specials in the county," said Will. "Let's grab us a bite."

We were seated at a booth toward the back and the waitress took our order in no time. As we waited for our food Doug spoke up.

"Okay, gentlemen, we've got two crank labs cooking dope—we're talking massive quantities from chemicals that are available from damn near any wholesale supplier. Our snitch gave us the locations but apparently he doesn't know when or how the stuff is moved. We've got surveillance on both places, but there's a heavily wooded area north of the larger place. Now this particular lab is surrounded by a tall cinder block wall with a heavy steel gate and there are armed guards posted on the roof and at the perimeter. The smaller lab should be a piece of cake to get to. It's just a small house, but the big one . . ."

"What were ya plannin' on doin'?" I asked.

"Well," Doug said, "the judge will issue a warrant on probable cause, but we've got to hit the fortified lab first. If the small one gets busted and the other place finds out about it, they'll fold up shop and we lose 'em."

Our food arrived and Doug said, "We'll take a look at the place and you'll see what I mean."

We finished lunch, then drove north on U.S. 67 for about forty minutes, then took a side road past thick trees and bushes surrounding rural houses set far apart from each other. After winding our way back into a small subdivision, we came to a cross street. Doug nodded toward the house on the far left corner, which barely showed over the top of a forbidding wall, nearly forty yards from corner to corner and skirted by low shrubbery.

As we passed by, I carefully studied the features of the place and got a glimpse of the dense trees behind it. The gate was toward the back at the end of a driveway that ran between the wall and a vacant lot. On the other side of the lot was a residential construction site. All three properties were at the edge of the woods.

"So now you see what we're up against," Doug said as he looked back at me.

"Shoot," I said, "I don't see no problem gettin' in. Of course, we gotta take care of a few things first and . . ."

"You planning on parachuting in there?" Doug asked with a laugh.

"No," I said matter-of-factly. "Lemme explain somethin' to ya, Doug. I can get us in there, but we're gonna have to do our homework and you're gonna have to pull some strings downtown."

I grabbed a pencil and notepad, then went forward and crouched between the two men up front as we drove.

"Okay, here's the dope lab," I said as I scribbled out a crude map of the area. "Here's the vacant lot next to it and the gate is back here between the two properties. Now, instead of havin' fifteen cars converging on the place, we'll have all your men . . ."

After I told them my plan, both men started grinning.

"I'll be damned," said Will. "That's great, Tex!"

"That's too damn simple," Doug said, shaking his head, laughing and looking at the sketch. "I love it!"

I went over the details of my plan a little more as we drove back to Little Rock. When we got to the sheriff's office, Will dropped us off at Doug's car.

"I'll tell ya what, Tex," Will said with a laugh as we got out of the van, "you're either certifiably crazy or a genius."

I waved to him with a smile as he drove off. Then we took off in Doug's vehicle.

"If ya don't mind," I said, "I'd like to stop by the funeral home for a few minutes to pay my respects alone."

We went to the mortuary and Doug waited in his car.

"I won't be but a minute," I said to him as I went inside.

I walked up to a man in a real fancy suit who stood rigidly in front of a desk talking to a receptionist.

"My name's Ray Brown. I'd like to pay my last respects to Edward D. Long. Where can I . . ."

The man stared at me for a second, then nodded and led me to a room off the main hallway. He opened the doorway and motioned for me to enter. Then he closed the door and left me alone. I walked up to the closed coffin and bowed my head. I stood in silence for a minute or two, and after a few private words of good-bye, I looked up.

"We'll get 'em, Ed," I said with a frown, my voice cracking slightly. "You can count on it."

I sat quietly on the way back to the motel. As we pulled into the parking lot Doug said, "I'll get the ball rolling. We should have the warrants and equipment day after tomorrow." We stopped near my room.

"I'll pick you up tomorrow at nine," he said as I got out.

I waved back and shut the door. That night I ordered supper from room service and watched a movie on television, then went to bed early.

That funeral service the next morning seemed about the longest forty minutes of my life. The church was filled with police officers from all over the county—not to mention Ed's fellow agents from the Drug Enforcement Agency. After the service was over, me and Doug jumped in his car and followed the procession to the cemetery.

All the cars parked one behind the other along a road lined on our left with tall oak trees. The cheerful beauty of the rolling hills covered in green grass and trees filled with singing birds seemed to be smothered by the stone markers set in orderly rows for as far as the eye could see. There were many sad faces that day gathered around the coffin draped with an American flag.

The next day after breakfast I called Doug on his car phone.

"How's she goin', Doug?"

"The judge isn't available today," he said, "but I've been assured I'll have the warrants by tomorrow noon."

"What about the blueprints to the house?" I asked.

"You were right," Doug said with a laugh, "they had 'em on record downtown. Those'll make things one hell of a lot easier for us. Oh, yeah, I talked to the boys in Public Works about blocking the water and sewer. At first they thought I was nuts, but after I explained your plan they said they'd have a crew out there whenever I said."

"Good, good," I said, "and what about the . . ."

He cut me off in midsentence. "At first," Doug said, "my boss was kinda surprised, to put it mildly, and he was hemmin' and hawin' about the cost, but he wants to get those bastards as much as anyone, so he okayed it."

"When you figure on movin'?" I asked.

"There'll be a briefing at ten A.M. tomorrow," Doug said, "and as I said, we should have the warrants by about noon, so when I get those I'll have the water crew get in position with one of our radios. I expect we'll move by late afternoon."

After I hung up the phone I called Becky at work just to talk, then spent the rest of the day swimming and reading a book by the side of the pool.

When I woke up the next morning it seemed to be only slightly lighter outside than it was when I went to bed. As I got ready I kept thinking about the bust and how it should or could go down, playing it over and over in my head in different ways and preparing myself for what might happen. I had breakfast in the motel coffee shop and took it easy on the caffeine. I paid the cashier, then walked all the way to the back of the property where I'd parked my Mack.

I pulled my eighteen-wheeler out on the road and drove over to the Drug Enforcement Agency parking lot. Then I went inside for the briefing.

Doug stood at a large black chalkboard scratching lines and squares, Xs and arrows with an occasional bloodcurdling screech of chalk on slate. It was almost like a football coach planning the big game.

"This dope lab is surrounded by a seven-foot cinder block wall, the steel gate is kept locked, and there are armed men posted along the perimeter as well as the roof. Once we're inside the compound this will be a standard entry. We'll have two men on the front door with the battering ram, then each room will be secured one at a time. Given the nature of this operation, we will have the cooperation of the Public Works Department, who will cut off all water and sewer to the premises to prevent the loss of evidence."

He picked up a stick with a rubber tip—it looked like a miniature pool cue—and turned to the blueprint that was leaning on an easel to the right.

"I want you men to familiarize yourselves with the layout of this place. It'll save time and possibly lives. This first lab is substantially larger than the second. The second lab has no wall and there should be a lot less difficulty with that one. We will hit the second immediately after the first is secured."

A hand rose in the second row and Doug nodded to the man. "How will we get into the compound?" he asked.

Doug smiled and pointed toward me. "I'm going to let this gentleman tell you that, since this was his plan."

When Doug introduced me to the group of men who were to be on the entry team with me, some of them gave me sideways looks as though they had their doubts about my credentials. Things like that don't bother me unless they get in the way of the bust.

"I'm happy to be a part of this operation," I said. "I'm just sorry about the circumstances that brought me here. I'll lay it out real plain for y'all. I've got a Mack eighteen-wheel truck parked out there, and what we'll do is, instead of having all of y'all tear on up to the place in plain-wrapper vehicles, you men will be inside the trailer of my rig and . . ."

The men were smiling, nodding, and laughing among themselves as I filled them in on the rest of it. When I sat back down Doug answered a few questions from the group. Then he adjourned the briefing and made some phone calls.

After lunch Doug came over to me. "Tex, I've got the warrants," he said with a smile. "The water crew is in place and the truck you ordered is on its way."

"Good to hear it," I said.

"This is agent Tillman," Doug said. "He'll be driving the equipment truck and he'll have this M16 with him to cover the entry team." The man held up a rifle all decked out with a scope and heavy barrel.

"That works for me," I said as we started walking.

The men were assembled in a large open office separated into workstations by cloth-covered partitions and bordered on all sides by glass windows. Doug gave the word for everybody to saddle up and get moving.

As I walked outside with the driver and the rifleman I saw another semi parked behind mine. I was met by a man in sneakers, blue jeans, a tan shirt with his name and company logo sewn on over the pocket, and a matching cap. He was holding a clipboard and his lower lip bulged out to one side damn near past the end of his nose.

As I walked up to the man he spat a long stream of dark brown juice onto the grass next to the walkway. He looked up at me and smiled, exposing heavily stained teeth and a black wad of tobacco between his cheek and gum.

"You Brown?" he asked, shading his eyes from the afternoon sun.

"Yeah," I said as he handed me a clipboard. "You folks doin' some excavatin'?" he asked as he pointed to the line on the invoice I was to sign.

"In a manner of speakin'," I said with a laugh. "So this rig's ready to roll?"

"Yes, sir," he said as I walked toward the vehicle, "and, ah, I left the engine in my truck runnin' for ya."

As we walked toward the vehicles I turned to the agent who was to drive the other truck.

"So you know where to go?"

"Yes," the agent said, "I've been fully briefed."

"I hope you know how to use that peashooter," I said to him, pointing to the M16, "'cause ya might have to shoot over my head."

He smiled and nodded, then walked to the other vehicle.

Doug walked over to me and said, "Give these boys a smooth ride, will ya?"

"Don't you worry," I said with a laugh, "I'll drive that rig like I'm haulin' crates of eggs stacked tall and loose."

Seventeen agents, half of them with riot shotguns, piled into the trailer of my Mack semi through the door on the left side. I got into the cab of my rig and we were all on our way. Doug followed in an unmarked car along with a paddy wagon and three other cars for the return trip.

With my handheld walkie-talkie I monitored A channel as we all headed northbound on U.S. 67. We'd been on the road for about thirty-five minutes when word came over the radio.

"This is Blue Leader," came Doug's voice. "We're approaching ground zero. Support units are to fall back. Outlaw, do you read me, over?"

"I read ya," I said.

"It's your baby from here on in, over," said Doug.

"Ten-four, Blue Leader," I said. "I will give the word when I'm in position, over."

"Roger that, Outlaw. Blue Leader out."

We wound our way back through narrow streets, past quiet houses and dense green woods. I parked the Mack just across the street from the fortress toward the far corner of the wall. The other truck passed by and romped over the curb to the left just past the dope lab. I jumped out of my truck as the agent stopped at the back of the vacant lot about a hundred feet from the steel gate and parallel to it.

I walked quickly over to the trailer, which was only a foot and a half off the ground between axles. I stepped up onto the bed and climbed into the seat of a big John Deere bulldozer. I fired up the massive engine of the earthmover, then pulled out my walkie-talkie.

"This is Outlaw," I said. "I'm in position, repeat, I am in position. Do you copy?"

"Roger that, Outlaw. You got the ball . . . run with it, over."

I looked up at the back window of the truck as I buckled up and the rifleman looked at me and nodded. As I sat there gunning the engine I noticed a couple of men on the roof inside the compound, but they didn't seem to pay much attention to me since there was construction going on behind me.

I put the radio away, pulled out my .45 auto, and rolled the bulldozer down off the side of the trailer. Its monstrous tracks bounced as they hit the dirt. I picked up speed and slowly barreled toward the gate. As I got within fifty feet of the entrance, out of the corner of my eye I saw the door of the trailer fly open. The agents poured out of the vehicle and ran toward me along the edge of the wall.

Sparks flew as the front blade of the dozer hit the heavy steel bars with the screech of twisting metal. Sections of the block wall toppled to the ground on both sides in a cloud of gray dust. The thunderous clap of a gunshot came from the rooftop in front of me. The bullet slammed into the steel plating two feet from my right leg and screamed as it richocheted past me. Almost at the same instant I heard a burst of automatic fire from behind me, as sections of the gunman's torso seemed to explode in a cloud of red mist. He slumped backward like a rag doll as the men swarmed past me through the breach in the wall.

Agents fanned out on either side of the building and many of them ran in behind two men carrying a three-foot length of four-inch steel pipe that was filled with cement and had handles welded onto it. The door flew off its hinges in splinters when the agents smashed the battering ram through it. Within minutes the agents had rounded up eleven prisoners, marched them outside, and laid them facedown on the pavement.

CHAPTER 11

As I backed the bulldozer out through the rubble and debris, four blue Ford LTD sedans with blackwalls screeched to a halt outside the premises. The paddy wagon pulled up to the gate as I drove back across the vacant lot. My heart was pumping a mile a minute. I raised the blade of the bulldozer as I approached the side of the trailer, slowed down just a little, then romped onto the bed. The eighteen-wheeler jostled from side to side with the impact and I bounced in my seat so hard I thought my fillings would come loose. I secured the dozer onto the trailer then hopped down and headed over to the house. Doug was standing at the open door of one of the sedans talking into the radio. He turned and saw me, then finished up and signed off.

"Tex," he said with his hand held out to me, "what can I say . . ."

"Listen," I said as we shook hands, "save your breath. I did this for Ed. You just get that other house, ya hear?" I asked as I started to walk toward my truck.

"You take care of yourself," he hollered, "and if I can do anything at all for you down the road, just don't hesitate to ask, hear?"

I waved back at him as I headed down the driveway. I ran across the street, jumped up on the side of my cab, opened the door, and swung in. Nearly three days of hard driving got me to the edge of Laredo just as the sun fell out of sight in a deep red blaze of glory. I parked the Mack in its usual spot by the barn and shuffled on over to the house. As I opened the door my dog, Boo-Boo, started jumping up for attention with her tail wagging to beat the band. I hung up my hat and saw Becky sitting on the couch in front of our color television.

"Hi, hon," I said. "I'm gonna soak in the tub before supper and . . ."

"I already ate," she said without turning away from the set, "I couldn't count on you showin' up."

"Becky," I said, "I called you from Dallas this morning and told you I'd . . ."

She turned to me with a look that could peel paint.

"Raymond Brown, you're gone so much I just don't know when I'll be graced with your presence around here."

I forced a laugh to keep my anger in check. "Lemme explain somethin' to ya, Becky," I said as I sat down next to her. "First of all, I know your job helps us out some, but I am earnin' the bread-and-butter money to keep a roof over our heads. More importantly, I'm tryin' to make a difference out on the street. Every dope smuggler we take off the streets and every ounce of dope we confiscate means there'll be fewer kids gettin' their hands on the stuff."

"My family thinks you're with the Cowboy Mafia," she said with her arms folded, looking at me sideways. "I tried to tell them you were workin' for the government, but they don't believe me. And that time you got arrested for stealing back the stagecoach . . ."

"I repossessed it," I said, "and remember, after the new evidence came in, those charges were all dropped. My slate is clean." I moved a little closer to her and started gently rubbing her shoulder. "I know your folks mean well," I said, "but you knew the line of work I was in when you married me. Tell ya what. I talked to Don

Austin up in Dallas on my way down here and he's got a case for me. I promise ya that we'll go on a vacation when I get back. Okay?"

She nodded in agreement but she didn't exactly light up with excitement. I went into the other room and took a long hot bath, then went to bed. I woke up the next morning before the sun had a chance to show itself and quietly got ready so as not to wake my wife. After I had my coffee I went out to the barn, saddled up one of my horses, and went riding. By the time I got back Becky had gone off to work. I poured myself a cup of coffee, then went to the phone and dialed.

"Department of Public Safety, Dallas, can I help you?" said the operator.

"Mornin', ma'am," I said, "can I speak to Don Austin please?" I'd been on hold for about half a minute when Don picked up.

"Good morning, Don," I said.

"You're up bright and early this morning," said Don.

"Shoot," I said, "I've already been out ridin' fences this mornin'."

"Well, that's pretty ambitious of ya, Tex," he said, laughing. "Okay, I'll meet you tomorrow at the Red Ryder Truck Stop in Victoria at . . ."

"I'll be there in the morning," I said anxiously.

"Hold on," he said. "Let's make it tomorrow evening at six." I got off the phone and went out to the Mack to get all my stuff out of the sleeper. I threw the dirty stuff in the hamper and put away my dress clothes, then I filled my duffel bag with clean stuff and stowed it back in the cab of my rig. After dinner that night I thought it'd be a good idea if I helped Becky with the dishes. We finished up, then I grabbed my coat and headed for the door. I stopped short as I was about to turn the knob, went over to Becky, and laid my hands on her shoulders.

"Remember now, we're goin' on a long vacation when I get back, just you and me." I gave her a big hug and a kiss, then left.

All trace of daylight was gone by the time I got onto U.S. Highway 59, which took me northeast to a town called George West, halfway between Laredo and Victoria. I parked at a truck stop and called a good friend of mine named Jimmy Kelner. Jimmy had retired from the Drug Enforcement Agency about a year or so before and I'd been too busy to do much visiting with old friends. He was glad to hear from me and agreed to come down and have coffee with me.

I was sitting in a booth next to a window with my feet up on the seat when I turned and saw Jimmy walk in. His hair was almost solid white, with a few strands of black running through it, and his face seemed to hide his age. He had the habit of ducking through any doorway, and with good reason; he stood six foot eight inches tall in his bare feet. I once saw him lift the back end of a Plymouth station wagon four feet off the ground on a bet.

"Tex," said Jimmy as he came over to the booth. "It's been a long time." I stood up and shook his hand and he gave me a big bear hug.

"Too long," I said as we sat down.

"How's Becky?" he asked, grinning from ear to ear.

"Well," I said with a sigh, "we had kind of a spat last night. Nothin' real serious. It's the first time we've had any problems to be honest with ya."

"If ya don't mind me sayin' so, Tex," said Jimmy, "this business keeps a man away from home one heck of a lot. It's not like being a nine-to-five cop, where ya go home every night. That kind of thing can put a real strain on a marriage, and you're talkin' to a man who knows first-hand."

"I hear ya," I said, "but even when I'm home for a spell, she's workin' or her mother comes over or takes her shoppin' or whatever. It always seems to be somethin'. Oh, and that's another thing. She says her folks think I'm a doper because of the people I've been seen with and the money I've been makin' and all."

"Damn," said Jimmy as he shook his head with a

frown. "Yep, when you work deep cover that can happen, and if ya bust your tail to convince them otherwise word could get out and your life wouldn't be worth a plugged nickel."

"I hear that," I said, "but y'know, maybe I should slow down and spend more time with Becky. I told her we'd go on vacation after I got back from this case." We talked about Ed's death and I filled Jimmy in on the case I was just on, then I started to get up from the table.

"Excuse me a minute, Jimmy. I'm gonna go call Becky just to let her know where I'm at and to talk a little." I went to the pay phone and dialed but got no answer. I tried the number again to make sure I had it right. Still no answer.

As I came back and sat down, Jimmy said jokingly, "Damn, that was quick. You must be one fast talker."

"That's damned strange," I said. "It ain't like her to be out at this time of night."

"Oh, she's probably visitin' with her mama," he said as he looked at his watch. "Well, I've got to get home before I have domestic troubles of my own." Jimmy paid the tab for the coffee and we went out to my Mack.

"This your truck?" asked Jimmy. "Shoot, I remember when you first got this beast, and to be honest with ya, Tex, I had to fight hard to keep from laughing. As I recall, this fender was all twisted and the whole rig was painted a kind of pale red. This thing looks damn near showroom quality now." Jimmy wanted to see the inside of the truck and I told him he was more than welcome. He climbed up into the driver's seat and sat there looking around while I stood by on the pavement below.

"Look at this," he said with amusement, "the man's got a television set in here. Can you imagine that? Hey, Tex, lemme pull this air horn, just one time."

I laughed. "Okay, you asked for it," I said as I put my fingers in my ears.

He pulled the cord, the horn blasted, and Jimmy covered his ears with a frown. The piercing sound of the air horn actually shook my teeth.

"Damn," he said, laughing, "where in the hell did you get that thing?

"Believe it or not," I said with a smile, "it's off a passenger train."

"Yeah," he said, "I believe it." He climbed back down and we shook hands and said our good-bye with a promise to keep in touch. I continued north on Highway 59, and it didn't seem like two hours had gone by when I reached the city limits of Victoria, Texas. I found a spot that looked like it was safe to park for the night, then I crawled back in the sleeper, curled up in a blanket, and turned on the television. I woke with the television hissing at high volume, showing the violently swarming particles of static. It seemed like a hive of bees was loose in my truck. I shut off the idiot box and looked at my watch. It was way too early to get up so I went back to sleep for a few hours.

I finally got up and drove to the Red Ryder Truck Stop. I backed into a parking slot at the far end of the lot, then walked over to the restaurant to get some breakfast. After I ate I borrowed a bucket and cloth and washed off the cab of my black Mack B61. That old Mack always drew a lot of attention from truckers who'd been in the business awhile. To the drivers, that kind of truck was almost like a rare vintage car that a person doesn't see too often, and I had a few of the guys come by and admire her. I spent the day shining the paint job on the cab and talking with people I'd never seen before and might never see again. What I was really doing was making contacts. I figure in this business, it never hurts to have a friendly face recognize you when you're in a bind.

A long shadow covered the parking lot as the sun slowly crept behind the building at the west end. A white sedan pulled up to my truck and sounded its horn lightly. I looked out past my right fender and saw Don Austin waving me over. I motioned to him that I'd be a second, locked up my truck, then ran over to his car and got in. We drove to a nearby bar, where we took a booth toward the back.

"What are ya havin', Tex?" Don asked as the waitress came over to us.

"I'll take an iced tea," I said.

"C'mon, Tex, at least have a beer or somethin'," he said.

"I need to stay sharp for these deals, Don," I said, "but thanks anyway." The jukebox was playing loud country music, so we weren't worried about being overheard.

"We've got a man who's been working deep cover on this case for weeks," Don said, "and he's got a line on a dope operation out of Seadrift, Texas—where they bring the stuff in on fishing boats. What we're going to do is this. We'll have you and our agent haul a shipment for them to find out where the operation is based."

I nodded and stirred my tea as he continued.

"Ross McFadden is the man you'll be working with. Ross says there's going to be fifteen hundred pounds of marijuana coming in by boat tomorrow." We talked a while longer. Actually he talked and I listened. Finally, Don settled up the tab and drove me back to my truck. I told him what motel I'd be staying at and we arranged to meet there the next day.

After I checked into the motel, I got on the phone and called home just to see how Becky was doing. I started to worry when I got no answer. I dialed again and let the phone ring about fifteen times, but still no answer. I woke up at about one thirty in the morning and tried to call her again and let it ring off the hook. I went back to bed but had a restless night's sleep. The next morning I got up later than I normally do. I called Becky's workplace at about the time I figured she'd get there. One of the women Becky worked with answered the phone and told me that my wife wouldn't be in that day.

After lunch, Don and two other men came to my room. He introduced me to them. Jay Stilwell was Don's superior and Ross McFadden was the agent I was to work with. Ross was tall and lean and he looked like a college kid, but I noticed a few gray strands showing through his full head of curly brown hair. We went over some of the final details, then I told Ross to wait in my Mack while I checked out of my motel room.

"Let me grab that for ya," said Ross, reaching for my duffel bag.

"Thanks," I said as I handed it to him. After I turned my room key in, I went out to my truck and we got going. As we drove through Victoria I noticed that we were being followed.

"Hey, Ross," I said, "there's a blue van keeps showin' up in my rearview."

"Those are my people," he said as he leaned forward to see through the side mirror. "They've got orders to hang back when we get to Seadrift. We've also got a plane overhead." We took Route 185 southbound to the small coastal town of Seadrift. Looking out onto the waters of San Antonio Bay from the cab of my Mack, I could actually see the curvature of the earth at the horizon. The water was a deep blue and its surface sparkled as the waves caught the afternoon sun. I saw huge white birds hovering motionless in the air over ivory beaches, swooping gracefully down to pluck small fish from the shallows.

Ross tucked his hand-held radio in the sleeper under my mattress as we pulled up to a warehouse on the waterfront. With the engine running, we waited about five minutes, then Ross spoke up.

"I was told just to drive up and wait. Tell ya what, Tex, honk that horn." I looked over at Ross and grinned as I reached for the cord. The shrill blast from the air horn made him jump just a little.

"Damn," Ross said with a laugh, "I didn't know they made truck horns that loud."

"They don't," I said with a smile.

"That ought to get their attention," Ross said.

Just as he spoke, a door opened and a man dressed in blue coveralls came over to my side of the cab, climbed up to the window, and looked in at us. The man reminded me of a tough old bulldog. His face was wrinkled and pushed inward and he had only a few strands of greasy hair combed back over his spotted, weathered scalp. The teeth he had left in his head were yellow, worn, and crooked, and his breath overpowered the smell of the docks.

"Who sent ya?" he barked.

"Augie," said Ross.

The old man looked at the both of us for a second, then said, "All right. Back it up to the side of the building over there." He pointed to a wide pier with no rails—just an occasional post at the edge for boats to tie up to—then he jumped down and went back inside. I swung the rig around, then kicked the clutch, threw her in reverse, and headed for the outer edge of the dock. As we slowly rolled backward over the heavy wooden planks I casually glanced at the rearview mirrors and noticed that Ross was getting edgy.

"Man, don't put us in the water," he said as he looked sideways at the mirror on his side.

I quickly jerked the wheel over and back to get his attention and laughed as he hung on for dear life. He laughed with me when he realized I was kidding. I spun the wheel and brought the tail end of the trailer to bear on the loading bay.

I stopped about thirty feet from the platform, then turned to Ross and said, "Why don't ya open up the doors and we'll get this show on the road." He nodded to me, then opened his door, and as he swung out on to the top rung, the old man we just talked to hollered up at us.

"You two just stay put," he said. "We'll handle the loadin'."

Ross just waved at him and got back in the cab. With the engine still running, we both watched the mirrors, and on my side I could see men carrying large bundles wrapped in plastic. After the truck was loaded, the old guy came over and climbed up to Ross's window.

"Pull it forward some," said the old man, "so they can

close 'er up." He hung on to the rail on the side of the rig as I eased the beast forward. The old man watched the back end till he got a signal. He told me to stop, then he reached in and handed Ross a package.

"Here ya go," he said, "five thousand dollars. A man driving a black Corvette will meet you at the El Rancho Barbecue at the junction of highways 80 and 820 on the west end of Fort Worth. He'll take ya to the place and you'll get the other half of your cash when ya deliver the load."

He turned away and started to climb down, then quickly popped his head back in the window.

"And by the way," said the old man, "we put our own padlock on it so that there ain't no problems."

As I pulled away from the building, Ross said, "This is some slick operation they've got here."

"Not for too long," I said with a smile.

"You got that right," he replied.

"This your first time in an eighteen-wheeler?" I asked.

He nodded and laughed under his breath. "It sure beats hell out of a damn U-Haul."

We went back up the road and got on U.S. Highway 77 northbound. For a while neither of us said anything; then I broke the silence.

"Ya ever notice how the sun looks different in the afternoon than it does in the morning?" I asked. "It's almost like it's burning out as it moves across the sky."

"What?" Ross said with a frown.

"I figure it's the air temperature and the dust and all," I said, looking out my window to the west. "Ya ever think about things like that?"

"You must be pretty damn bored," he said, laughing under his breath.

"No, it ain't that," I said, "but drivin' the long haul gives a man a lot of time to think and to see the world around him. Ya get a chance to see all different types of land and plants and weather. Sometimes ya go through a whole handful of climate changes in the same day.

'Course, ya gotta keep your eyes on the road, but ya still see a lot."

We had dinner in Waco, Texas, then we took Interstate 35 north to the western fork and headed on into Fort Worth. When we came to Interstate 20, I took the westbound exit, then drove until we reached Interstate 820 for the final leg of the trip. When we got to Highway 80, I saw the bright neon sign that read EL RANCHO BARBECUE, and I took the exit and pulled into the lot.

"You go ahead and climb in the sleeper, Ross," I told him, "get some shut eye. I'll just catch a few winks here in the saddle."

"You sure?" he asked. "I don't want to put you out."

"Shoot," I said, "I could sleep leanin' up against a fence post if I had to. Go ahead."

The next morning I went into the restaurant and ordered two tall coffees to go. By the time I came outside the black Corvette was parked alongside my rig.

"It's good to see you boys are here on time," said the driver of the sports car as I handed the coffee up to Ross. "Y'all just follow me. Okay?"

I waved to him and ran around to the other side, then climbed in and got the engine going. We followed the Corvette south along Interstate 820 to the southeast loop of Interstate 20, then back on Interstate 820 northbound. He took us damn near full circle around the city of Fort Worth, and there's no doubt in my mind that the dopers had eyes out there to try and see if we were followed. Luckily our spotter plane allowed the ground surveillance units to hang back. Finally we reached Interstate 35 and drove about forty miles to Sanger, Texas. We followed a lonesome road for several miles past open range dotted with tall shade trees, cattle, and hills covered in greenery and outcroppings of sharp rock and boulders. We arrived at a large gate set on pillars of hand-fit stone masonry. The bar steel doors were left open, and as we passed through I turned to Ross.

"You see that?" I asked.

"See what?" he replied.

"They got cameras monitorin' the gate," I told him.

"Shit," said Ross, pounding the side of the console between us. "That makes it a whole different ball game."

We drove down a smooth hard-packed dirt road past small brick buildings, scattered trees, and a large single-story house with a low-pitched roof surrounded by well-manicured landscaping. The Corvette parked to the side of the main house and another man walked out and motioned for me to stop. Just past the house I saw a water tank and three large steel-sided storage barns. The man who'd stopped us walked over to my side and hollered up at me.

"Back it up to that barn on the end and just stay put," he said, pointing to my right.

As I maneuvered into position I carefully studied the layout of the place. I saw rifle barrels trained on us from windows of the main house and there were armed men on roofs around the compound. When I noticed the tail end of an airplane to my left, I turned to Ross and said, "They got a plane behind those buildings. We need to get the call letters and it'll be on your side, between those first two barns, on our way out."

I came to a stop with the tail end of the trailer toward the door of the barn and waited with the engine running. They opened up the back and I saw several men unload the bundles and stack them inside the structure.

"This place is guarded like Fort Knox," Ross said in a low tone.

"Yeah," I whispered, "it's gonna be a hard one to take down." While they were emptying the trailer, a man walked over to my side and handed up a package similar to the one we'd been given at the dock.

"Here's the rest of your money," the man said. I heard the doors slam, then the man waved us on. "All clear," he said.

We both took a good look at the airplane and got the numbers from the tail as we slowly drove past the buildings. As we headed down toward the gate, a pickup truck passed us on its way into the place. Ross reached back under the mattress, got his walkie-talkie, and spoke into it.

"Nine two, six to nine forty, do you read me? Over."

"We read you, nine two six," came the response, "go head."

"Delivery is complete, repeat, delivery is complete. The compound is heavily guarded. They have at least one surveillance camera positioned at the front gate. We saw an aircraft on the premises and observed a truck with a trailer enter the gate. Over."

"Ten-four, nine two six, we have the area in sight. It looks as though the vehicle that just arrived is being loaded. We'll have an eye in the sky follow him. We're going to hang back and see what develops. You are to rendezvous in Denton at the Seventy-Six Truck Stop. Nine forty out."

After he finished talking on the radio, I pounded on the dashboard.

"I got it!" I shouted. "That pickup truck with the trailer just breezed on into the place . . . well, all we have to do is . . ."

Ross slapped his knee and laughed. "Damn," he said. "This is gonna be a good pop. It could mean a promotion. We're gonna seize the plane, the property, the bank accounts, and . . ."

"Just hold on there, son," I said with a frown. "Don't start the celebration just yet. It ain't over till it's over." I followed Interstate 35 south for about fifteen miles to the city of Denton. We pulled into the truck stop and I backed the Mack into a slot out behind the fuel pumps. We'd barely set foot onto the blacktop when a small blue van stopped right in front of us. Ross got in the front seat as I slid the side door open and jumped inside.

"Tex," said Ross, "this is Alan Richards. Alan, this is Tex Brown." We shook hands, then drove away.

"I just wanted to tell ya," Alan said, turning to Ross,

then looking back at me, "you two did a fine job. We've got them right where we want them. Any vehicle that leaves the place will be followed, and whoever they contact—we'll have us that many more defendants." Alan started shaking his head. "But with the surveillance cameras and armed guards," said Alan, "it doesn't look like we're gonna surprise them."

"Tex came up with something that I think might work," said Ross. "Go ahead, Tex."

"Well," I said, "as Ross told y'all over the radio, there was a truck with a trailer that passed us and went on into the place. I figure if we could put your men in a similar rig, they could scoot right on past the cameras and guards. It'd at least give 'em an edge on the deal." Alan smiled and nodded and kept his eyes on the road.

"As a matter of fact," said Alan, "we have a one-ton pickup and horse trailer at the yard. We seized it about two months ago."

I grabbed a clipboard and asked, "You mind if I write on the back of this?"

Alan nodded with a wave of his hand as I leaned forward and drew a map of the compound for him. I marked the positions where the guards were posted and gave detailed observations of the buildings, trees, heights, distances, angles, and anything else I could think of about the place.

"All right," said Alan. "We've got a command post behind a hill overlooking the doper's setup. I'll discuss this with the other agents and radio headquarters." Alan drove us north toward Sanger on Interstate 35, then we took a dirt road that looked as though nature was trying to claim it back. It was more like two paths side by side separated by clumps of scrub brush.

We wound our way through open range toward a group of tall hills. Finally we started to climb a hill with small dense trees and bushes scattered from foot to crest. We reached a clearing and parked next to two Chevy Blazers. An agent sat in the front seat of one of the vehicles with his leg dangling out the open door and a microphone in his hand.

We each grabbed a pair of binoculars, and as we got out of the van Alan shouted to the agent. "Hey, Bill, grab yourself some lunch. I brought us some sandwiches and sodas."

With a large paper sack in hand, Alan motioned for us to follow him, and we walked up the hill. As we approached a low rock formation at the summit, Alan stopped and looked back at us.

"I want you men to stay low when we get up here," he said with his hand held out at us. "We're a good seven to eight hundred yards from the compound, but I don't want to take any chances." We came upon three agents peering over the rocks through field glasses. We crouched down as we reached the top and sat down beside them. Alan introduced me to the other men, then handed out sandwiches and drinks to everybody.

After lunch they discussed my plan and decided to go with it. Alan contacted headquarters by radio and had the truck and horse trailer sent up along with additional manpower and equipment.

The mild afternoon breeze became a chill wind as the sun dropped out of sight. Alan went down to the vehicles and brought back an armload of blankets, a thermos full of coffee, and a small metal case. The container was black anodized aluminum and it looked like a cross between an attaché case and a lunchbox. Alan pressed a button next to the handle and I heard a loud hissing sound as if gas were escaping from or rushing into the box. He then opened two clasps on either side of the handle and lifted the lid to reveal a large rifle scope fitted into a gray foam lining. Alan pointed out a few do's and don'ts about handling a starlight scope and the fact that it's a six-thousand-dollar piece of equipment.

"Yeah," I said, "I've worked with these before."

"Oh, one other thing," said Alan. "Starlight can detect infrared but not the other way around, so if you see a red glow down there you should be all right—just don't make any sudden moves. If you see a green glow, I want you to shut off the device immediately. Starlight will detect starlight and if you can see them, they can see you."

Alan and three of the other men drove back to Denton for the night, where they were to meet with additional agents the next morning and brief them on the plan. Bill Thompson stayed with Ross and me, and we kept watch in four-hour shifts. We couldn't make a campfire, so we bundled up with blankets. I took the second watch and all was quiet down below. When I got up the next morning the sky was clear and bright, the air was crisp and clean, and my body was cold and stiff. We didn't have any more coffee so I settled for a diet cola. Ross and I kept an eye on the dopers.

Via radio, Alan finally gave word that the men were on their way. Ross kept Bill up-to-date on the movements of the guards with his walkie-talkie, while Bill relayed the information to Alan on the more powerful radio in his vehicle. The sun was behind us as we watched the place, and the mountain's shadow had all but pulled away from the doper's compound below us when I noticed a vehicle approaching the gate from the long, narrow stretch of road to our left. It was a royal blue one-ton pickup with a tarp covering the bed and it was hauling a horse trailer that was longer than the truck itself.

As the rig pulled through the gate, I saw what must have been a dozen police cars about a quarter mile down the road. Through the binoculars I kept my eyes trained on the truck and trailer as it moved through the compound.

The doors in back of the horse trailer opened as the rig passed the first set of buildings. Agents armed with M16's jumped out of the trailer in pairs and fanned out along the tree line. Others ran behind the buildings to await the order to move in or the sound of gunfire. When the truck pulled to a stop in front of the barn on the far right, the tarp covering the bed flew off and four agents hopped up with their weapons trained on the unsuspecting guards.

More men piled out of the trailer as the whole assault team kicked in the doors of each building and stormed inside them. A whole string of police vehicles barreled on through the gate and surrounded the place. The dopers surrendered without a shot being fired.

CHAPTER 12

Bill and Ross drove me back to my Mack at the Red Ryder Truck Stop, and then I followed them down into Dallas. Back at Department of Public Safety headquarters I gave a deposition and filled out payroll forms. I called home while I waited for the paperwork to be processed. I got no answer, but by this time I'd decided not to keep worrying, since it was Becky's day off. After I collected my paycheck, Ross McFadden, Don Austin, and Jay Stilwell took me to lunch along with five other agents. We sat at a group of tables toward the back of a restaurant where cops from all over town ate. I sat back and listened to the guys howling, laughing, and carrying on about the bust.

"Hey, Tex," Ross said, smacking me on the shoulder, "a bunch of the boys are getting together for drinks later. You up for it?"

"No, man," I told him, "I got a long road ahead of me, and I figure if I leave right from here I'll make it by tomorrow morning with a short stopover." We'd all finished eating and the plates had been cleared, but the men were still sitting around telling their war stories. I excused myself from the table with a wave of my hand and was followed out the door by a rousing chorus of good-byes.

Camping out in the hills without a campfire and hardly

a wink of sleep had tied my neck and shoulder muscles up in knots. About all I could think of as I drove southbound on Interstate 35 was having Becky give me a back rub followed by a long hot bath when I got home. About four hours out of Dallas, I stopped at the Gas-n-Eat Truck Stop to fill my thermos with coffee, then I pulled off at a rest area just south of the city. I dragged myself into the sleeper cab and collapsed onto the pillow.

My windup alarm clock buzzed right in my ear and jolted me out of a sound sleep. The countryside around me was covered in a faint orange light as I slid into the driver's seat, poured myself some coffee, and got back on the road. As I reached Laredo my stomach started growling, so I decided to have breakfast at one of the local restaurants rather than dirtying up the dishes at home. I pulled my Mack into the parking lot of the Sunbeam Diner and went inside. Before I sat down at a table, I went to a pay phone and tried home again, but still got no answer. When I went over to the hostess's station to be seated, I heard somebody shouting from across the room.

"Tex, c'mon over." I saw an older man waving to me and after a second I recognized him as Roy Smith. He was sitting with three other neighbors of mine at a large table and they all started waving me over, so I joined them. I had just settled into the chair when Joe Chavez, a sheriff's deputy, came over to the table.

"You are Raymond Brown?" he asked.

"You know I am, Joe," I said. "What's the matter with you?"

He hung his head, then looked up at me.

"I saw your truck out there, so I . . . Tex, my job ain't always easy, and some duties are tougher than most, and . . ." Joe reached into his jacket, pulled out some papers, and handed them to me. I frowned up at him and looked around at my friends, who stared blankly at me.

"What'n the hell is this, Joe?"

Joe looked down, fumbling with his hat as if he was searching for words. "Ah, I gotta get going," said Joe, and skedaddled out of the diner as I fumbled with the papers he'd handed me.

"What is it, Tex?" asked Roy. I looked at the papers, then slumped back in my seat and took a deep breath.

"Divorce papers," I said with great effort. I don't think any words could describe the level of pain and humiliation I was feeling at that moment. The men sitting with me mumbled words of sympathy to me, and that made me feel worse.

"If you'll excuse me, boys, I don't feel much like eatin' right now," I said as I got up from the table.

Roy put his hand on my shoulder and said, "You all right to drive, Tex?"

"Yeah . . . thanks, Roy."

"Well, lemme at least walk ya out, then."

The two of us went to the parking lot, and when we got to my rig, Roy said, "Tex, if ya need anything—anything at all—me and the missus will be there for ya."

"I appreciate that, Roy," I said as I slowly climbed up into my truck.

As he started to walk away, Roy added, "I'll check up on ya from time to time."

I waved to him as I shut the door, then started the engine and pulled away. Of all the journeys I'd taken in that truck, the short trip home from that restaurant seemed like the longest. From a distance my house looked lonesome. The trees on either side had few leaves and the branches moved slowly in the wind. The barren limbs seemed to shroud the place in a cold, stark shadow. Thin dust clouds whisked along the dirt road, spiraling past the front porch as I drove up and parked.

I found the door unlocked and when I opened the door I felt my temperature rise and my heart skip a beat. The place was a wreck. Drawers and cupboards were left open, the framed pictures we had on the walls were either gone or smashed on the floor and there were dirty dishes and papers and trash all over the place. The television, the appliances, and just about everything of value was gone. I picked up a cushion from the floor, set it back on the couch, and sat down on it. I just sat and stared mindlessly at the junk pile I used to call my home. My dog wasn't even there to keep me company. I grabbed the phone and dialed Becky's work number.

"Laredo Medical Group, may I help you?" said the woman on the other end.

"Hello, I'd like to speak to Becky Brown, please," I said in as calm a voice as I could muster.

"Who can I say is calling?" she asked.

I took a deep breath and said, "This is her husband."

"She left a message that she does not want to talk to you. Good-bye," she said, quickly followed by a click and a dial tone.

I felt like tearing the cord out of the wall and throwing the phone out the window, but I took a few deep breaths and paused to collect my thoughts, then I tried again. The woman threatened to call the police and file charges of harassment against me if I didn't quit calling, and then she hung up on me again. I don't know why, but I just laughed out loud and said to myself, "So much for open-minded discussion."

The next call I made was to my lawyer's office, which referred me to a good divorce attorney in Laredo. I called the attorney's office and got an appointment to come in the next day. The bed had been stripped and all the linens were gone, so I got in my old pickup truck and drove to Laredo, where I got a motel room for the night. The following morning, I parked in front of a renovated three-story brick building and went inside. It was an old building completely done over with modern art, earth-toned wall covering with pastel trim and short pile carpeting. In the lobby near the staircase I saw a directory, and I had to search for a second to find out which way the office was.

Rather than wait for an elevator, I climbed the stairs to the third floor and walked past doors with gold lettering and people with fancy suits carrying leather cases. I finally found the office.

"Hi, I'm here to see Mr. Stafford," I said as I took off my Stetson.

"Just have a seat, sir," she said. "He'll be with you in a moment." While I waited, I looked at a Hollywood-type magazine that was on the table next to me. As I leafed through the pages, I couldn't help but laugh at all the petty bullshit about who was sleeping with who or how silly the clothing they wear looks on them. When I got to a section about the divorce cases and custody battles and all the pain and hardships that go with them, my heart sank to my gut.

Just then the secretary interrupted to usher me into a spacious office with shag carpeting, leather furniture, and a massive oak desk with patterns carved into the edge. One wall of the office was filled with thick hardcover books on fancy shelves; another wall was covered with framed pictures, diplomas, and trophys. The wood trim on the sills of the two large windows behind the desk had fancy carvings at the corners and appeared to be original turn-of-the-century woodwork.

"Bill Stafford, Mr. Brown. Good to meet you. Call me Bill," he said as we shook hands.

"Ray Brown, you can call me Tex—everybody does."

"All right, Tex, have a seat," he said. "Now, what can I do for you?"

"My attorney, Joe Albertson, recommended you to me," I said. "My wife just left me. She took most everything we had in the house. The place looks like a tornado hit it."

Stafford leaned forward, folded his hands on the table, and said, "You may not like what I'm going to ask you, but . . . were you having an affair?"

"No, sir, I'm not, never did," I told him.

"Is your wife having an affair?" he asked bluntly.

I crossed my legs and settled into the chair. "To be honest with ya, I really don't think she is. I guess the main thing that broke us up was we didn't communicate near enough. My job kept me away for days at a time.

Speakin' of my job—I know what I say won't leave this room—I work as an operative for the government on undercover cases, and I can't afford to have any publicity about that. My life rides on that. Anyway, I ain't hiring you to rake her over the coals. I'd be happy just to get my eighteen-wheeler, my pickup, and my dog out of the deal."

"I think we can do a little better than that," he said with a smile. I gave Bill a list of character references and a stack of papers that Joe Albertson had told me to bring. We discussed the case while Bill looked at the documents, then he picked up the phone and called the clerk of the court to get on the calendar for a hearing.

With a few words of encouragement, he walked me to the door. "Okay, Tex, remember, the preliminary hearing is in nine days," said Bill. "I'll meet you at the courthouse at nine A.M., and if I have any questions to ask you in the meantime I'll be in touch."

I spent the next nine days doing any- and everything I could to take my mind off the bombshell Becky had dropped on me. I went fishing for a couple of days, washed and waxed the Mack, and worked with my horses. I didn't even have the heart to clean up the house, so I continued to sleep nights at the motel in Laredo.

When we got to court, Becky did her best not to look at me, let alone talk to me. Both of our attorneys presented their cases. When Bill Stafford finished his speech and sat down, I tapped him on the shoulder and whispered, "I want to say a few words before the judge."

Bill frowned and shook his head. "I don't think that's a good idea. Just let me . . ."

"No. I just wanna speak my mind. Tell the judge," I said.

Bill stood up and said, "If it please the court, my client would like to say a few words."

"This is only a hearing, counselor," said the judge, then he looked over at Becky's lawyer, "but if there are no objections . . ."

The judge nodded to me then I stood to face him and

said, "Your honor, I'm not going to say anything about the case or lay any blame for what happened. I'm the type of man that don't need a television or a blender. I'm man enough to admit that this thing hit me hard. Right to the bone it hit me, but I ain't gonna go home cryin' in my pillow. Anyway, my point is, I've got no kinfolk left on this earth and it'd mean a lot to me if I could have my dog, Boo-Boo, back."

The judge looked over at Becky's attorney and asked, "Is that something your client would agree to, Mr. Karnes?"

Becky's lawyer, Karnes, leaned over and listened as she whispered with sharp hand gestures and shook her head. Karnes finally stood up and said, "Your honor, my client wishes to keep the dog."

"Your honor," I said, "I think I can give Boo-Boo as good a home and maybe better."

The judge paused and looked over at Becky, then back at me, and said, "I've scheduled the divorce proceedings three months from now and this is a matter that will have to be resolved at that time."

"Can't I at least get to visit Boo-Boo between now and the court date?" I said.

"Well, Mr. Brown," said the judge, "I don't think we have a legal precedent covering visitation rights where a dog is concerned." Laughter rose from the courtroom and the judge slammed his gavel down a few times to quiet the crowd, then he turned to my lawyer. "Mr. Stafford, I assume you will file the necessary motions for your client?"

After the hearing, Bill took care of some paperwork, then he met me out in the lobby.

"Say, Tex, that must be some kind of dog by the way you were talking," Bill said. "What is it—a guard dog, a Doberman maybe?"

I just smiled and said, "Naw, it's a Pekingese."

"Ya mean one of those little toy dogs? Well, maybe you can train it as an attack dog and carry it in a shoulder holster."

"Look, Stafford," I said. "You're workin' for me and I don't appreciate you jokin' about me."

He held his hands out defensively and said, "Hey, I'm sorry. I didn't mean to offend you, I . . . I wasn't thinking."

"Well, anyway. My wife bought the dog and I became attached to it," I said as we walked toward the parking lot. "Sometimes I took Boo-Boo along with me on the road, and bein' as small as she is, she's good company on the long haul." Bill wrote the next court date on one of his cards, we shook hands, and I drove back to the ranch. Cleaning up the house was more than just a tedious chore, it was a nagging reminder of a failure in my life. That empty house left a real hollow feeling in my gut. I figured I just had to get out of there for a while and just be by myself. I threw some camping gear into my pickup, then grabbed some guns, ammunition, fishing tackle, and drove to the northeast corner of my ranch. The fresh air and solitude did me a lot of good. I got in some target practice and fishing for the few days I was there. I didn't forget my problems, but I was able to put a few things into perspective. When I got back to the house the phone was ringing, but I didn't pick it up in time. A few minutes later the phone rang again and I grabbed it.

"Hello?"

"Hello, Tex. This is Jimmy Kelner."

"Hey, Jimmy," I said.

"I'm real sorry to hear about you and Becky," said Jimmy.

"I appreciate that, Jimmy," I said. "Word really travels fast in these parts, don't it?"

"Actually, Tex, I read about the case in the newspaper," he said.

My eyes widened with surprise. "What?" I gasped.

"The story's about your dog more than the divorce itself," said Jimmy. "Yeah, they're makin' a big deal about it because it's the first custody battle over a dog . . . at least, in the state of Texas, anyway. But listen,

Tex. I think it's great, what you're doin', and I know the folks I've talked to are behind ya."

I got a lot of calls like that the rest of the day, until I finally unplugged the phone. I decided to get out and enjoy myself. I drove up to Las Vegas for a few weeks and had a good old time playing poker, then traveled around to visit some old friends. I kept in touch with my attorney and he finally told me I could see my dog. I had to go to my lawyer's office to be with the dog because of the court order and I visited Boo-Boo only a few times in the three months before the trial. Boo-Boo looked thinner than usual and Bill said the house that she was staying at had no air conditioning. Radio stations were making jokes about the "canine custody battle" and "the fight for Boo-Boo," as they called it. The jokes really hurt Becky, according to some mutual friends of ours, who told me that she was taking a lot of ribbing about the whole deal. During the divorce proceedings, when the judge awarded Boo-Boo to me, I saw a look of sadness on Becky's face.

"Your honor, excuse me. Can I say something?" I asked as I stood up.

The judge looked over at Becky's lawyer then nodded to me.

"Thank you, your honor. I know I've pushed for the custody of our dog Boo-Boo, and I really do have feelings for the dog, but now I can see how much Boo-Boo means to my wi . . . I mean to Becky. I'll let her take the dog after all, your honor."

After court was adjourned I walked across the street to a diner and grabbed a cup of coffee. I didn't know what to expect when I saw Becky walking down the aisle toward my booth.

"Tex," said Becky, "can I sit down a minute?"

"I don't see why not," I said with a wave of my hand. The afternoon sun lit her face and I could barely see her lower lip trembling as she began to speak.

"Tex, I . . . I think I should . . . apologize to you," she

said. "I know I should've talked this thing through with you, but I was mad and confused and . . ." Tears welled in her eyes and she laughed a little as she wiped her eyes with a napkin. "You're gonna think this is crazy, Tex, but . . . can I come back home?"

My eyebrows raised. I didn't know whether to laugh, cry, or spit. "Now, hon, we just got divorced," I said, "and I don't wanna go and tie the knot at the drop of a hat—not that I ain't willin' to give us another shot, mind ya."

We lived together for the next nine months. I stayed at the ranch and worked at horse breeding so I could be at home. I guess maybe I wasn't ready to gather moss at the time. We grew further apart until finally tempers flared and she talked about moving out. I told her to go right on ahead. I even helped her pack.

After Becky left, I took off for three days to clear my head. I was even half thinking of calling Duke McMann and getting back in the saddle again. When I got home my door was open about half a foot. As I walked closer I saw large splinters on the floor and the lock was busted open. I staggered through my house like a zombie. The television was smashed in. Glass was everywhere. The refrigerator was tipped over onto the kitchen floor. All my case files, newspaper clippings of cases I was on, and my scrapbook were destroyed. Even pictures of some of the horses I'd owned were smashed and torn up. I could hardly see straight and I was trembling beyond control.

I picked up a floor lamp by the base and smashed it into the front door, then threw it against the wall of the living room. I pulled out my .45, flicked off the safety, and started screaming at the top of my lungs. I came about a heartbeat away from emptying the magazine of my automatic into the toppled refrigerator. I put the pistol on safety again, tucked it back in my belt, then grabbed the refrigerator at the top end and stood it back up.

After I cooled down a bit I called the Laredo Police

Department and reported the crime. They didn't come up with any solid leads, so there were no suspects. I hired some men to help with the clean-up and repair operation, and when I finally got things in order I called Duke McMann at the Department of Public Safety.

"Hello, Duke, it's Tex."

"Well, hello, Tex," Duke said in his usual gruff voice. I told him about the recent events and he expressed his condolences to me. Then he said, "It might do you a world of good to get back to work. Get yourself back on track. I've seen men end up as head cases over personal problems."

"Duke, just tell me where and I'll go," I said.

To the sound of paper shuffling in the background he said, "I'll make a few calls and get back to ya." Within an hour, Duke called me back and gave me the phone number of a man named Bobby Summerell at the Department of Public Safety office in Laredo. I gave Summerell a call and arranged to meet with him the next morning.

As I drove my pickup into town, the morning sun shone brightly beneath layers of dark clouds. The clouds seemed to change color as they quickly rolled and swirled through the cool, clean air. I really found it hard to imagine that there was enough water to fill a lake floating above my head in those clouds at that very moment. I parked in front of the Department of Public Safety office and went inside. I was directed to Bobby Summerell's office, where I introduced myself, we shook hands, and got the formalities out of the way.

"Now, Tex, this isn't a major case, but I think that your experience will be invaluable," Bobby said as we both sat down. "I've got a new man, and I'd like for you to kind of show him the ropes a little bit."

I sat back in the chair, crossed my legs, and said, "I can handle that. What's the job?"

"We've got a line on a local dealer named Mike Munsell, who works out of a house on the south side of town," said Bobby. "The guy deals quantity, but he's not what we'd consider major league. We figure we can hang a heavy rap over his head and get him to turn his source."

Bobby picked up the phone, punched three numbers, and said, "Bumper, would you come into my office right away?" Bobby hung up the phone, then said to me, "The man you'll be working with is named Walter McNeeley. He goes by the name of Bumper—you'll see why. He may seem a little slow, but he's a good man." The door opened and in walked a tall man dressed in jeans, boots, a red flannel shirt, and a Stetson. He was overweight but seemed to be built pretty solid. His arms swung as he lumbered awkwardly into the office. Bobby introduced us, then gave me the address of the doper.

As we were leaving, Bumper said slowly in a heavy drawl, "We'll go in my car."

"No we ain't," I said sternly, "you'll ride with me."

Bobby held up his hand and said, "Bumper, you just follow Tex's lead. Do whatever he tells you to do. All right?"

Bumper nodded to him and we went out to my pickup truck. We drove over to the address and I slowed to get a good look at the house as we passed by.

"Hey, ya passed on by the place!" Bumper said anxiously.

I frowned at him and said, "Look, will ya trust me on this? I know what I'm doin'."

"I guess I'm just nervous, is all," he said.

I explained what I was doing as we drove around the block. "Okay, the way we're gonna do this is, we'll watch the place for as long as it takes and wait till somebody enters or leaves. That way you can see what you're gettin' yourself into. It also makes the guy think you just happened to get there at that particular moment and gives you an edge. If you just walk up to a dope house cold, it can get ya dead." I parked the truck about seventy yards away from the house and waited. While watching the place we talked a little bit and I found out that Bumper had been transferred from Highway Patrol.

"What kind of piece ya carry?" I asked. He reached

down, pulled up his left pant leg, and started to pull out his gun. "Don't take that out, man," I said abruptly. "Somebody sees that and they're gonna know we're the law." I took a deep breath and continued. "Look, I ain't tryin' to be a hard-ass with ya, but it's little mistakes that can get a man killed."

Bumper rolled his pant leg back down, sat back up, and said, "I can appreciate that, Tex. I'm sorry."

"That's another thing," I said. "Never apologize. Especially not when you're under cover. It's a sign of weakness."

He nodded humbly, then said, "Anyway, it's a Star PD in .45 auto. I like it because it's compact."

"Spanish gun, huh?" I asked.

"Yeah," he said. "I ain't had any problems with it so far. It's a good shooter."

"Well, that may be," I said, "but as far as I'm concerned, I won't have anything but a Colt with me when I'm puttin' my life on the line. I carry a Colt Government Model in .45. And I gotta insist you carry that piece in your belt when the bust goes down. Your size makes it a heck of a lot tougher for ya to reach down to an ankle holster. What ya do after the bust is your business, but when you're with me . . ."

At that moment a one-ton truck pulled up in front of the doper's house. I fired up the engine, pulled away from the curb, and barreled down the street.

"Anybody asks you, you're from Oklahoma City," I said, "but don't talk unless ya have to . . . and keep your eyes open."

I pulled in behind the doper's truck as a tall, thin, blond-haired man was crossing the sidewalk.

"Mike?" I yelled as both of us got out of the car. "My name's Tex, and this here's Bumper. Edwin from San Antone told me about ya . . . said we might be able to do some business."

"Now, how do I know you ain't cops?" said the doper, squinting as the noontime sun showed itself between the clouds.

I cocked my head, folded my arms, and smiled. "First of all, I'm too ugly," I said, then I pointed to Bumper, "and he's too damn big . . . and ugly."

Munsell laughed and said, "Okay, what can I do for ya?"

"We're lookin' to score some weed," I said. "Big quantity."

"I got two hundred and fifty pounds comin' in tonight," said Munsell. "How much d'y'all want?"

I paused for a second then said, "We can handle the whole thing. What's the price?"

Munsell folded his arms and said, "Five bills per."

"I gotta make a livin' too, man," I told him. "That's too damn high."

"Okay, man," the dealer said, shaking his head with his hand up. "Four eighty-five, and that's the bottom dollar."

I looked at Bumper, then back at the doper. Testing the stuff was for TV cops. Even if he was selling hay, we'd get him on the intent to sell. "Works for me," I said. Munsell nodded and said, "Okay, ah, meet me here tomorrow morning."

"Ain't no way I'm gonna do business in somebody's house," I said. "It's gotta be done out in the open. It's safer that way . . . for everybody. There's a grocery store near Clark and Meadow. We'll meet at the west end of the building. Eight thirty in the morning."

The man agreed and we shook hands. As we drove away from the place, I turned to Bumper and said, "Okay, I'm gonna drop you off at the mall near the college just in case we're followed. Laredo ain't that big a town." I parked the pickup in the mall parking lot and the two of us went to a pay phone. I took out my notepad and pen and worked out some quick figures, then called the Department of Public Safety.

"Bobby, it's Tex. The deal is set for tomorrow morning at eight thirty. The location will be the west end of the grocery store near Clark and Meadow. The man's bringin' two hundred and fifty pounds and the price we agreed on is four hundred eighty-five dollars per pound. That comes to a hundred twenty-one thousand, two hundred fifty dollars."

"Good work, Tex," said Bobby. "Where are you at now?"

"I'm at a pay phone in the mall at Park and San Bernardo," I said.

Bobby paused as if to write down directions, then said, "Okay, I'll meet you there tomorrow morning at six-thirty sharp. I'll have some money for you to show them and I'll give you a final briefing."

"I sure wish you wouldn't say *final*," I said with a laugh. "By the way, Bumper needs a ride."

"Just have him call a cab," he said. "See ya tomorrow, Tex."

I filled Bumper in on the details and double-checked to make sure he had cab fare, then drove off. I could've gone back home, but I had my fishing rod and tackle box with me, so I went to Casa Blanca Lake for the night.

I woke the next morning in the front seat of my pickup with my windup alarm clock buzzing in my ear. On the way into town I stopped at a convenience store for a coffee to go. Bumper was waiting for me at the mall when I arrived and Bobby got there shortly afterward.

Bobby handed me a briefcase full of money and said, "Okay, Tex, you know the routine. We'll be watching from a distance. When you see the dope, give a signal. Ah, take your hat off, and we'll move in. Got it?"

We drove to the grocery store and waited for about an hour and a half, until Munsell and three other men arrived in a brand-new Ford one-ton pickup with a snap-down tarp covering the bed. Munsell parked his truck next to mine and the four men got out.

"You got the cash?" said Munsell. With the case full of money in my left hand and my right hand resting on my hip near the grip of my Colt, I said, "Lemme see the weed first." Munsell nodded to his men, who unsnapped the tarp on the back of the truck to reveal bales wrapped in green plastic piled right up to the top of the bed. I went over for a closer look, took out my hunting knife, and cut open one of the bales. I grabbed one of the green buds, smelled it, then handed the money to Munsell.

"That looks like damn good smoke," I said as I took my hat off.

"Yeah, it's Colombian," said the doper.

In the distance I saw the squad cars start to move in, and suddenly, to my right, Bumper reached down, tugged on his pant leg, and went for his gun. As he straightened himself I reached back for my Colt. Bumper called out like he was in trouble. As if in slow motion, the gun slipped from Bumper's hand and tumbled to the pavement. I saw the muzzle swing up toward me just as the weapon was about to hit, so I dodged to the left as I drew my pistol. Sparks flew up at my face as the short-barreled .45 belched a huge flame. The blast sent a shock wave through me that felt like I hit a brick wall doing ninety. I was still standing, so I leveled my Colt at Munsell's head and yelled, "You're under arrest. Nobody move."

Bumper scurried over and picked up his weapon as the cars moved in.

CHAPTER 13

The doper froze wide-eyed at the sight of my .45. Squad cars screeched to a stop all around us. Two of the suspects started to run and Bumper grabbed one and spun him around onto the pavement with his pistol pointed at the man's ear. As the prisoners were being frisked by uniformed officers, I locked my weapon on safety, put it back in my belt, and checked my shoulder for blood. The shirt was torn by the bullet, but I wasn't bleeding. My shoulder was sore and I was shaking slightly from the adrenaline and the thought of just how close that half-ounce slug had come to splattering my brains. Bobby came rushing up to me as the dopers were being cuffed and led to the police cruisers.

"Tex, I heard a shot! What in the hell happened?" he asked anxiously.

I was standing against the truck rubbing my shoulder and shaking my head. "I told him . . . I sure as hell told him, and he said he wouldn't, but sure as shit . . ."

"Tex, what happened?" said Bobby.

I looked up angrily at Bobby and said, "I am never in my life gonna work with that man ever again. He damn near got me killed . . . and maybe himself or somebody else to boot." I took a real deep breath, pounded the quarter panel of the truck with my fist, and said, "I told the man to carry his pistol in his belt on this deal—I wasn't just sayin' it to make conversation—but he carried it in an ankle holster anyway. When he went for his gun, he dropped it and it went off." I showed Bobby the bullet hole in my shirt. "I think it's time to get out of this business."

Bobby rested his boot on the tire of my truck, took off his hat, and said, "Tex, I've known you for a lotta years and . . . and you should think this through. Hey, listen, Tex, I ain't goin' to get all mushy on ya, but we need ya, man."

I said, "I appreciate that, Bobby, but I think I'd rather not leave this business feet first, if ya know what I mean." I started to walk around to the driver's side of my pickup.

"Do me a favor, Tex," said Bobby. "Don't let word of this get to Duke. Bumper's a good man—we all make mistakes."

"For cryin' out loud, Bobby. I told the man he shouldn't be usin' an ankle holster." I kicked the front fender of my truck, then tore my hat off and pointed it at him. "You just damn sure better be prepared to do some real fast talkin' if somebody dies next time that man don't follow directions."

After I took care of the paperwork at headquarters I drove back to my ranch. As soon as I got in the door I called a friend of mine named Gary Sheridan. Gary owned a truck dealership up in San Antonio and he told me he'd put the Mack in covered storage and sell it for me on consignment. The following morning was gray and sunless. I took two steel ramps out of the barn, set them up on the back end of my refrigerated trailer, and drove my pickup truck inside. I climbed out the window of the pickup, slid the ramps into the trailer and secured them, then got behind the wheel of the Mack for the last time. During the long trip north to San Antonio I felt like I was taking a horse I loved to the glue factory. As I rolled the B61 Mack into that dark storage building it was almost like laying the beast to rest in a huge tomb.

I rolled my pickup truck out of the trailer, then turned

the keys over to Gary and left the black Mack behind without giving her a second look. As I drove south on Interstate 35 I felt very alone in the world. Sure, I had friends and people I could visit with, but that just wasn't the same as family. Even the Mack was like family to me in a way, because it represented a way of life—a way of life that I felt had torn up my home and damn near got me killed. Of course, that wasn't the only time I'd been shot at or had a close brush with death, but something just told me to get the hell out of Dodge, as the saying goes.

When I got to Dilly, Texas—halfway to Laredo—I pulled into a truck stop owned by a friend of mine named Tom Wilson. I sat down at a booth in a second dining room that had been added on a few years earlier. When the waitress came to take my order I said, "How're you doin', Arlene? Bring me an iced tea and tell Tom I'm here, would ya please?"

A few minutes later, Tom came to my table and we shook hands.

"Good to see you again, Tex. Hey, listen, there's a guy that comes in here once in a while that looks suspicious. I think he might be into somethin' dirty," said Tom as he sat down across from me.

"Tom, I ain't in that business anymore," I said, "but I appreciate all the help you've given me over the years."

"You're retirin'? I can't believe that," he said.

"I just came back from retirin' the Mack," I said, "and I'm on my way back home to try and sell what I got left."

"Are things that bad?" he asked.

"Man, it's over between Becky and me. I'm gonna leave the border and start all over."

"That don't make no sense, Tex," Tom said. "You ain't that old."

"Yeah, well, I'd like to live long enough to get old," I told him. "Some rookie damn near got me killed the other day. But it ain't just that. There are only about twenty people in south Texas who know what I really do for a livin'. About all of Becky's family think I'm crooked or runnin' dope. And the same goes for a lot of the folks in Laredo. I just ain't gonna live with all that hate, Tom."

"I hear that," he said. "Say, listen, Tex, I ain't had lunch yet. Have you ordered anything?"

"I sure ain't," I said.

"Well, lemme run back in the kitchen and fix us up a couple T-bones. How does that sound?"

After lunch Tom walked me to the parking lot. Tom's wife, Mary, pulled up as we left the restaurant and we talked for a bit. I started off toward my pickup, then I stopped short and said, "Say, Tom, I'll just bet your kids would love to have a horse for their very own."

Tom just gave me a puzzled look.

"I got an old Appaloosa mare that they can have if you'll come and get her. She's the last of the Joker-B mares—a real prizewinner in her day—and . . ."

"Now, hold on, Tex," Tom said, "I can't accept a gift like that. It just wouldn't be . . ."

I held up my hand and cut him off in midsentence. "Tom, now hear me out. You've done right by me for all these years, and besides, I can't take her with me. Yours would be the best home I could find for her. All I ask is that she gets a decent burial when her time comes." He agreed to pick up the horse, we shook hands, then I got back on Interstate 35 and headed back to the house.

I made quite a few phone calls that day to people I'd worked with in the past. I let them all know that I was hanging up my guns, in a manner of speaking. I wasn't calling to tell them not to look me up anymore. These people were my friends and I promised to keep in touch with all of them.

I'd made up my mind rock solid to get out of undercover work, but each time I said good-bye to one of my friends in law enforcement something gnawed at me in a way I couldn't explain. For the next five days I scrambled all over town to sell or trade the rest of my belongings. I was able to trade a Lincoln arc welder that I had for a camper shell that fit my pickup truck just right. Whatev-

er I couldn't sell, I gave away to friends. I threw a
mattress in the bed of the truck and put dark curtains on
the windows of the camper. The camper shell was damn
near tall enough to stand up in and it had a compartment
that hung over the cab of the pickup that gave me a fair
amount of storage space. I had a stud horse with a lot of
years ahead of him. I didn't want to sell the horse, so I
called around and finally made a deal to lease the animal
to a stable up in Oklahoma City. When I had all my gear
packed up in the camper and my stud horse loaded into
the horse trailer, I gave Duke McMann a call to let him
know my plans.

"Yeah, Bobby told me that you were leavin'," Duke
said. "I'll tell ya what, Tex, we'll put you down as being
on an extended leave of absence. I'm leavin' the door
open for ya."

"I appreciate that, Duke," I said. "Don't worry, you
ain't heard the last of me." All the buildings on the place
were stripped bare and I was all packed and ready to go.
Just as I was leaving I thought I'd make just one last call.

"Hello, Becky? This is Tex. Listen, Becky, I'm leavin'
town for good and I figured you and me should go to
dinner one last time and say good-bye on good terms."

"Dammit, Tex!" said Becky. "I still got people funnin'
me about the dog and the trial and all—and I just heard
that you sold everything and you didn't even bother to
ask me if I wanted anything."

"Well, Becky, you didn't ask me if I wanted a divorce
or not, either. Hey, look, I needed the cash because I'm
starting from scratch. I'll meet you at the Red Barn Grill
out by the interstate. Okay?"

During dinner, Becky and I talked about some of the
good times we'd had during our marriage and I told her a
little bit about my plans for the future. She said I'd be
back working for the government before too long, but I
just told her I'd made up my mind. We parted company
as friends. As I got onto Interstate 35 northbound I
figured I'd never see the town of Laredo ever again. It
would have been at least a twelve-hour trip to Oklahoma

City driving flat out, but I didn't feel like pushing myself so I stopped over in Dallas and spent my first night in the camper. After I dropped the stud off at the stable I headed south on Interstate 35. I arrived at my friend J. D. Stovall's ranch in Waco, Texas as the sun was setting.

"Hey, I appreciate ya lettin' me keep my horse trailer at your place, J.D.," I said.

"I'm more than glad to help ya out, Tex," said J.D. "Yer welcome to keep it here for as long as ya like."

"Well, I won't need to leave it that long," I said. "I'm plannin' to buy and sell horses."

"You need a place to board 'em?" he asked.

"Thanks, J.D. I'll let ya know if I do," I said. "What I'm plannin to do is arrange to buy a horse over the phone from people I know, then turn right around and line up a buyer and I turn a quick profit. I'm also plannin' to do the same with watermelons, lettuce, and other produce. I'll hire drivers to haul the stuff for me."

"You got an office somewheres?" asked J.D.

"No. There's a truck stop in San Antonio where the restaurant has telephones at every booth. I can work there," I said. "I'll just spend the day makin' calls, bullshittin' with the drivers and flirtin' with the waitresses."

"Well, shoot, Tex," said J.D. with a laugh, "I think I'll join ya."

For the next seven months my business prospered. It wasn't nearly as exciting or as interesting as undercover work, but I was able to relax a little and enjoy myself. Living in the camper was comfortable and it allowed me the freedom to go to the races, horse shows, or any damn place I wanted to go. I was at a horse show in San Antonio one day when I saw a girl that I just had to get to know. The way the sunlight caught her long, silky brown hair really grabbed my attention. She had an hourglass figure and skin that looked as smooth and soft as a baby's. I walked up to her and introduced myself. When I looked into her dark, piercing eyes I damn near melted.

She told me her name was Lynne. I asked her out and we went to dinner that night. We courted for the next three months until I finally popped the question. The wedding was held in a nice quiet chapel and she was prettier than words could describe in her wedding dress.

After the honeymoon we settled down in a mobile home south of San Antonio. I gave Duke McMann a call to let him know how I was doing.

"Well, it sounds like you've got your head straight," said Duke. "You ready to go back to work?"

"I hadn't planned on it, Duke," I said, "but I do kinda miss the action a little. I'll have to get back to ya on that."

I talked it over with Lynne. She told me that she only wanted me to be happy and if working for the government made me happy she was behind me all the way. I started working undercover again, but I didn't spend nearly as much time away from home as I did during my first marriage. Three months after we got married Lynne told me I was going to be a father. I was so pleased and excited I ran outside the trailer and hollered at the top of my lungs till my eyes went watery. When my daughter was born, Duke McMann was at the top of the list of people to call with the good news.

"Congratulations, Tex," said Duke, "I'm real happy for the both of you. Look, Tex. I know you haven't been back to work for that long, but you should think of your family. I never thought I'd be telling you this, but you should get away from this business. Go raise your family someplace where you don't have to worry about some doper you sent to the penitentiary getting out and coming after you."

"Well, shit, Duke. Texas is more than my home—it's a part of me. I'd hate like hell to leave."

I knew Duke was right and after a long discussion I agreed to leave the state and settle down out west. We bought a nice little two-bedroom house in Tucson, Arizona, and I got back into the business of buying and selling horses and produce. Our daughter, Ryan, was getting bigger every day. She was about the cutest, happiest little baby I could ever wish for. Parenthood was probably one of the biggest challenges in my life, but I wouldn't have traded it for anything.

One day a large brown sedan with blackwall tires and two radio antennas pulled up to my house. Two men wearing suits and wire-rimmed sunglasses came to my door. They identified themselves as agents from the Federal Task Force on Organized Crime and showed us their badges. I invited them in and we sat in the living room.

"My name is Bill Wilkins and this is my partner, Frank Travis. I'll get right to the point, Mr. Brown . . ."

I held up my hand and cut in. "I'd feel more comfortable if y'all called me Tex."

The agents smiled at each other, then Bill continued. "Our superiors have been pleased with the work you've done for us in the past and they've taken another look at your files, and quite frankly, Mr. . . . I mean, Tex—they're impressed, and they feel it would be invaluable to have an operative who isn't hindered by certain legalities when conducting investigations, if you catch my meaning."

"Well, fellas," I said, "it ain't that I don't appreciate the offer, but I think I'll have to turn y'all down." After trying to get me to reconsider, the men left. Damn near every month agents from the task force came to my house to see if I'd change my mind and each time I politely refused.

Having a truck stop nearby with phones at every table allowed me to get out of the house to conduct my business. I'd sometimes find myself looking out the window admiring some of the trucks out on the lot and thinking back to some of the good times I'd had on the road. When I sat down with the newspaper and coffee every morning I couldn't help but read about large drug raids in different parts of the country, and it made me feel like I was missing something. One morning I got a call from a friend named Ron Sellway with the Federal

Task Force on Organized Crime. We made small talk for a while about our families, then Ron got to the point.

"If you come back to work for us, Tex, we will buy you an eighteen-wheel rig, tractor, and trailer. It'll be in your name, and you can pick out whichever truck you want. We'll pay all your expenses and you can bring your family along with you from time to time. We'll cover all motel bills. And before you make any decisions, I think you might be interested to know that, rather than keeping you in one state, you'll be working all over the country. Coast to coast, man. You can just about write your own ticket. How 'bout it, Tex?"

I smiled at the thought and paused for a second. "Look, I'll kick it around and get back to ya, Ron."

Lynne was cooking breakfast when I told her about the offer. She turned to me with a smile and said, "Well, that sounds exciting. I don't think you should pass that up, Ray. You know you won't be happy until you get back on the road."

I called Ron right back and accepted the job.

"That's great, Tex. Glad to have you aboard. Now go truck shopping. That's an order," he said with a laugh. "After you get one picked out, call me and I'll have a plane ticket waiting for you at the airport. You'll fly here to Fort Worth, pick up the paperwork and a cashier's check for the full amount of the purchase price."

I knew of a truck dealership up in Phoenix and Lynne was anxious to get out of town for a few days, so we packed a bag and the three of us drove north on Interstate 35 for two hours. We reached Phoenix around lunchtime and stopped for a bite to eat. All three of us went to the truck dealership and I took my time looking through almost all the vehicles on the lot. I'd narrowed it down to three rigs, but Ryan was getting tired and a little cranky so we drove to a motel for the night.

The next morning we went back to the lot and I finally chose a white Kenworth cab-over with a double-wide sleeper cab. I dropped Lynne and Ryan off at a motel, then caught a round-trip flight to Fort Worth from

Phoenix Sky Harbor International Airport. I arrived back in Phoenix later that afternoon, picked up Lynne and Ryan at the motel, and we went back to the truck dealership. After all the paperwork was done, the man handed me the keys and papers. The Kenworth was sitting right out in front of the building waiting for me. I stopped outside the door of the office, folded my arms, and just looked at the rig, then I walked around to the other side of the cab and continued to stare at the vehicle.

Lynne walked over to me with Ryan cradled in her arms and said, "What's wrong, Ray? You should be on top of the world. You've got yourself a brand-new truck. It is yours, isn't it?"

Lost in thought, it took a second for me to answer. "Huh? Oh, yeah, it's mine all right," I said. "I ain't thinkin' about that. What's buggin' me is, I ain't thought up a name for the rig, and it's important 'cause it'll be my handle. It's bad luck to drive a truck off the lot without naming it, ya know."

Lynne smiled and said, "I didn't know you were superstitious."

"Well, I ain't really. It's more like . . . tradition."

"Worry about that later," she said. "It's almost sundown. It'll be dark soon."

I slapped my hands together and hollered, "That's it! You just named it. Sundowner!"

Lynne and Ryan got into the pickup and I followed them to the motel in my brand-new Kenworth. I was like a kid with a new toy that night, sitting in the cab admiring the nice, clean interior, getting to know the layout of the instruments, and talking on the citizens band radio. I knew I'd have plenty of time to sit behind the wheel of the rig, so I tore myself away and spent the rest of that happy evening with my family.

After breakfast the next morning we checked out of the motel and drove both vehicles to a truck stop just off Interstate 17, near Van Buren Street at the south end of town. I found a sign painter at the truck stop and hired him to paint SUNDOWNER on the side of my cab. The job was finished by noontime and I figured we'd have lunch while the paint dried a little. I held little Ryan's hand as we walked out to the parking lot. She was jumping up and down and pointing at my new truck.

"I think our daughter wants to ride in the KW with me for the trip home," I said.

"She's a big girl now," said Lynne. "I think she can ride with Daddy if she behaves. Will you behave with Daddy, Ryan?"

Ryan eagerly nodded and I carried her up into the cab of the truck and set her in the passenger seat. Lynne pulled up next to the Kenworth and rolled down her window.

"I'll see ya down there, Ray," she said with a wave of her hand.

"Turn on your CB," I said. "Make sure ya got it on channel nineteen. All right?" She waved to me and we headed down the on ramp to Interstate 17 southbound. As we drove out past the sharp, craggy mountains bordering the southern edge of the valley, I grabbed the microphone of my CB radio and said, "Breaker one-nine. This here's the Sundowner. Come back to me, Cactus Flower."

"I read you, Sundowner," said Lynne. "How's the truck feel to you?"

"It ain't the black Mack, but it's not a bad truck," I said modestly with a smile so wide I thought my face would split in two.

"I thought the Texas Outlaw was your handle," said Lynne.

"Naw, those days are gone," I said. Suddenly another voice cut into our frequency.

"Breaker one-nine, you got the Wind Rider north-bound. Say, pardner, are you the Texas Outlaw? I've heard of that black Mack you was just talkin' about."

"Ten four," I said, "I was at one time, but I'm in this white KW now. The name's Sundowner."

When we got home I brought in our luggage. Lynne

had just tucked Ryan in for a nap. I held my wife's hands firmly, looked into her eyes, and whispered, "Let's go on a short road trip in the new truck. Just the two of us. It'll be real romantic."

The corner of her lip curled in a sensuous smile and she called a girlfriend to baby-sit Ryan. We packed a cooler full of sodas and sandwiches and drove to Mount Lemmon, just west of Tucson. The scenery was magnificent from the cab of my new Kenworth tractor rig. We fell in love all over again as the trees and hills rolled past us. In the dark early morning hours as Lynne slept next to me, I lay awake, full of excitement at the thought of fighting crime in all those cities from coast to coast.

Case Dispositions

Chapter 1 - Defendant in border patrol shooting/ kidnapping (name not given) served ten to fifteen years.

Chapter 3 - Gene Byrd, father of girl who was kidnapped, has never been brought to trial and has never returned to the U.S.

Chapter 4 - Seven hundred pounds of marijuana was seized. H, five to ten years; M, ten to fifteen years. Eighteen defendants, Gomez's truck and house were seized, along with five cars.

Chapter 5 - All charges against Tex were dropped in the stagecoach case after new evidence was presented.

Chapter 6 - Bail jumper received six to fifteen years.

Chapter 7 - In the rape case, the two men were escaped convicts. One man received thirty years, the other got life in prison.

Chapter 8 - Truck theft ring—six defendants. One got fifteen months, two got three years, four got ten years.

Chapter 9 - Big Bend shootout—no defendants. College student was killed.

Chapter 10 - No data on large crank lab. Small crank lab—one hundred seventy-five pounds of crack and six barrels of chemicals used in drug manufacture were seized. Four defendants.

Chapter 11 - Drug shipment from Seadrift to Sanger—1,250 pounds of marijuana were seized at Ranch; seventy-five pounds were seized when truck delivered to Abilene.

Chapter 12 - Four defendants, two hundred fifty pounds of marijuana seized.